Chekhov
FOUR PLAYS

A Smith and Kraus Book
Published by Smith and Kraus, Inc.
One Main Street, PO Box 127, Lyme, NH 03768

Copyright ©1996 Carol Rocamora
All rights reserved
Manufactured in the United States of America
Cover and Text Design by Julia Hill
Cover painting of Chekhov by his brother, Nikolai Chekhov, courtesy of the State
Museum of Literature, the Chekhov Museum.
First Edition: October 1996
10 9 8 7 6 5 4

The Library of Congress Cataloging-In-Publication Data
Chekhov, Anton Pavlovich, 1860–1904.
        [Plays. English. Selection]
        Chekhov: four plays / translated by Carol Rocamora. —1st ed.
                p. cm. — (Great translations series)
        Includes bibliographical references.
        ISBN 1-57525-065-9
        1. Chekhov, Anton Pavlovich, 1860–1904—Translation into English. I.
Rocamora, Carol. II. Title. III. Series: Great translations for actors series.
PG3456.A19R63   1996
891.72′3—dc20   96-36228
                        CIP

Chekhov
FOUR PLAYS

Translated by Carol Rocamora

Great Translations Series

SK
A Smith and Kraus Book

Contents

Preface vii

Notes from the Translator ix

Introduction by Carol Rocamora 1

The Plays

    The Seagull 37

    Uncle Vanya 91

    The Three Sisters 143

    The Cherry Orchard 213

Chronology of the Plays 271

Biographical Chronology 272

Glossary 276

Pronunciation Guide 286

Selected Bibliography 292

Preface

CHEKHOV AND THE CENTENNIAL

"We cannot even imagine what the theatre will be like in a hundred years," Anton Chekhov once said to his fellow writer Alexander Kuprin, just after the turn of the century.

The period 1996–2004 marks the centennial anniversary of the premieres of Chekhov's four major plays. A new collection of translations is a way of celebrating this centennial, and a way of keeping the plays alive today.

The purpose of this collection is to provide fresh, new translations for actors, theatre artists, audiences, and lovers of dramatic literature. The plays were translated to be read, performed, and enjoyed. In the contents of this book, you will find new translations of the four major plays of Anton Chekhov: *The Seagull, Uncle Vanya, The Three Sisters,* and *The Cherry Orchard.* The following supplementary information has been provided: an introduction with background and biographical information of interest and relevance to the major plays, a chronology of Chekhov's life and dramatic works, a brief glossary and pronunciation guide for each play, and a selected bibliography.

ACKNOWLEDGMENTS

These new translations were begun in April 1991 and completed in October 1995. Premiere productions of these new translations were performed in The Chekhov Cycle from 1993–96, under the auspices of the Philadelphia Festival Theatre for New Plays, at the Annenberg Center. For the support of the new translations and productions, I wish to acknowledge with deepest appreciation the following sources: the Annenberg Foundation, the ARCO Chemical Company, the Arcadia Foundation, the Knight Foundation, and the William Penn Foundation. For support of my travel to Russia in 1992 and 1993 to research these translations I would like to thank the International Theatre Institute, my host Dr. Anatoly Smeliansky at the Moscow Art Theatre, and all his colleagues who assisted with my visits. I also wish to extend the following special thanks to: Lauren Bon, Alan and Nancy Hirsig, Stephen D. Cohen, and Harry Cerino and his associates, for their understanding of the value of new translations; to George Pahomov, Morton Benson, and Vera Zubarev, for their valuable advice; to Anne Denlinger and the Bryn Mawr College Library, for their resources; to members of the Board of Directors of the Festival Theatre, the Annenberg Center, and Mary Harden, for their support; to Janet Neipris and all my colleagues and students at NYU Tisch School of the Arts, for their support and enthusiasm; and to my husband, James A. Katowitz, for his encouragement. Finally, I would like to thank all the theatre artists in the Philadelphia and New York communities listed on the title page of each play, who helped breathe life into these translations for the first time.

Notes from
the Translator

"I have been translated into all languages, with the exception of foreign ones."

Chekhov to Tikhonov, 2/22/92

"Why don't I know foreign languages? It seems to me I could translate literature superbly. When I read other translations, I keep altering and transposing the words in my mind, and I experience a sensation of something light, ethereal, like lacework."

Chekhov to Suvorin, 5/10/91

In this collection, I have striven to create living translations for purposes of reading and performance, which are both faithful to the original Russian language, while at the same time fluid for the contemporary American actor and accessible to modern audiences.

There are so many vital features to Chekhov's dramatic language. It is the translator's challenge to bring all these elements into harmony and balance, while at the same time creating living texts which the contemporary American actor can use and enjoy.

I have first and foremost sought to preserve the poetry and music of the language as it is in the original. Chekhov's language is beautiful and rich in rhythm, rhyme, alliteration, and onomatopoeia, and the preservation of these qualities has been a first priority.

Second, I have sought to preserve the period flavor of the language, which reflects the grace and style of the original. One example of this is retaining the formal use of the Russian names and patronymics, a challenge for the contemporary American actor, but once mastered, greatly enhances the color, musicality and 'Russianness' of the language in translation. A pronunciation guide is included at the end of the translations, and one will note the many variations of a character's name used in direct address throughout a play (for example, Andrey Sergeevich, Andrey Sergeich, Andryusha, Andryushka, Andryushenka) which again adds so much richness to the dialogue.

I have also sought to preserve, wherever possible, the punctuation and the syntax of the original, as a way of protecting one of the strongest features of

Chekhov's dialogue — its natural flow. Both the longer passages and the colloquial dialogue have their own special and distinct rhythms. If the actor "goes with the flow" of the language, and follows the phrasing, he or she will find the rhythm and the special energy of the character's speech, and through it, find an important aspect of the role.

There are numerous allusions to literature and music in the plays, reflecting Chekhov's broad knowledge of Russian and European culture. Their usage is illumating to the texts, and they add a sense of context and tradition to the plays. Like the patronymics, they also add color and richness to the dialogue. For these allusions, I have supplied a simple and practical abbreviated glossary for each play. There are also French and German expressions, and quotations from the Latin, all preserved from the original.

A special note for directors: Again, the stage directions are all Chekhov's own original ones. Of interest to directors will be the lyrics to occasional songs which characters sing throughout the plays. I have listed their sources in the glossary to each play. In many cases they are lyrics to Russian 'romances,' popular love songs of the day. The melodies of these 'romances' were sometimes taken from the music of great composers; the lyrics, similarly, were often taken from existing poems by noted poets of the day. Directors may find it difficult in some cases (as I did) to trace the actual melodies; in any event, I have preserved the original lyrics which Chekhov chose, to give the director an indication of the quality of the moment.

The supplementary information, including the glossary and the pronunciation guide, are all designed to enhance the practical usage of the texts.

In general, a modified form of the popular standard transliteration system has been used in these translations, in both the texts and the bibliography. Where there are exceptions, it is for the purpose of making it easier for the actor's use.

A final 'mea culpa' to the author for any slight liberties I may have inadvertently taken, or any errors, which do not do him justice. I have sought to show his texts the reverence and respect they deserve.

AN INTRODUCTION TO CHEKHOV,
THE DRAMATIST

There are many fine biographies and critical studies of Chekhov's plays avail-able to the actor. This introduction provides a very brief overview of the life of Chekhov, the dramatist, and some background information about the writing of the four major plays. For further insights into his life and work, there is a selected bib-liography at the end of this collection.

Anton Chekhov's four major plays: *The Seagull, Uncle Vanya, The Three Sisters,* and *The Cherry Orchard* — four plays that have influenced twentieth century drama — are all the more remarkable for the fact that there are only four of them, that they are a small part of a much larger, diverse body of liter-ary oeuvre, and that they are the work of a modest man who lived remarkably few years, who devoted his life to so many other endeavors, who had very little faith in his abilities as a dramatist, and who from a very young age knew that his life would be short.

For the contemporary theatre artist, audience member, and lover of theatre to understand these remarkable plays, to experience their riches, to unlock their mysteries, to appreciate their position in dramatic literature, it is useful to find their genesis in the man himself and in his extraordinary life, to know their con-text in his larger body of work, to have a sense of their place in a rich literary tradition, and to know the times in which they were written. Then, we can gain a fuller appreciation of the passionate cry of Konstantin Gavrilovich in *The Seagull* for 'new forms' — the forms which these four new plays of Anton Chekhov created for the contemporary theatre.

A SHORT BIOGRAPHICAL SKETCH

"Autobiography? I have a disease — 'autobiographophobia.' To read any sort of details about myself, or worse, to write them for publication, is true torture for me."

Chekhov to Rossolimo, 10/11/99

"Do you need my biography? All right, here it is. I was born in Taganrog in 1860. I graduated from Taganrog Grammar School in 1879. In 1884 I graduated from medical school at Moscow University. In 1888 I received the Pushkin prize. In 1890 I made a journey to Sakhalin, across Siberia and returned by sea. In 1891, I completed a tour of Europe, where I drank excellent wine and ate oysters. In 1892 I had a good time at V. A. Tikhonov's nameday party. I began to write for the journal *The Dragon Fly* in 1879. My collected works are: *Motley Stories, In the Twilight, Tales, Gloomy People,* and a tale, *The Duel.* I have also sinned in the realm of drama, although in moderation. I have been translated into all languages with the exception of foreign ones. However, I have already been translated into German, a long time ago. The Czechs and Serbs also approve of me, and the French don't think too badly of me, either. I experienced the mysteries of love at the age of thirteen. With my colleagues, both medical and literary, I remain on excellent terms. I am a bachelor. I would like a pension. I still practice medicine, to the extent that, in the summertime, I even perform an autopsy or two, although I haven't done one now in a couple of years. Among writers, my preference is Tolstoy, among doctors — Zakharin.

However, all this is nonsense. Write whatever you like. If you have no facts, substitute something lyrical."

Chekhov to Tikhonov, 2/22/92

Anton Pavlovich Chekhov (1860–1904) was the son of a shopkeeper, grandson of a serf, doctor, humorist, short story writer, letter-writer, landowner, humanitarian, environmentalist, loyal son and brother, supporter of his family, husband (for three short years), aesthete, ironist, Russian. All the facets of this rich life, which filled forty-four short years, are to be taken into account for what they contributed to his special vision as a dramatist. A variety of fine biographies are available for the appreciation of this extraordinary life: by Ernest J. Simmons, David Magarshack, Henri Troyat, V. S. Pritchett (listed in the bibliography), among others, all providing different and valuable perspectives.

A chronology of his life and major works is offered in this collection. To understand his development as a dramatist, Chekhov's life readily divides itself into four and one-half decades. Chekhov was born in 1860 in Taganrog, a southern Russian town on the Sea of Azov, the son of a shopkeeper. His father's father was a serf in the Voronezh province, and had purchased the freedom of his family in 1841, a good twenty years before the abolition of serfdom in Russia. By dint of hard labor, his peasant grandfather Yegor Chekhov managed to save 3500 rubles to purchase the freedom of his eight-member family at the rate of 500 rubles per head (his master included one of Yegor's daughters 'for free' in the bargain). Pavel Yegorovich, Chekhov's father, opened his own grocery shop in Taganrog, where he required the services of his six children — Aleksandr, Nikolai, Anton, Maria (Masha), Ivan, and Mikhail. It was in this grocery store that the vivid scenes of Chekhov's early life played themselves out — including long hours of labor, often severely restricting time for school preparation, and mandatory practice for church choir conducted by his father, which frequently began before dawn. Chekhov's father often beat the children — and the description of Lopakhin in the opening scene of *The Cherry Orchard* of the beating by his father's hands is hauntingly reminiscent of Chekhov's own experience. The memoirs of Aleksandr, Chekhov's eldest brother, also depict, however, a close and lively family life among the siblings during these early years, filled with family theatricals, practical jokes, and general merriment, mostly engendered, authored, and enacted by Anton himself, as an antidote to paternal tyranny. It was in these early years that the humorous muse — and the love of theatre — was born in Chekhov.

The main event during the '70s — the Taganrog period, the second decade of Chekhov's life, was the relocation of his family. His father's business failed, the bankrupt Pavel Yegorovich fled with his family to Moscow in 1876, leaving Anton behind to complete his studies, supporting himself by tutoring. For three brief years, Chekhov was completely on his own. While he planned for a medical career, he also had a passion for writing. In 1877–78 he sent a number of short comedic pieces to his brother Aleksandr in Moscow, who submitted them for publication. Among them also was a full-length play, and some literary historians speculate that the lost manuscript, allegedly entitled *Bezotzovshchina (Fatherless)*, was an exorcism of the paternal demons which haunted Chekhov in his early years. (In later life, remarkably, Chekhov forgave his father — his only overt form of protest against his pious father could be said to have been his rejection of organized religion. Chekhov took responsibility for supporting his parents and siblings throughout his life.)

In 1879, Chekhov joined his family in Moscow in their poor basement flat and entered medical school at Moscow University. Compelled to support his studies and his family, he began to write sketches for humorous journals. The decade of the 1880s, the Moscow period, marks the period of greatest productivity in Chekhov's literary career, and his remarkable rise to fame and popularity in which he jokingly called 'le tout Moscou,' From 1880–87, while living in Moscow, Chekhov contributed almost four hundred humorous sketches and short stories to numerous literary publications of the day under a variety of 'noms de plume,' including 'Antosha Chekhonte,' 'My Brother's Brother,' 'A Doctor without Patients,' 'A Man without a Spleen.' He received his medical degree in 1884 and installed his family in a house on Sadovo-Kudrinskaya Street in Moscow; a museum remains there today, a faithful preservation of the modest little rose-colored house (Chekhov once said it looked like a "chest of drawers") where the young Dr. Chekhov lived with his large family, practicing medicine and literature at the same time. His fame grew; he acquired a noted publisher, Suvorin, the prestigious Pushkin Prize in 1887, acceptance among the Moscow 'literati,' and widespread popularity.

But most significantly, during this decade of Chekhov's twenties, amidst this flurry of literary activity and success, the long shadow of consumption was cast, which was eventually to take his life. In 1884, at the age of twenty-four, Chekhov experienced his first hemorrhage; in 1886, his second. This increasing awareness of his impending illness was coupled with a growing 'ennui' with the Moscow 'literati.'

> "I have hundreds of friends in Moscow, and among them dozens of writers, but I cannot recall a single one who has read my work or who thinks me an artist. There is in Moscow a so-called 'literary circle': talents and mediocrities of all ages and varieties, who gather once a week in a private room of a restaurant and exercise their tongues. If I were to go there…they would laugh in my face. In the five years that I have been published in the newspapers, I've become accustomed to their opinion of my literary mediocrity, I've even started to look down on my own work myself. And still, I keep on writing!… [Anyway] I am a physician, I'm up to my ears in my medical work, so that no one has been troubled more than I by the proverb about chasing two hares…All my hope is in the future. I am only twenty-six years old. Perhaps I shall still manage to accomplish something, although time flies by so rapidly."
>
> *to Grigorovich, 3/28/86*

This feeling was combined with what Chekhov saw as a failure at that which he loved most of all, but which did not come as easily to him: the writing of plays. During the eighties, Chekhov wrote a number of short works, all comedies and all well received. But it was the three full-length plays written during this period and his frustration at the lack of their critical acclaim that finally propelled him into escaping from Moscow and the life of success which had now become a spiritual prison for him.

The decade of the 1890s — Chekhov's thirties — the Melikhovo period — marks the turning point from humorist to serious dramatist. Following a hiatus of two years, in which he traveled to parts of Asia and Europe, he purchased a dacha in Melikhovo, where he vowed to retreat and write. Even though his entire family followed him there, and despite the many distractions of practicing medicine and country life, he managed somehow to write *The Seagull* and *Uncle Vanya* and lived there in contentment until he experienced a major hemorrhage in 1897. In 1898, his father died; in 1899, his ill health forced him to sell his Melikhovo dacha and move to Yalta, his beautiful prison by the sea in the Crimea.

During the final years of his life (1900–04), the Yalta period, Chekhov wrote *The Three Sisters* and married Olga Knipper, the leading lady of the Moscow Art Theatre. Meanwhile his health gradually declined. During the writing of his final play, *The Cherry Orchard*, there were days when he could barely write a few lines. His physicians finally prevailed and sent him abroad to Germany for further treatments. He died at a spa in 1904 in Badenweiler, Germany, in exile from the Russia he loved.

CHEKHOV THE DRAMATIST

During his short, prolific life, filled with so many other activities, Chekhov managed to write over 4000 letters, almost five hundred short stories, about a dozen short plays, and seven full length plays. The last four, *The Seagull, Uncle Vanya, The Three Sisters,* and *The Cherry Orchard*, constitute the canon of the major plays. A chronology of his full-length and one-act plays is included in the supplement of this collection of translations.

THE 'MOSCOW PERIOD': 1880–1890

It is clear from reading the extraordinary body of Chekhov's letters that all his life he maintained a passionate love-hate relationship with playwrighting and the theatre. We know of his love of theatre from his domestic and school theatrics during the Taganrog period, his early attempts at playwrighting during those days, and how thrilled he was to have reviewed a production of *Hamlet* in Moscow at the age of twenty-two. And yet playwrighting was a struggle for him, while his short stories came naturally, indeed they seemed to pour out of him, almost one every other day during certain periods of the early eighties, when he was discovering how successful they were and how lucrative a source of income they were in support of his family. So, as the desire to write seriously for the theatre grew during his twenties in the Moscow period, so did the frustration with his own ease at writing in the humorous vein.

> "I cannot recall one single story on which I worked more than a day; *The Huntsman,* the one you like so much, was even written in a bath-house! As reporters dash off their notes about fires, so I write my stories, mechanically, unconsciously, caring nothing either about the reader or myself."
>
> *to Grigorovich, 3/28/86*

On the other hand, he was so ashamed of his first playwrighting attempt in 1880–1, the sprawling, unwiedly, unfinished manuscript now known as *Platonov* — it was rejected for production by a Moscow theatre — that he intended to destroy his copy (fortunately, his siblings preserved the rough draft). With *Ivanov* (*A Drama in Four Acts*) (1887), his second full-length play of the Moscow period — it was commissioned by the prestigious Korsh theatre at the height of his popularity, and he boasted that he wrote it in less than two weeks — Chekhov held high hopes, excited by the prospects of his debut as a serious dramatist. But the public and critical responses were wildly mixed. Chekhov's brother Mikhail was present at opening night, and described the pandemonium: wild, ecstatic cheering, violent booing, fist fights in the buffet, patrons ejected from the theatre. Part of the problem, Mikhail pointed out, was that Chekhov was a famous humorist and thus the audience expectations were for a comedy, despite the forewarning of the play's subtitle.

However controversial, *Ivanov* had a great impact on the Moscow theatre scene, and enhanced Chekhov's reputation as a successful writer. Chekhov, however, was dismayed by what he perceived to be a misunderstanding by the critics and the public of his serious dramatic intentions, and, in particular of his central character, Ivanov, a portrait of a 'man of the '80s,' a liberal idealist who could not effect social change. Chekhov felt that he was continuing the Russian literary tradition of the 'superfluous hero,' established by Pushkin and Lermontov before him, and, moreover, offering a fresh new interpretation of this hero's spiritual state. Bewildered by the sharply mixed reactions, Chekhov's first response was to turn the blame upon himself.

> "I did not know how to write a play…If on paper my characters have not come out alive and clear, the fault is not in them but in my inability to express my thoughts. It means that it is still too early for me to start writing plays."
>
> *to Suvorin, 12/30/88*

Frustrated by what he perceived to be his failure as a serious dramatist, Chekhov turned his energies to the writing of short comedic sketches — 'shutki' (literal translation: 'jokes') or 'vaudevilles,' named so after the French form popular in Moscow theatre at the time.

> "So now I'm a very popular vaudevillist, am I! My God, how they grab them! If in all my life I somehow succeed in scribbling a dozen empty trifles, I'll thank God for it. I have no love of the stage…This season, I'll write a vaudeville and that will keep me happy till the summer. Now, is that what you call work? Really, is there any passion in that?"
>
> *to Shcheglov, 11/2/88*

And indeed, he did write almost a dozen vaudevilles in his lifetime — more, if those lost in the early years are counted. These seemed to pour from him as effortlessly as "oil from the depths of the Baku," as Chekhov put it to Suvorin, his publisher *(12/23/88)*. "I could write a hundred a year." Between 1886–1888, he wrote his most well-known ones: *On the Harmful Effects of Tobacco, Swan Song, The Bear, The Proposal,* among others, garnering him more critical acclaim and praise, particularly for the latter two, from his contemporaries (including Tolstoy, for whom *The Bear* became a favorite). Yet again, he harbored resentment at the ease with which the humorous muse brought him success, and the difficulty he had in the serious vein.

> "No matter how hard I try to be serious, nothing ever comes of it, and all my serious efforts are mingled with insipidity."
>
> *to Polonsky, 2/2/88*

> "I think that if I were to live another forty years, and read, read, read, and learn to write talentedly — i. e., concisely — at the end of that time I would fire on you all with so great a cannon that the heavens would tremble. But for now I am but a Lilliputian, like the rest."
>
> *to Suvorin, 4/8/89*

Even with the popularity of the vaudevilles, Chekhov entered a period of reflection on literature and on his own spiritual state as a writer. His letters of this period (1888–89) contain more writings on literary theory than in any other period of his life, and in them, glimmerings of the voices of Treplev and Trigorin, and the soul of Chekhov the mature dramatist of the four major plays to come. (They also include a campaign against criticism of the day — perhaps in response to what he perceived as the critics' misunderstanding of his serious attempt at playwrighting).

> "There are moments when I completely lose heart. For whom and for what do I write? For the public? But I don't see the public, and I believe in it less than I do in ghosts; it is uneducated, uncouth, and its best elements are unscrupulous and insincere to us [dramatists]. Whether the public needs me or not — I can't figure it out…Write for money? But I never have any money, and having grown accustomed to living without it, I remain almost indifferent to it. For money, I write almost apathetically. Write for praise? But praise only irritates me."
>
> *to Suvorin, 12/23/88*

Chekhov struggled to rewrite *Ivanov* for its St. Petersburg production in 1889. Even though the rewriting process brought critical success, still it did not satisfy him. Clearly, he was frustrated that somehow the serious dramatist in him had not yet found voice, and that, in any case, the public was not ready to hear it.

> "I am worn out, and no honorarium can make up for the agonizing labor…Formerly, I didn't give a damn about my play and regarded it with condescending irony: I wrote it and to hell with it. But now when all of a sudden I found it in the works again, I realized what a bad job of writing it actually was…All week long I was fussing with the play, scribbling rewrites, corrections, insertions. I started hating my play to such a degree that I was ready to end it with [Edmund] Kean's words: 'Flog Ivanov, flog him!'"
>
> *to Pleshcheev, 1/15/89*

> "…it is hard to write a good play, and twice as hard to write a bad one. I would like to see the entire public merge into one person. Then you and I would sit in a [prominent] box at the theatre and hiss it off the stage."
>
> *to Suvorin, 5/4/89.*

It was the critical failure of his third full-length work, *The Wood Demon,* which premiered in 1889 at the Abramov Theatre in Moscow, that drove Chekhov to conclude the 'Moscow period' of his life. Perhaps as a reaction to what he saw as *Ivanov's* failure, Chekhov chose to experiment in another vein with *The Wood Demon,* a long comedy with a happy ending, as he called it. With its sharp and uniform critical failure (it had first been rejected with severe criticism by the literary committee of one Petersburg Theatre, members of which advised him to stick to storywriting), his worst convictions reconfirmed as to his dramaturgical skills, Chekhov forbade its publication.

Despite their lack of uniform critical success, and Chekhov's own discouragement, the three full-length plays of the 'Moscow period' are alive today, the latter two performed throughout the world as he wrote them, and *Platonov* most often in a variety of adaptations, *Wild Honey* by Michael Frayn being the one most known on the British and the American stage. They also remain of great interest because of their rich and colorful contents, which clearly identify them as predecessors of the four major plays. There are the country settings, the depiction of the landed gentry, the social, philosophical, and environmental issues, the love intrigues, and the colorful ensemble of characters. There are the central characters and their philosophical and moral struggles, most notably Platonov and Ivanov, spiritual antecedents of the characters of the four major plays. There is the balance of tonalities — the comedic and dramatic, tinged with farce and melodrama — with which Chekhov was experimenting, a balance which found a mature resolution in the later works. And then, there is the fascinating and mysterious transformation in later years of *The Wood Demon* into one of his major plays, a story to be told later in this introduction.

Thus, bored by the superficialities of fame, peeved by the Moscow literary scene, unfulfilled by his own success as a humorous writer, wounded by the criticism of his plays, frustrated by what he saw to be his failures, and grieved by the death of his brother, Nikolai, of consumption — Chekhov sought an escape from his dramaturgical efforts. He wished to purify himself of the only source of bitterness in his life to date: the theatre.

In 1900, Chekhov made the historic journey across Siberia to the island of Sakhalin off the Pacific coast, to study the penal colonies and penal codes. In seeking to give expression to another side of himself, the doctor and humanitarian, the journey which concludes the 'Moscow period' was nonetheless born of spiritual need for Chekhov the serious playwright, a need which was finding a voice even before the opening of *The Wood Demon.*

"I was on the right track [in the writing of *Ivanov*], but the execution wasn't worth a damn. I should have waited!…One must be mature — that's the first thing; and second of all, one must have *a feeling of personal freedom,* and that feeling has only recently begun to develop in me. I didn't used to have it; its place has been successfully filled by my frivolity, carelessness, and lack of respect for my work."

to Suvorin, 1/7/89

"I should like to be a free artist, and I only regret that God hasn't given me the strength to become one…My holiest of holies is the human body, health, intelligence, talent, inspiration, love and *the most absolute freedom* — freedom from violence and lying, in whatever forms they may take. That is the program I would follow if I were a great artist."

to Pleshcheev, 10/89

This urgent reach for spiritual freedom which marks the culmination of the Moscow period is further expressed by Chekhov in a letter to his publisher:

> Write a story about this, will you… how a young man, the son of a serf, a former shopkeeper, choir boy, school boy and student, taught to respect rank, to kiss the priests' hands, to worship the ideas of others, to be grateful for his daily bread, to appreciate a beating, who went to school without galoshes, who got into fist fights, who tortured little animals, who loved to dine at the home of rich relatives, who played the hypocrite before God and men for no reason at all other than the recognition of his own insignificance, — write how that young man is squeezing the slave out of himself drop by drop, and how he wakes up one fine morning and feels that in his veins there flows no longer the blood of a slave, but true human blood…"

to Suvorin, 1/7/89

The journey to Sakhalin provides a special landmark for Chekhov the dramatist, the beginning of a six year hiatus in serious full-length playwrighting. For it was on this journey and in the years to follow that Chekhov gained this vital feeling of personal freedom, which, more than the acquiring of technique and skill, permitted the four major plays to be born. As his character

Konstantin Gavrilovich would say six years later in Chekhov's first major play, *The Seagull*:

> "…it's not about forms, old forms or new forms, it's about writing, not bound by any forms at all, just writing freely, from the soul".
>
> The Seagull, *Act IV*

THE MELIKHOVO PERIOD: 1892–1899

> "I do not intend to write dramas. I don't care for the work."
>
> *to Suvorin, 11/11/93*

The six year hiatus between *The Wood Demon* (1889) and the completion of the first draft of *The Seagull* (1895) was a period of great personal growth for Chekhov, a period in which his quest for freedom found expression. His arduous journey by land to Sakhalin, and back by sea, took over a year and had a significant spiritual impact on him; the separation from Moscow life was crucial in giving him the perspective he knew he needed for his growth as a dramatist. Once back in Russia, wanderlust overtook him again, and he left for western Europe. Finally, in 1892, he fulfilled a dream: the purchase of an 'estate' (actually, a picturesque 'dacha' on several hundred acres of land) about fifty miles southeast of Moscow, a place he chose to do his writing away from Moscow and his family (who, of course, joined him there, subsequently). Once installed in Melikhovo, he joined vigorously in the fight against the cholera epidemic, practicing medicine from his tiny estate. His social consciousness inspired by the Sakhalin trip, he threw himself into social reform efforts in Serpukhov, the district in which his estate was located, building schools with his own funds, and starting other programs to benefit the peasant population. During this period, his productivity in short story writing decreased to a handful a year (it had been in the dozens during the '80s).

Above all, it was the love of Melikhovo which filled Chekhov during this period — the love of nature and of the Russian countryside, and it was this spirit that was to enrich and inform the plays he wrote there, *The Seagull* and *Uncle Vanya*. It is an enchanting place: Would that every actor performing Chekhov might be able to visit it, for the country setting, so alive in the plays, is inspiring!

> "Imagine this: 575 acres, 432 of them wooded, two ponds, a scraggly stream, a new house, an orchard, a piano, three horses, cows, a spring-less carriage, a drozhky, carts, a sleigh, hotbeds, two dogs, birdhouses for starlings, and other items…and it's farewell to Moscow! Come see us, Sasha, you can stay in the chicken coop …There are fish in the ponds, mushrooms in the woods, the air is fresh and pure…I shall try to pay off the mortgage in four years."
>
> *to Aleksandr Chekhov, 2/23/92*

It is still lovingly preserved with its original furniture, colorful wallpaper, family photographs, memorabilia, and all the domestic and personal accoutrements — even the family 'lotto' game! The small, charming rooms are flooded with light, the colorful gardens are delightful, the pond (not nearly as large as Nina's lake) nonetheless is appropriately moody and evocative, the woods are mysterious and beckoning. The presence of the writer who loved his 'estate' so dearly is still felt.

Many of Chekhov's Moscow artist and literary friends flocked there during the early Melikhovo years (1892–95) (some weekends, guests would sleep on the floor of the hall) to enjoy the idyllic surroundings and to walk through the woods — he had a large bell installed on the grounds which tolled at midday to summon everyone to lunch. Chekhov could never refuse their company, an invitation for distraction from his work which was to plague him all his writing life, but an area in which he remained hopelessly vulnerable. The beauty of nature, which Chekhov romanticized in his plays of the '80s, was now a real part of his life. And his appreciation of nature and his surroundings was also augmented by another factor — the shadow of his ever-present illness.

The Seagull

> "Yes, I shall write a play…I don't feel like writing a drama, but I don't have an idea for a comedy yet. I'll probably sit down and write a play in the fall…"
>
> *to Suvorin, 4/18/95*

> "I'm going to write something strange."
>
> *to Suvorin, 5/5/95*

How Chekhov conceived of *The Seagull* is not notated in his letters; unlike *Ivanov* and *The Wood Demon*, for which he wrote letters of lengthy 'explication du texte,' he wrote none, other than a series of letters in October – November, 1895, marking his progress on the manuscript. The following letter is the first mention of it.

> "Can you imagine it — I am writing a play which I shall probably not finish before the end of November. I am writing it not without pleasure, though I abuse the conventions of the stage terribly. It's a comedy, there are three *[sic]* women's parts, six *[sic]* men's parts, four acts, landscapes (view over a lake); a great deal of conversation about literature, very little action, lots of love."
>
> *to Suvorin, 10/21/95*

But it must have already been taking shape in his dramatic imagination. Indeed, events in the lives of his fellow artists and friends who visited him in Melikhovo served as a rich resource for the play. They lie like hidden treasures in much of his correspondence from 1892–95. In the early spring of 1892, for example, Chekhov wrote to his publisher, Suvorin, describing a hunting expedition he took with his friend Isaac Levitan, the gifted, depressive landscape artist, in which Chekhov described with sang-froid the shooting of a woodcock: "One less beautiful, loving creature on this earth," wrote Chekhov, "while two fools returned home and sat down to supper." *(4/8/92)*. Subsequently, Levitan attempted suicide twice, and the second instance led Chekhov to an estate in the north, near the Finland border, by a lake filled with seagulls, where Levitan was staying. This visit was in the summer of 1895, two months before Chekhov sat down to start the first draft.

Biographers and literary historians enjoy supplying detail of the lives of numerous artists and friends close to Chekhov during the Melikhovo period, which may have contributed to the conceptualization of *The Seagull*. In addition to Levitan, there were no less than three young ladies named 'Lydia' in Chekhov's life at the time, details of whose lives appear in the play: Lydia Mizinova, a friend of Chekhov's sister Masha, whose unrequited love for Chekhov drove her into the arms of a writer, Potapenko, resulting in the birth of their illegitimate child who subsequently died (Potapenko, also a friend of Chekhov, accused Chekhov of patterning the character 'Trigorin' after him); Lydia Yavorskaya, an actress who was fond of embracing Chekhov at soirées and proclaiming that he was "the last page of her life"; and Lydia Avilova, an intense young short story writer who pursued Chekhov for his mentorship and bestowed upon him a love-gift engraved with a line from his short story *The Neighbors,* saying: "If ever you have need of my life, then come and take it." Some suggest that the inclusion of these personal details from the lives of Chekhov's friends was an aspect of Chekhov-the-practical-joker now matured into Chekhov-the-playful-ironist. But some of the subjects took these messages from the stage to heart, and the effects were sometimes inadvertently cruel, as in the case of two of the Lydias who loved Chekhov deeply and who felt his rejections keenly. To what extent one may chose to emphasize these biographical details as a source of inspiration for *The Seagull* — indeed, to what extent one may also theorize that Treplev and Trigorin are aspects of Chekhov the writer himself, it is of interest nonetheless in understanding the mysteries of Chekhov's own creative processes as a dramatist. It can also delight an actor's imagination with the thought that Chekhov was carefully crafting his roles with rich and colorful detail from people whose lives he knew intimately.

All these details from Chekhov's life — the beautiful surroundings, the stimulation of his fellow artists, the love affairs of his friends — served to provide rich material for his dramatist's imagination. But a deeper source of *The Seagull* is in Chekhov's own love of art: his lifelong passion for literature, his fascination with creativity, his obsession with the creative process, his own tempestuous love affair with the theatre, and all the energy these passions brought to bear. He was ready to breathe dramatic life into the literary theories he had been expressing in his letters of the Moscow period, into all the dreams and frustrations of his life as a writer and artist. His dramatic imagination was poised to take flight.

From the correspondence in late 1895, when Chekhov finished the first draft, behind the characteristic tone of self-deprecation and flippancy, there is a sense of excitement and anticipation that he had written something new.

> "I began it 'forte,' and ended it 'pianissimo' — contrary to all the rules of dramatic art. It came out more like a long tale. I am more dissatisfied than satisfied with it, and reading over my newborn play, once again I am convinced that I am not a dramatist at all. The acts are very short, and there are four of them…I'll send you a copy. Only don't let anyone else read it."
>
> *to Suvorin, 11/21/95*

During the next months, Chekhov waited nervously while it was typed, then sent it to his publisher, Suvorin, and next to the Theatre and Literary Committee (a censoring body), before whom plays must appear before they might be staged at imperial theatres. They gave approval in September 1995 with requests for minor revisions (for example, Chekhov had to omit certain references Konstantin Gavrilovich makes to his mother in Act I, which included her smoking, drinking, and living openly with "that novelist").

The ill-fated story of *The Seagull*'s first production is legendary in theatre history. By September it was too late to be included in the prestigious Maly Theatre's repertory for the current season, where Chekhov had hoped to have it staged, so it was offered to one of the actresses in the Alexandrinsky Theatre in St. Petersburg for her benefit performance — Levkeeva, a popular comedic leading lady of the day. It is surprising that Chekhov would ever have agreed to it, and equally so that the actress would choose it, but since he was the author of popular farces, and had titled *The Seagull* 'a comedy,' she therefore agreed without reading the play. It was to appear on a double bill, with the actress appearing in a comedy to follow Chekhov's play, which meant that the audience's expectations were for an evening of popular and broad entertainment. The play had only nine days of rehearsal; on the fourth day, the actress playing Nina was replaced by the well-known and gifted actress Vera Kommisarzhevskaya, who, according to Chekhov, was the only one in the cast who had any sense of his play. Thus in an atmosphere of artistic disunity, ill-preparation, and utter dread, Chekhov attended the disastrous opening night on October 17, 1896, where, after hearing the boisterous, derisive laughter during Nina's speech in the play-within-the play of Act I, and the responses to the subsequent acts, he took refuge in the dressing rooms and ultimately fled the theatre. He returned to the flat of his publisher at 2 AM, and left early by train for Melikhovo the next day. In a series of letters over the following two months, he wrote of the horrors of opening night, his sense of humiliation at the public ridicule, his indignation at the poor performances, but most of all, a sense of personal injury deeper than any of his 'failures' in the '80s:

> "Stop the publication of my plays. I shall never forget last evening...I shall not have that play produced in Moscow, ever. *Never* again shall I write plays or have them staged."
>
> *to Suvorin, 10/18/96*

First-hand accounts of this legendary opening night fiasco abound — in addition to Chekhov's own letters, there are the memoirs of his publishers, critics, and one of the Lydia's — the ever-hopeful Avilova, who eagerly awaited Chekhov's message from the stage. (As an ironic postscript to the locket which

Lydia gave Chekhov and which was used as a stage-prop in the play, Chekhov ultimately gave it to one of the actresses in the production).

A further irony of the first premiere is that, because the opening night audience was filled with Levkeeva's admirers, expecting a Chekhovian vaudeville, they derided the play. But by all reports, there were sold-out audiences at the second and third nights, packed with members of the Petersburg intelligentsia. Chekhov began to receive ecstatic reports of an artistic triumph! Traumatized by his first-hand opening night experience, he ignored them.

> "I feel nothing but loathing for my plays, and it is an effort for me to read the proofs. Again you'll say that this is silly, and unreasonable, that it is from conceit, pride, etc. etc. I know, but what can I do, tell me? I would gladly rid myself of that stupid feeling, but I cannot, I simply cannot. The reason is not that my play was a failure; indeed, that is true of most of my plays and every time it's like water off a duck's back. No — on October 17th, it was not my play, but I myself who failed."
>
> *to Suvorin, 12/14/96*

Equally as melodramatic is the contrast between the disastrous premiere of *The Seagull* and the jubilant opening night of the second production. While Chekhov was nursing his dramaturgical wounds and returning to short story writing, in May 1897, a momentous meeting took place at the Slavyansky Bazaar, a famous Moscow hotel, between playwright-director Vladimir Ivanovich Nemirovich-Danchenko and producer-actor Konstantin Sergeevich Alekseev, a. k. a. Stanislavsky. From that historic meeting (purportedly to have lasted almost eighteen hours), the Moscow Art Theatre was born — a nucleus of actors dedicated to creating a new school of acting, to break from the old, established conventions of the stage. Nemirovich was passionate about the genius of *The Seagull*, saying it was the only new play which excited him and that Chekhov was the only contemporary author of value, and pleaded with Chekhov to permit the Art Theatre to stage it in their inaugural season. Chekhov reluctantly agreed after a flurry of correspondence, and *The Seagull* was placed in the repertoire of the Moscow Art Theatre's first season in 1898. The cast would include a young actress (a student of Nemirovich) named Olga Knipper, later to be Chekhov's leading lady and wife, in the role of 'Arkadina,' and Stanislavsky as 'Trigorin.' The play was directed by the theatre's co-founders. Knipper wrote in her memoirs of the company's passion for the play, of how the play captured the actors' imagination completely and, indeed, became a part of their lives. This bond between the playwright and the company was to last throughout the collaborations on the four major plays, and remain in the hearts of the actors long after Chekhov's death.

The Seagull had its second premiere on December 17, 1898, and was a resounding success. The memoirs of Stanislavsky and Olga Knipper both describe the melodrama of opening night. The anxious cast had all taken valerian drops (the same prescription of Dr. Dorn in the text) to calm themselves, and were stunned when, after the curtain fell on Act I, there was a tumultuous roar of applause from the audience, and the actors stood on the stage before a hastily raised curtain, tears streaming down their faces. (Their memoirs differ only on the point of when the ecstatic erruption from the audience occurred — after Act I or III!) That night, the Art Theatre became 'Chekhov's Theatre,' and the relationship was forged that was to influence the canon of Chekhov's major plays as well as a company which would have a major presence in twentieth century theatre.

And yet, Chekhov never quite recovered from the fiasco of the first premiere. He lapsed into a new kind of detached anxiety about playwrighting, never trusting the affirmation of this exhilarating triumph and the promises it held for the future. Somehow, he could never overcome his sensitivity to the vicissitudes of the theatre.

> "My *Seagull* is being performed for the eighth time now in Moscow, and the theatre is filled to overflowing every night. They say that the play is unusually well-directed, and that the actors play their roles beautifully...Even so, I haven't the slightest desire to write any more plays. The Petersburg theatre cured me of that."
>
> *to Kommisarzhevskaya, 1/19/99*

Uncle Vanya

> "My plays are being printed with amazing slowness...two full-length plays are not yet included in any collection: *The Seagull*, known to you, and *Uncle Vanya*, unknown to anyone on earth..."
>
> *to Suvorin, 12/2/96*

Of all the major plays, *Uncle Vanya* is the one mentioned least in Chekhov's correspondence. Indeed, the actual date of the writing of *Uncle Vanya* remains a mystery in literary history — a mystery, one suspects, deliberately created by its author who may have been protecting himself from what he perceived to be his chronic failures as a serious dramatist. Though some literary historians place it earlier, most speculate that it was written sometime between November 1895 after the first draft of *The Seagull* was completed, and December 1896, when Chekhov first mentions it to his publisher. There is a second reason for this reticence — the text of *Uncle Vanya* is drawn significantly from the text of *The Wood Demon*, his earlier work, whose critical failure had wounded him so deeply in 1889. Among the changes: Dramaturgically, Chekhov reduced the number of characters from thirteen to nine, preserving seven of the original characters but reworking most of them significantly; he rewrote Acts I and IV; he reduced the length of the play by more than one-third; he removed numerous operatic and other musical allusions; and importantly, he altered the tone from a 'romantic comedy,' as he called it, to a far more contemplative play. Of significance is the metamorphosis of the two pivotal characters: Uncle George, who had shot himself at the end of Act III in *The Wood Demon*, becomes Uncle Vanya, who now shoots at the professor and misses, and Dr. Khrushchov (meaning a kind of 'beetle') becomes Dr. Astrov (meaning 'star') — details which only begin to suggest the significant spiritual transformation of both characters.

Of greatest significance is the transformation of the play's setting in the eyes of the dramatist: the country setting as a place for romance in *The Wood Demon* metamorphoses into 'scenes from country life' in *Uncle Vanya*, a place where the hardships of provincial life and the spiritual isolation and loneliness are now dramatized. And this transformation comes, it seems, from Chekhov's life in Melikhovo. Whereas during the '80s he visited the country only in the summertime, and in a social context, vacationing with his family or as a guest on the estate of a literary admirer, now he was in residence, fully participating in country life, managing his estate, planting and harvesting, sowing rye, tending the vegetable garden, planting orchards, managing the accounts, paying off the mortgage, participating in the community, cognizant of all the issues of peasant life. His letters dating from '92 to '96 are full of descriptions of nature surrounding his beloved 'estate,' his many humanitarian and philanthropic activities in the Serpukhov district of his estate, and his hands-on experiences as a country doctor. While they still reflect his love of nature, they are also tempered with the realities of country life which he experienced first-hand both as a landowner and a doctor — the difficulties of managing an estate, the horrors of the cholera epidemic, the misery and the intransigence of the peasant population, the violence, the alchoholism, the squalor of their lives. As soon as he arrived in Melikhovo, Chekhov was appointed as a cholera doctor, supervising care of twenty-five villages, four factories, and a monastery.

"As a cholera doctor, I see the sick, and sometimes I am overcome by it all, but really and truly, they are three times easier to bear with than discussions of literature with visitors from Moscow."

to Shcheglov, 10/24/92

Thus the ravages of the epidemic, the terrible weather, the impassable country roads, the brutal peasant life, the burdens of the estate — all the realities of country life, experienced first-hand by Chekhov himself during the Melikhovo years from 1892–1896, transformed *The Wood Demon* into *Uncle Vanya*. It also transformed Chekhov's romantization of nature in the 1880s into a broader perception of nature not only as a place of beauty, but also of isolation and mystery, a place of forces sometimes beyond the control and comprehension of man.

The play was first produced in 1897 in the provinces — Odessa, Kiev, Saratov, and Tbilis, with positive responses. Then, after the exhilarating success of *The Seagull* in '98, the Moscow Art Theatre begged Chekhov for the rights to produce *Uncle Vanya* in its '99 season. Chekhov had already promised it to the Maly Theatre, but they demanded changes in the text as a condition for production (for example, the theatre's literary board considered it improper for a character on stage to shoot at a professor with a doctoral degree!) Chekhov flatly refused to make changes, and gave permission to the Moscow Art Theatre to produce it, with Olga Knipper cast as 'Yelena' and Stanislavsky playing 'Astrov.'

Although the theatre continued to be a source of anxiety for him, he was, on the other hand, fascinated with all aspects of pre-production. He insisted on being informed and involved in the everyday life of the company during rehearsals, demanding reports even when he was away from Moscow. Stanislavsky was, as usual, over-extended; he was working as an actor and director in other productions of the company's repertoire (as well as managing his family factories); he frequently missed rehearsals and Nemirovich had to remonstrate him to learn his lines, not to knock props and furniture about during rehearsals, and not to indulge himself in "actor moments." And his interpretation of Astrov differed from Chekhov's intentions: "When he directs, he's an artist, but when he acts, he's just a rich young merchant who wants to dabble in art…" Chekhov wrote to Olga Knipper *(10/4/99)*.

Uncle Vanya opened at the Art Theatre on October 26, 1899. Though reviews were mixed, the audiences were much moved, and it was considered the second great success in the collaboration of Chekhov and the Moscow Art

Theatre. The artists of the theatre were bound more than ever to the work of Anton Chekhov.

Chekhov saw neither of the two openings of his plays, *The Seagull* and *Uncle Vanya,* at the Moscow Art Theatre. In March of '97, following the completion of *Uncle Vanya,* he experienced his most violent hemorrhage to date, causing him to face the realization of the seriousness of his condition, and prompting doctors to urge him to move to the South. With reluctance, Chekhov gave up his medical practice at Melikhovo, and started to spend longer periods of time in Yalta, convalescing. Following the death of his father in 1898, he moved permanently to Yalta in the late fall of '99. However, he came to Moscow in the spring of '99 and a performance of *The Seagull* was put on especially for him at the Moscow Art Theatre. Chekhov was excited by the production — but not particularly pleased with Stanislavsky's interpretation of Trigorin (he was too reserved to tell Stanislavsky of his displeasure to his face, but simply said that his costume was wrong — that Trigorin would wear scuffed shoes and baggy trousers, and that his fishing rod would be handmade, observations that seem superficial but which, in Chekhov's characteristically laconic, subtle style, hinted at vital insights into the heart of the character).

Chekhov saw *Uncle Vanya* performed in Yalta in the spring of 1900, when the Moscow Art Theatre, to celebrate the centennial and to honor their beloved author, toured through Yalta and presented *Uncle Vanya* there. They brought with them the swing and the bench from Act I, which they placed in his garden near his orchard of almond trees.

THE YALTA PERIOD: 1899–1904

"I feel I've been living in Yalta for a million years."

to Korobov, 1/29/00

The Three Sisters

"I promise to be a splendid husband some day, but give me a wife who, like the moon, does not appear in my sky every night. P. S. — I won't write any better for having gotten married."

to Suvorin, 3/23/95

The writing of *The Three Sisters* was very much entwined with the growing love affair between Chekhov and Olga Knipper during the year 1900. Indeed, it is interesting to note that the first two major plays, *The Seagull* and *Uncle Vanya,* were already written before the Art Theatre sought to obtain their rights. This distinguishes *The Three Sisters* as the first of the major plays which Chekhov wrote expressly for the Art Theatre and the members of its company.

In the spring of 1900, to celebrate the centennial, the Moscow Art Theatre toured through the south of Russia, performing *Uncle Vanya* in Yalta for Chekhov. It was an exciting time — the first year of the centennial, and Gorky, Tolstoy, Bunin, Kuprin, Rachmaninov and other writers and artists flocked to Yalta to join Chekhov and the Moscow Art Theatre in celebration of the beginning of a new century. Chekhov entertained the troupe nightly till three each morning; he was exhilarated, exhausted, and in love again, with the theatre and with Olga Knipper.

A few months later, Olga returned to Yalta, and biographers delight in pointing out that the subsequent correspondence reflects a new intimacy between them (from "you" to "thou"). After the visits of the Art Theatre company and Olga, Chekhov was left alone to face his feeling of spiritual exile.

> "…I am again in Yalta, in my prison. A cruel wind is blowing, the cutter isn't running, the sea is tossing violently, people are drowning, there is no rain, everything is drying up, everything is withering — in fact, since you left, it has been absolutely awful here. Without you I shall hang myself. Be well, and happy, my good little German. Don't get depressed, sleep soundly, and write to me more often. I kiss you passionately, passionately, four hundred times."
>
> *to Olga Knipper, 8/13/00*

Separation from the Russian countryside he loved in Melikhovo was painful enough, but now the distance from Moscow was insurmountable. Moscow was where Olga was, where the Art Theatre was, where the glamorous literary and theatre life (for which Chekhov had such an abiding ambivalence) was.

But there was also the growing realization that his declining health might make it a permanent place of exile, and this realization called out for expression. The yearning call "to Moscow," which was to become the three sisters,' was not to be theirs alone, but Chekhov's, too.

> "My sweet, I don't know when I am coming to Moscow, I just don't know, because, if you can imagine, I am actually writing a play right now. Well, not a play, but a sort of muddle. There are a great many characters, — perhaps I shall get frustrated and give it up."
>
> *to Olga Knipper, 8/14/00*

While the actual writing of *The Three Sisters* occurred from August to October 1900, the first mention of it in Chekhov's correspondence is in late 1899, in a letter to Nemirovich, reporting that he had the plot for a new play, but would not begin writing until he'd finished several stories he'd been working on (one being *On Official Duty*, begun just after he had moved to Yalta, in which he was already developing the 'Moscow theme'). Naturally, the Art Theatre was eager to have a new play from Chekhov for its third season (1900–01), since its first two seasons had been so greatly enhanced by his work. The Moscow Art Theatre now was publically recognized as 'Chekhov's theatre,' and he as its dramatist.

In the correspondence from August to October 1900, Chekhov reported enormous difficulty with the writing of the play: his chronic frustration with the process, his continuing doubt of his dramatic skills, his concern that the play was dramaturgically awkward and more novelistic than theatrical, that it had too many characters, that it was boring, unclear, even vulgar, and so on. He wrote to his brother that this was the most difficult play to date in the writing; in another, he reported that one of the sisters had developed a limp, thereby slowing the process even more! Moreover, he complained of constant interruptions by admirers in Yalta, a phenomenon which was to plague him through the writing of *The Cherry Orchard* as well, though he was too sensitive and discreet to refuse his eager visitors. His correspondence to Olga Knipper during the time was laced with innuendo, half-teasing half-serious, that perhaps he'd let the play sit for a while, and let it breathe, "like a pie put out on the table" *(9/28/00)*, since he wasn't sure it would be ready for the current season. And yet, the play was already announced for that season, so the company was desperately eager to have it. Perhaps all these machinations and complaints had become Chekhov's own defense against writing in the medium he both loved and dreaded.

As for other sources of *The Three Sisters* in Chekhov's dramatic imagination, Chekhov wrote to Gorky *(10/16/00)* that *The Three Sisters* takes place in a remote Russian "provincial town, like Perm" (which is actually a town on the Kama River in the Ural Mountains, over 800 miles from Moscow, not even as far as Yalta is from Moscow). According to Mikhail, Chekhov's younger brother, the source of Chekhov's knowledge of the military was in a town called Voskresensk near Moscow, where Ivan, another of Chekhov's brothers, was a teacher in an elementary school. In this town, where the Chekhov family came for their summer holidays, there was also a military battery. The family became close with the officers, according to Mikhail (one of the officers reportedly proposed to Masha, Chekhov's sister).

The source of the three sisters themselves is another story, particularly the character of 'Masha,' whom some biographers feel is of particular significance — her mercurial moods, her rages, her depressions, her beauty, her intelligence, her artistic temperament — because she is so close to the essence of Olga Knipper herself. The biography *Chekhov's Leading Lady* makes wonderful reading for any actress playing Masha, and the extent of the derivation of Masha in Olga Knipper herself can be the domain of the actress's own imagination. (Evidently, even the details of Dr. Chebutykin's prescription to cure baldness came from Olga Knipper's uncle himself, who, like Chebutykin, also loved to drink. And the love song which Masha and Vershinin sing in the third act was one which Olga herself told Chekhov that a former lover used to sing to her — another one of Chekhov's little dramaturgical 'messages' similar to Nina's locket). The Chekhovian roles Olga Knipper had played — 'Arkadina' and 'Yelena' — were written before they met. But 'Masha' was the first role he wrote expressly for her.

> "Ah, what a part there is for you in *The Three Sisters*. What a part! If you give me ten rubles you can have it, otherwise I'll give it to another actress."
>
> *to Knipper, 9/28/00*

Chekhov attended the first reading by the Moscow Art Theatre in the fall of 1900. He was quite upset by the actors' response of perplexity and confusion, and could not understand why they felt the tone was so dark.

> "*The Three Sisters* is finished, but its future, at least its immediate future, is unknown to me. The play has turned out to be dreary, drawn-out and awkward... The mood, as they say, is gloomier than gloom... The play is as complicated as a novel, and the mood of it, they tell me, is deadly."
>
> *to Komissarzhevskaya, 11/13/00*

Originally, Chekhov had hoped to be present during rehearsals at the Moscow Art Theatre for *The Three Sisters*.

"Four crucial female roles, four young intelligent women, — I can't leave that to Stanislavsky, no matter how much respect I have for his talent and understanding. No, I'll have to keep an eye on rehearsals."

to Olga Knipper, 10/15/00

Now, however, discouraged by the response of the company, frustrated with anxiety over the upcoming rehearsals, and plagued by ill health, Chekhov retreated to Nice, where he mailed rewrites to Nemirovich. He wrote to Olga daily, begging for details of the rehearsal process, wary of Stanislavsky, who was again directing, and whose tendency to interpret Chekhov's plays as tragedies, to pace them slowly, and to overload them with sound effects not indicated in the text, elicited Chekhov's strong disapproval. Stanislavsky wrote copious and enthusiastic correspondence about the rehearsals' progress. At the eleventh hour, Stanislavsky took over the role of Vershinin, under Nemirovich's direction.

Masha, Chekhov's sister, reported that she wept with emotion at the dress rehearsals; Chekhov, overwrought with anxiety, fled from Nice to Italy, so that he was unreachable on the opening night, January 31, 1901. Indeed, the news did not reach him of the opening until February 15, after he had returned to Yalta. Despite mixed reviews, Olga was singled out for praise by the critics, the run was sold out, and the play was considered a success for the Moscow Art Theatre. Again, despite the criticism, the 'literati' and the theatre community recognized the newness of the plays of Anton Chekhov.

On May 25, 1901, following Moscow and St. Petersburg productions of *The Three Sisters*, Chekhov and Olga were married in a church outside Moscow. There are confusing and ambiguous reports of the details surrounding this event. Evidently, the couple planned a reception where Chekhov's family awaited them — then deliberately didn't appear, went to a church at a separate location, and were married with no witnesses from the family to whom he had been devoted all his life. The ceremony proceeded, despite the curious fact that Chekhov had somehow failed to bring his passport from Yalta, a document needed for the marriage ceremony.

"My darling, how hard it was for me to write that play."

to Knipper, 10/12/03

"Ich sterbe." *7/02/04*

The Cherry Orchard was by far the longest in writing of any of the four plays — ten months in duration. That was because of the constant interruptions due to visitors and his declining health. The long shadow of his illness was darkening.

That Chekhov knew this would be his last one is perhaps the source of inspiration for this play, and possibly one of the causes for his procrastination in the writing of it. Many distractions presented themselves. Following his marriage in the spring of 1901, Chekhov fell ill again and had to return to Yalta, while Olga returned to Moscow to the Art Theatre. That winter, both Gorky and Tolstoy came to the Crimea, providing a welcome diversion. Following Olga's visit to Yalta in early 1902, she suffered a miscarriage, and then contracted peritonitis; Chekhov was therefore preoccupied with her care while she convalesced during the summer of 1902 on Stanislavsky's estate near Moscow. (Actually, while there, Chekhov ran across an eccentric English governess, whom some think is the prototype of Charlotta. Stanislavsky claims that the setting in Act I of *The Cherry Orchard* was inspired by the drawing room on his estate, where Chekhov spent time during his visit).

It was during 1902 that Stanislavsky renewed his pressure on Chekhov to write a new play for the Art Theatre — a comedy for which Chekhov had an idea as early as the fall of 1901, and had already mentioned to him. What he was hiding from Stanislavsky and from Olga, behind his characteristic playfulness, his persistent complaints of 'ennui' and self-doubt, was the fact that the labor of writing a play, with his sharply declining health, was now a physical torture for him.

"No, I'm not writing my play, and I don't feel like writing it, there are too many dramatists around nowadays, and anyway, writing plays is a boring, depressing and ordinary occupation…"

to Knipper, 3/16/02

"That I am going to write my play is as certain as two times two equals four, only if I'm well, of course; but whether it will succeed, whether anything will come of it — I really don't know…. Ach! what masses of subjects there are in my head, how I'm longing to write, but I feel there is something missing, somehow — either in my surroundings, or in my health… I should not be living in Yalta, that's what! I may as well be in Asia Minor."

to Olga Knipper, 1/23/03

Instead, in late 1902, he turned to a dramaturgical task which had some special consolation — the chronic rewriting of his vaudeville *On the Harmful Effects of Tobacco,* now in its sixth draft, and the writing of a short story, *The Bride.* The latter was to be his last story, and it took him months to write it. As he used *On Official Duty* for *The Three Sisters,* so he used *The Bride* to explore a theme of *The Cherry Orchard* — the twilight of the beautiful, gracious estate life in Russia. (The story tells of an idealistic young granddaughter who leaves her grandmother's estate and goes to Moscow in pursuit of a young student who has awakened her social consciousness: prototypes of Anya and Trofimov).

Chekhov felt the end of his own life approaching, but he also felt keenly the turning tides of a new century. Tolstoy once remarked that Chekhov was one of the most 'Russian' of all the writers he knew. As a writer, Chekhov was close to the heartbeat of Russia; he recognized, in his nondidactic way, the end of an era for Russia and the dawn of a new one. This dual consciousness — of the ebbing of Russia's life and of his own — is evident in his initial vision of the play: an old lady, an old manservant, an orchard all in white, and ladies in white dresses. Part of this initial vision also included the most haunting sound effect which Chekhov put in any of his plays, an actual sound he remembered from his youth: While fishing near the Don once, he heard a strange far-off sound, which he thought was coming from the sky, but which turned out to be a falling bucket in a distant coal mine shaft. He had never used this recollection before; it was as if it were somehow meant to be saved for this final vision (as he had saved so many details from his life for his plays and stories). Chekhov pointed out the new play's superficial differences from its predecessors — no gun, no doctor, and no love. But there were larger issues. Perhaps this insistence that the play be called a comedy reflects a wish to recognize the beginning of a new century with a vision of optimism and hope: "Good-bye, old life!" "Hello, new life!" as Anya and Trofimov, his two young characters, say. And yet, in the subtle mixture of comedic and dramatic tone of the play, he was making his own sober prediction about a future he knew he would not live to see.

From February till October of 1903, while he struggled with the writing of the play, Olga may have not realized how seriously ill Chekhov was. She repeatedly pressured him, along with Stanislavsky and Nemirovich — even remonstrated him for what she termed his laziness, to finish it in time for the upcoming season. In fact, there were days when he could only write a few lines, owing to the increased feeling of weakness, headaches, and the constant coughing. His letters during this period are particularly touching; they do not communicate the agonizing doubts about his dramaturgical abilities as before, but rather constant apologizies for his illness, pleas that his wife no longer be angry with him for his slowness, and reassurances to all that the play was forthcoming.

Chekhov mailed the manuscript from Yalta to the Art Theatre in October; Stanislavsky telegraphed Chekhov immediately that, upon the first reading, the company wept copiously, further irritating Chekhov, who insisted he had written a comedy. Then followed a series of letters to Knipper, Nemirovich, and Stanislavsky, giving brief but extremely detailed descriptions of the characters, as well as specific casting recommendations. Of all the four major plays, Chekhov's correspondence on *The Cherry Orchard* is of most value as a resource for theatre artists, in terms of his own specific vision of the play and the characters. The role he first thought of for Olga Knipper was Varya, then Charlotta (Chekhov didn't think Olga should or could play the part of 'an old woman,' and was irritated that despite his advance notice, the theatre had not found an older actress for the role. Olga proceeded to play it beautifully, by all critical reports, and it was a role she was to repeat throughout her life). He wrote the role of Lopakhin for Stanislavsky, who refused to play a merchant (even though he came from a merchant family! Stanislavsky chose Gaev, the aristocrat, for himself). Fearing a negative response by critics, Stanislavsky decided to schedule the opening night on January 17, 1904 — Chekhov's birthday, to celebrate the twenty-fifth anniversary of his work as a writer, hoping that the sight of the ailing dramatist would soften any potential critical blows. The reluctant Chekhov had to be summoned from his Moscow flat and coerced on stage, coughing, after the third act, for a forty-five minute testimonial on opening night. Despite the audience's emotional response to his much weakened appearance, Stanislavsky's plan was not altogether successful. Again, the reviews were mixed.

Chekhov died six months later, and never wrote another play after *The Cherry Orchard*. He had in mind a new play: about a group of arctic explorers on a voyage, with the spirit of the hero's lover haunting him on board, and the ship crushed by polar ice, but he never lived to write it. Even a month before he died, despite all the accolades which his four major plays had brought him, he persisted in feeling misunderstood as a dramatist. Weeks before his death, he wrote to Olga about *The Cherry Orchard*:

> "Why do they insist on calling my play a drama on the posters and the press announcements? Nemirovich and Stanislavsky absolutely do not see what I wrote, and I am ready to give you my word, however you want it, that neither of them has ever read my play carefully, not even once…
>
> *to Knipper, 4/10/04*

Three months after the opening of *The Cherry Orchard,* in response to his declining health, Chekhov's doctors sent him abroad to Germany with Olga Knipper. They took up residence in a spa in Badenweiler. The story of his death and burial reads like one of his own ironic stories. On the night of July 2, Chekhov asked his wife to summon the German doctor. "Ich sterbe," he said, and asked for a glass of champagne. He drank it, and died peacefully. His body was shipped to Russia by train in a car marked 'oysters' (one of his favorite indulgences). The train was met in the Moscow station by a military band (not for Chekhov, but for a high-ranking military official on the same train); he was buried in the cemetery of the Novo-Devichy Monastery, the same place as the mother of Olga, Masha, and Irina.

CHEKHOV AND THE DRAMATIC FORM

> "We need new forms. We must have new forms, and if we don't, we may as well have nothing at all."
>
> *Konstantin Gavrilovich, in* The Seagull, *Act I*

> ". . . I began it 'forte' and ended it 'pianissimo' — contrary to all the rules of dramatic art."
>
> *to Suvorin, about* The Seagull *11/21/95*

> " . . . I have written such a farce."
>
> *to Knipper about* The Three Sisters, *12/15/00*

"I haven't written a drama [*The Cherry Orchard*], no, it's a comedy and, in places, even a farce."

to Lilina (Mme. Stanislavsky), 9/15/03

"The last act is gay — yes, and the whole play is gay, lighthearted, carefree."

to Knipper 9/20/03

Chekhov's major plays take place in his own times, and are set on country estates (or in the case of *The Three Sisters*, in a grand house in a provincial town). His plays are inhabited primarily by the landed gentry and other members of the educated and privileged classes. While his settings and their inhabitants may not have been new to the Russian theatre, his treatments of them were. Seen as a whole, these four plays had a new and distinct presence all their own on the Russian stage.

Clearly, both the public, the critics, and the actors of Chekhov's times, who saw and performed in his major plays, recognized their 'newness.' And despite his persistent doubts as to his own abilities as a serious dramatist, Chekhov, too, knew that he was writing in 'new forms.'

This 'newness' is challenging to describe. Chekhov broke free from the conventions of Ostrovskian drama and its standards of plot and characterization, which had influenced the Russian theatre since the 1850s. But how do we define this 'newness'? The terms 'realism' and 'naturalism' as applied to Chekhov's plays, which one encounters in literary history and criticism, can be problematic, because the definition of these terms changes with every decade and with the appearance of more 'new' writers for the stage, whose work challenges us to redefine our terminology. Chekhov himself scoffed at the description of his plays as 'realistic', saying that one could hardly surgically remove a nose from a portrait, substitute it with a real one, and still call it 'art.' His contemporaries recognized the 'newness' of his plays and expressed it in a variety of ways: Stanislavsky and Nemirovich thought them to be unique, and praised their freshness and simplicity; Gorky noted the originality of the form and the broad scope of the ideas; Knipper, from the actors' perspective, spoke of the remarkable world of the Chekhovian play, and how actors loved to live in it.

Chekhov himself put it best, when he said he strove to put "life as it is" upon the stage: what he set out to do in *Ivanov* in the '80s and had to struggle for almost two decades to give it expression in the later, major plays.

"Artistic literature is called artistic for the very reason that it depicts life as it really is. Its aim is truth — absolute and honest."

to Kiseleva, 1/14/87

I think the sense of 'newness' lies in a unique combination of dramatic elements: the four-act form; the deliberate lack of strong dramatic plot or action; the life of an ensemble on stage; the remarkably rich character portrayals, so detailed, so subtlely and gracefully drawn; the atmosphere evoked by a very specific 'mis-en-scène'; the simple details of everyday life, but surrounding them, the sense of a much vaster landscape; and, finally, the tragicomedic tone.

Chekhov introduced a new notion of dramatic action, in seeking to depict "life as it is" on the stage. To achieve this, he refined his craft, purging it of some of the more conventional melodramatic features of his plays of the '80s. In the major plays, there are no 'Ivanovs' who shoot themselves onstage. All significant action takes place offstage, while onstage, there is "life as it is": arrivals, sojourns, departures, and the trivial details of daily existence — tea-taking, card-playing, small domestic events and entertainments, and a great deal of talking. Chekhov also introduced 'living characters' to the Russian stage — which he had been struggling to do in his plays of the '80s — full, human characters with rich inner lives, with emotional and psychological complexities, with spirituality, and at the same time, with colorful outward 'behavior.' For the Moscow Art Theatre, whose founding purpose was to create a new school of acting for the Russian stage, the challenge which these new plays and characters presented was ideal.

Chekhov also brought a strong new visual aesthetic to the Russian stage. His 'mis-en-scènes' in the major plays are sharp and specific for each of the four acts, with reference to time of day, season, climate, light, sound, and the strong presence of nature and the elements. Serving as the backdrop to the detail of everyday life, these richly textured settings created a mood, as Stanislavsky said — they paint the larger picture of each play, as the story moves from act to act, from exterior to interior (or the reverse), as spaces contract, empty and darken, as weather changes, as time passes. Specific scenic elements: a small stage, a mounted seagull, a samovar, a piano, a clock — and specific sounds: a night watchman knocking, a lonely gun shot, a breaking string, an axe falling against a tree — stand out in sharp relief. Like a pointilist painter, Chekhov introduced a new aesthetic, one of detail, translucence, and depth, and his plays have an evocative 'atmosphere' all their own.

Above all, it was the 'tone' of the Chekhov play that was new. For the contemporary ensemble performing the plays, the 'tone' is the most important aspect to achieve — and yet the most illusive. To strive for this tone, an appreciation of the comedy-drama conflict between Chekhov and Stanislavsky is particularly useful. Chekhov insisted to his dying day that all his major plays were comedies. He titled *The Seagull* and *The Cherry Orchard* as such, he called *Uncle Vanya* 'scenes from country life' and *The Three Sisters* 'a drama', though in the case of the latter, he later clarified his intention and insisted that it was a comedy, too.

Whether Chekhov's plays were comedies (he being alone and adamant in this opinion) or dramas, even tragedies, as Stanislavsky maintained, is a topic that has provoked misunderstandings and misinterpretations of Chekhov's plays then and today. The debate was alive throughout the production of the four major plays at the Moscow Art Theatre, and intensified following the reading of *The Three Sisters*, when some actors commented that it was a drama, even a tragedy. This frustrated Chekhov terribly. According to Stanislavsky, Chekhov sincerely thought he had written a comedy and that because the actors had wept over it, the play was misunderstood and therefore a failure. The difference of opinion over whether his major plays were comedies or dramas came to a peak during the preparation for the production of *The Cherry Orchard*. In a telegram to Chekhov on October 21, 1903, Stanislavsky describes the thrilled response of the company and observers to the first reading of *The Cherry Orchard*, and how they were all moved to tears. This infuriated Chekhov. He blamed Stanislavsky for what he felt was a distortion of his comedic intent. When Stanislavsky pointed out the many references in the text to the characters who speak "in tears" or "through tears," Chekhov retorted that that was not what he meant. Some theatre historians maintain that his irritability on this subject, bordering on irrationality, was further exacerbated by his declining health. Perhaps, with *The Cherry Orchard*, he deliberately titled it a 'comedy' because he knew it would be his last work, and wanted to end his literary oeuvre as such. Perhaps he meant to suggest a subtle and special irony in his insistence on calling it a 'comedy'. One must continue to search for the author's intent behind this insistence, in order to do his plays justice on the stage.

Finding the special tone of the Chekhov play — also referred to by Stanislavsky as 'Chekhovian mood' — is combining all the aforementioned dramatic elements. It also means dealing with both perspectives, the comedic and the tragic, and seeing them as coexistent, rather than mutually exclusive. Indeed, it was their disagreement that brought Stanislavsky to the realization he expressed in *My Life in Art*: that the characters in Chekhov's plays do not indulge in their own sorrow, but rather reach, as Chekhov did himself, for life, joy, and laughter. They want to live life to its fullest. It is their struggle in face of the insurmountable obstacles in life that is both comedic and tragic at the same time.

For theatre artists of every generation, understanding Chekhov the man and his very special vision of life will help to understand why he called his plays comedies, and why his plays conclude, as Astrov puts it, with "Finita la commedia!" — because the plays are his special vision of 'the comedy of life' itself. Thus, the characters live through the events of the play, laughing through their tears, as the directions indicate, and meanwhile, the larger world view — the tragicomedy of life which Chekhov has written — comes alive on the stage.

CHEKHOV'S PLACE IN DRAMATIC LITERATURE

> "*The Seagull* is nonsense, nothing about it is true... It is altogether very weak..." "Really, I can't stand your plays. Shakespeare wrote badly, but you write worse."
>
> *Tolstoy, commenting to Chekhov on his work*

> "'Do you know for how many more years I shall be read?
> Seven.'
> 'Why?' I asked.
> 'All right, seven and a half, then...but I only have six years left to live. Don't go telling that to the Odessa newpapers, though.'
> He didn't even live for six years after that, only for a little more than one."
>
> *from Bunin, 'Chekhov,' in* Reminiscences

Despite Chekhov's comments in his autobiographical statement, his plays have been translated into many foreign languages and staged all over Russia, Europe, America, Asia, and throughout the world. The Moscow Art Theatre to this day continues to have his plays in its permanent repertoire. A history of productions of his plays in Britain has been recently documented in *Chekhov on the British Stage.* One of many examples of his great influence on our own American theatre can be found in *The Actors' Chekhov,* a series of interviews with American actors who performed at the Williamstown Theatre Festival over several decades and who express the impact Chekhov has had on their work as artists. At this American theatre, as at so many others here and all over the world, the spirit of Chekhov is alive today.

How would Chekhov wished to be placed in dramatic literature? He himself gives an indication of the Russian writers whom he admired, and the great tradition from which he was proud to emerge. References in the actual texts of the four major plays abound: Pushkin, Lermontov, Gogol, Turgenev, Ostrovsky,

Tolstoy, among others. Chekhov came from a great dramatic tradition in the Russian theatre. By the time he came on the scene, however, there seemed to have been a kind of vacuum. Ostrovsky had died in the 1880s, leaving over forty plays as part of the accepted permanent repertoire of the Russian theatre. Tolstoy, Dostoevsky, and Turgenev's impact was primarily with the novel. The plays of Saltykov-Shchedrin and Pisemsky, Chekhov's contemporaries (they died in the 1880s), had not taken a stronghold in contemporary theatre. The strongest new trend in Russian literature when Chekhov arrived upon the theatre scene was the Russian symbolist movement, most expressed in poetry. Although to some extent one might say that Chekhov satirizes the symbolists (also known as the 'decadents') in his treatment of Konstantin Gavrilovich's play-within-the-play in *The Seagull*, the exotic elements of the symbolist movement nonetheless fascinated Chekhov, and one can argue that there is subtle strain of poetic symbolism in the four major plays.

It is hard to measure all the influences on Chekhov. He was so aware and appreciative of Russian and world literature, it flowed in his blood stream. And yet, his voice is distinctly his own. He respected many Western writers, including Voltaire and Maupassant; he held Maeterlinck, Gerhart Hauptmann, and Strindberg in high regard. But the dramatist he most admired was Shakespeare. In his passionate review of *Hamlet,* which he wrote on January 11, 1882 (at the age of twenty-two), he called out for Shakespeare to be performed everywhere in Russia, to let fresh air in on what was, in his young opinion, the stagnant Russian stage, and to serve as a stimulant for the Russian actor, who needed to be cultured in order to perform the works of this great dramatist. Shakespeare became the standard for Chekhov throughout his life as a writer, and the presence of Shakespeare is felt throughout his letters and in many of his plays — most vividly, in *The Seagull*.

> "Always remember that the writers whom we call eternal, or even just simply the good ones who intoxicate us, they all have one highly important trait in common: they are moving toward something, and they beckon you to follow, and you feel — not only with your mind, but with your entire being — that they have some purpose, like the ghost of Hamlet's father, who did not come to disturb the imagination without reason…The best of them are real and write of life just as it is, but because each line is filled with the awareness of this purpose, you feel more than life as it is — you also feel life as it should be, and this captivates you."
>
> *to Suvorin, 11/25/92*

Literary historians place Chekhov in the front ranks of contemporary dramatic literature. But ultimately, I think, from Chekhov's point of view, it was neither his place in dramatic literature nor the legacy of his work that concerned him. As he put himself with characteristic succinctness, early on in his literary career:

> "All that I write will be forgotten in five to ten years, but the path paved
> by me will be free and clear — in this lies my sole merit and contribution."
>
> *to Lazarev, 10/20/88*

Reading literary history and criticism of our century, Chekhov might find the adjective 'Chekhovian,' now so permanently incorporated into our theatrical and literary vocabulary, to be quite amusing. For Chekhov, the freedom of the writer in his own times to create his own 'new forms' is how he wished to be remembered.

CHEKHOV's WELTANSCHAUUNG

> "You ask: what is life? That's exactly like asking: what is a carrot? A carrot is a carrot, and nothing more is known about it."
>
> *to Knipper, 4/20/04*

Chekhov the humorist, Chekhov the doctor, Chekhov the humanitarian — all these aspects endowed him with a special love of life and an insight into its meaning. And this insight is the light that penetrates all of the four major plays. Viewing these four plays as a whole, one can appreciate the breadth and depth of his very special vision. The universality of his themes: love, art, nature, death, his passionate love of his country and his understanding of so many of its aspects, his perception of the passage of time, his subtle sense of history — all contribute to make him a lasting author for our times. And then, there is the humanity of his characters: their desires, their weaknesses, their limitations, their foolishness, their dreams and longings, their desperation, their valiant struggle to love, to endure, to have hope, to have faith — to understand, in the face of all obstacles, "why the cranes fly," as Masha says in *The Three Sisters*.

Chekhov as an adult rejected his father's religion. Through his art, he defined his own — humanism. Born of his practice as a doctor, the abuse he suffered as a child, his steadfast loyalty to his family and friends, his capacity for love, compassion, and forgiveness, and his sense of humor about his own frailties and those of others — this humanism pervades his work. His love of life, his true understanding of its intrinsic value — of the one lost patient whom Dr. Astrov laments — his sense of compassion for the human condition, his understanding of human nature and of human fallability — these are the facets of his humanism. He steadfastly refused to judge his fellow man, and sought to portray him, rather than to condemn him.

> "An artist must not be a judge of his characters or of what they say, but only an impartial witness…My only job is to be talented …to place my characters in the proper light and speak their own language."
>
> *to Suvorin, 5/30/88*

This is why the actors of the Moscow Art Theatre and actors of today love to play his roles — because they are so true to "life as it is," because they present portraits of full human beings with the full gamut of human behavior, because there is so much humor and truth in these portraits. That is why his plays and their characters have inspired a new understanding and appreciation of acting in our time.

> "A writer must be as objective as a chemist; he must free himself from subjectivity; he must know that dung- heaps play a very respectable part in a landscape, and that evil passions are as inherent a part of life as good ones."
>
> *to Kiseleva, 1/14/87*

ॐ.

> "How beautiful life will be in three hundred – four hundred years."
> *Chekhov to Kuprin,* Memories of Chekhov

One must also recognize that Chekhov was both a 'fin de siècle' writer *and* a writer at the beginning of the new century. Born one year before the emancipation of the serfs and dying thirteen years before the Russian revolution, Chekhov's life spans an extraordinary period of change in Russian and world history. The grandson of a serf himself, he lived through the reign of three tsars, he observed the slow decline of the Russian aristocracy — the landed gentry, the slow metamorphosis of the peasant class into an emerging working class, and the rise of industrialism. The first Russian revolution came one year after he died; the second one, twelve years after that. He knew the great artists of his time intimately, including Tolstoy, Gorky, and Rachmaninov; he was an outspoken champion of Dreyfus. Chekhov knew and felt history — this was part of his special vision. As a part of the Russian literary tradition, he, like his character, Trigorin, also felt "obliged to write about the people, about their suffering, and so on and so on." And although he never preached to us, the larger landscape of his plays is always there, subtle and pervasive, like the haunting far-off sound of a breaking string, dying away in the distance.

Thus, we perceive the remarkable Janus-like vision which Chekhov had of the century before, in which he lived, and the new century ahead — of events he foresaw and did not live to see. In retrospect, knowing what we know now of Russian and world history of our century, the speeches of Astrov, Vershinin, Tusenbach, Lopakhin, and Trofimov haunt us with their prescience.

Ever objective, Chekhov agreed with all his characters. Like Vershinin, he hoped for happiness on earth for generations to come. However, like Tusenbach also, he perceived that there are forces in the universe beyond our control, beyond our grasp and understanding, which determine this, no matter how we live our lives on earth, no matter how valiantly we prepare for future generations.

Ultimately, there is Chekhov the ironist, who sees the futility and absurdity of human endeavor, who sees the fierce truths of life beyond the efforts of man, beyond history, and who, in these gentle, evocative plays, says, like Chebutykin: "It doesn't matter, it doesn't matter."

This vision and insight were enhanced, in the end, by the fact that Chekhov, from age twenty-six, knew how short his own life would be. Only a man and a writer like Chekhov could have recognized this mortal fact as a gift with which to enrich his art, so that others might benefit from his vision.

"I hope that in the next world I shall be able to look back upon this life and say: 'Those were beautiful dreams...'"

Chekhov, The Notebooks

The quotes from Chekhov's letters, the notebooks, and from the reminiscences of his contemporaries have all been newly translated for this introduction.

THE SEAGULL

A Comedy in Four Acts

The premiere of this new translation was produced by the Philadelphia Festival Theatre for New Plays, Annenberg Center, opening night January 17, 1993; Scenic Designer, James Wolk; Lighting Designer, Jerold R. Forsyth; Costume Designer, Vickie Esposito; Sound Designer, Conny M. Lockwood; Stage Manager, Erica Schwartz; Musical Director, John S. Lionarons; Production Dramaturg, Michael Hollinger; Casting, Hilary Missan; directed by Carol Rocamora.

THE CAST (in order of appearance)

Treplev, Konstantin Gavrilovich . . . . Matt Servitto
Yakov . . . . Philip F. Lynch
Musician, Workman . . . . John S. Lionarons
Medvedenko, Semyon Semyonovich . . . . Frank Wood
Masha . . . . Jan Leslie Harding
Sorin, Pyotr Nikolaevich . . . . Don Auspitz
Zarechnaya, Nina Mikhailovna . . . . Julia Gibson
Polina Andreevna . . . . Carla Belver
Dorn, Yevgeny Sergeevich . . . . William Wise
Shamraev, Ilya Afanasevich . . . . H. Michael Walls
Arkadina, Irina Nikolaevna . . . . Marcia Mahon
Trigorin, Boris Alekseevich . . . . David Purdham
A Cook . . . . Ricki Gever
A Maid . . . . Sue Adelizzi

CAST OF CHARACTERS

ARKADINA, Irina Nikolaevna (Trepleva by marriage), an actress

TREPLEV, Konstantin Gavrilovich, her son, a young man

SORIN, Pyotr Nikolaevich, her brother

ZARECHNAYA, Nina Mikhailovna, a young girl, daughter of a wealthy landowner

SHAMRAEV, Ilya Afanasevich, a retired army lieutenant, manager of Sorin's estate

POLINA ANDREEVNA, his wife

MASHA, his daughter

TRIGORIN, Boris Alekseevich, a novelist

DORN, Yevgeny Sergeevich, a doctor

MEDVEDENKO, Semyon Semyonovich, a teacher

YAKOV, a workman

A COOK

A MAID

The action takes place on Sorin's country estate. Between the third and fourth acts, two years have passed.

The Seagull

ACT ONE

A part of the park on SORIN's estate. A broad avenue leads away from the audience deep into the park toward the lake. The avenue is obstructed by a stage, hastily constructed for a home performance, and the lake is therefore not visible. To the left and right of the stage are shrubs. There are several chairs and a small table.

The sun has just set. On the stage, behind the lowered curtain, are YAKOV and the other WORKMEN; the sound of coughing and hammering is heard.

MASHA and MEDVEDENKO enter from the left, returning from a walk.

MEDVEDENKO: Why do you always go around wearing black?

MASHA: I am in mourning for my life. I'm unhappy.

MEDVEDENKO: But why? *(Deep in thought.)* I don't understand…You're in good health. Your father — all right, he may not be rich, but he's not poor either. I'm much worse off than you. I earn a total of twenty-three rubles a month, and that's before they deduct for the pension fund, and you don't see me walking around in mourning.

They sit.

MASHA: It's not a question of money. Even a poor man can be happy.

MEDVEDENKO: That's in theory, but in practice, it goes like this: There's me, plus my mother, plus two sisters and a little brother, all on a salary of twenty-three rubles. Now, we have to eat and drink, don't we? What about tea and sugar? What about tobacco? You see, it's goes on and on.

MASHA: *(Looking at the stage.)* The play will be starting soon.

MEDVEDENKO: Yes. Nina Zarechnaya is performing in a play written by Konstantin Gavrilovich. They're in love with one another, and tonight their souls will unite in a single sublime artistic expression. And your soul and mine? They will never even meet. I love you, I can't bear to stay home and long for you, so I walk over every day, four miles here and four miles back, just to watch you sit around 'in mourning.' Well, who can blame you? I don't have any money, I've got a big family…Who would want to marry a man who can't even support himself?

MASHA: Nonsense. *(Takes snuff.)* Your love is touching, really it is, but the feeling's not mutual, and that's that. *(Offers him the snuff box.)* Here, go on, have some.

MEDVEDENKO: No, I don't feel like it.

Pause.

MASHA: It's stifling out…there'll be a storm tonight for sure. You know, you spend all your time philosophizing, or whining about money. For you, there's no greater tragedy than poverty. But for me, it's a thousand times easier to go around in rags, begging, than to…Oh, what's the use, you wouldn't understand…

SORIN and TREPLEV enter from stage right.

SORIN: *(Leaning on a cane.)* There's something about the country, my friend, I don't know what it is, but I shall never get used to it, no doubt about it. Last night I went to bed at ten, and woke up at nine this morning from the deepest sleep, feeling as if my brain had been stuck to my skull, or something to that effect. *(Laughs.)* And after lunch, it seems I dropped off again, and now I feel like a total wreck. Really, it's a nightmare, in the end…

TREPLEV: It's true, you're better off living in town. *(Sees MASHA and MEDVEDENKO.)* Everyone, when it's time to start, we'll call you, but for now, you're not supposed to be here. Would you please go?

SORIN: *(To MASHA.)* Marya Ilyinichna, would you kindly ask your papa to have his dog untied, otherwise she howls. My sister was kept up again all night.

MASHA: You can ask my father yourself, I'm not going to. Spare me, please. *(To MEDVEDENKO.)* Let's get out of here!

MEDVEDENKO: *(To TREPLEV.)* Let us know when it's curtain time.

They both exit.

SORIN: That means the dog will howl again all night long. The fact is, I've never been able to live in the country, not the way I'd like to. Once upon a time, I'd take a month's vacation, just to come out for a rest, that's all, but here they plague you with so much nonsense that after one day I couldn't wait to leave. *(Laughs.)* Always, it was such a pleasure to leave…But, now that I'm retired, and so on, where else is there to go, in the end? So, here I live, whether I like it or not…

YAKOV: *(To TREPLEV.)* Konstantin Gavrilovich, sir, we're going for a swim.

TREPLEV: All right, but be back in ten minutes for places. *(Checks his watch.)* It's almost time to start.

YAKOV: Right-o, sir. *(Leaves.)*

TREPLEV: *(Looking at the stage.)* Now this is a theatre! The curtain, the wings, and beyond, nothing but empty space. No scenery of any kind. An open vista stretching clear to the lake and the horizon. The curtain goes up at exactly eight-thirty, just when the moon is rising.

SORIN: Magnificent.

TREPLEV: If Nina is late, then of course the whole effect is lost. She should have been here by now. Her father and stepmother are standing guard, for her to get out of the house is like escaping from prison. *(Straightens his uncle's tie.)* Your hair and beard are a mess. You need a haircut, or something…

SORIN: *(Combing his beard.)* It's the tragedy of my life. Even when I was young, I always looked as though I'd been out drinking, that's all. Women never seemed to fall in love with me. *(Sitting.)* So tell me, why is my sister in such a bad mood?

TREPLEV: Why? She's bored. *(Sits down next to him.)* She's jealous. She's against me and the performance and the play, and that's because Nina is in it and she isn't. She doesn't know a thing about my play, and already she hates it.

SORIN: *(Laughs.)* Oh come now, really…

TREPLEV: Already she's in a "state," because here upon this pathetic little stage it will be Nina's hour, not hers. *(Looks at his watch.)* A psychological wonder — that's my mother. Unquestionably talented, brilliant, capable of - falling to pieces over a book she's reading, of rattling off all of Nekrasov by heart, of nursing the sick like an angel — but just try mentioning the name of Duse in her presence, and 'oh-ho'! No, we must sing her praise and hers alone — yes, sing it, write it, shout it — wild, ecstatic praise over her stunning performance in *La Dame Aux Camélias* or God only knows what play. But here, in the country, where you can't get that drug for her, she gets bored and evil-tempered, and all of us — we are her enemies, everything's our fault. And she gets so superstitious — she's afraid of three candles burning or whether it's the thirteenth day of the month. And stingy? She has 70,000 rubles in the bank in Odessa, that I know for a fact. But ask her to lend you anything, and she bursts into tears.

SORIN: You've gotten it into that head of yours that your mother doesn't like your play, and you're all worked up in advance, that's all. Calm down, your mother adores you.

TREPLEV: *(Plucking petals off a flower.)* She loves me, she loves me not; she loves me, she loves me not; she loves me, she loves me not. *(Laughs.)* You see, my mother doesn't love me. And why should she? She wants romance and adventure, a whole new life for herself, a gay, romantic life, and here I am, twenty-five years old, a constant reminder that she's not so young any more. When I'm not around, she's only thirty-two, and when I am, presto! — she's forty-three, and she hates me for it. She also knows I don't believe in the 'theatre,' such as it is. She adores the theatre — she thinks she's serving mankind and her sacred art, but if you ask me, our theatre of today is dull and narrow-minded. Every evening, when the curtain goes up, and there under the bright lights, in a room with three walls, those celebrated artists, those high priests of our sacred art, when they play it all out before us, how we mortals eat, and drink, and love, and go around wearing our clothes and leading our lives; when out of this vulgar scenario we are served up some kind of message or moral, however meagre, ready for our daily domestic consumption; when after its one thousandth incarnation all these plays seem to me to be the same, time after time after time the same, then I flee — I flee like Maupassant fled the Eiffel Tower, because it outraged him how enormously trite it was.

SORIN: Without the theatre, nothing is possible.

TREPLEV: We need new forms. We must have new forms, and if we don't we might as well have nothing at all. *(Looks at his watch.)* I love my mother, I love her very much, but she leads a chaotic life, forever carrying on with that novelist, her name all over the papers — and I've had it with her. Although sometimes I think it's my own mortal ego; I feel sorry for myself that I have a famous actress for a mother, and if only she were an ordinary woman, oh, how happy I would be. Uncle, can you imagine a more desperate and pathetic situation: Here she is, holding court in her own home, surrounded by all sorts of artists and writers, and there, in the midst of all these luminaries sits the only nobody — me, and why do they tolerate me, because I am her son. And who am I? What am I? I left the university in my third year, due, as they say, to "circumstances beyond one's control," or whatever the phrase is — with no talent, no money, and a passport announcing, loud and clear, that I am a member of the Kiev bourgeoisie. Yes, indeed, my father was a true member of the Kiev bourgeoisie, although he also happened to have been a well-known actor. And thus, it came to pass, when in my mother's living room, all these artists and writers bestowed upon me their benevolent attention, it dawned on me that what they really were doing was sizing me up in all my insignificance. I could read their minds, and how I suffered from the humiliation.

SORIN: By the way, tell me, please, what kind of a fellow is this novelist? I don't have a sense of him. Never says a word.

TREPLEV: Oh, intelligent, straightforward, somewhat aloof, I suppose. And very respectable. You know, not quite forty, already famous, and full of himself... As for his writing, well...what can I tell you? It's charming, it's witty...but...after Tolstoy or Zola, who wants to read Trigorin?

SORIN: Ah, my dear boy, how I love the literati! Once upon a time I wanted two things passionately: to get married and to become a man of letters. And what do you know, I didn't do either. Yes. And to have been a minor man of letters, now that would have been lovely, in the end.

TREPLEV: *(Listens.)* I hear footsteps...*(Embraces his uncle.)* I can't live without her...Even the sound of her footsteps is beautiful...I'm out of my mind with happiness. *(Crosses quickly to meet NINA ZARECHNAYA as she enters.)* My darling, my dream...

NINA: *(Agitated.)* I'm not late...Tell me I'm not late...

TREPLEV: *(Kissing her hands.)* No, no, no...

NINA: All day long I've been so upset, it was terrifying! I was afraid my father wouldn't let me come...But he just went out with my stepmother. The sky was red, the moon was rising, and I kept driving the horses, faster and faster. *(Laughs.)* But now I'm so happy. *(Presses SORIN's hand warmly.)*

SORIN: *(Laughs.)* So, we've been crying! No, no, we can't have that!

NINA: I can't help it...Look, I can hardly catch my breath. And I have to leave in half an hour, we must hurry. For God's sake, don't make me late, please don't! My father doesn't even know I'm here.

TREPLEV: Anyway, it's time to start. We'd better go call everyone.

SORIN: I'll do it, that's all. Right away. *(Goes off singing.)* "In France, two grenadiers!..." *(Looks around.)* You know, once when I started singing, just like this, one of the deputy prosecutors said to me: "Your Excellency, what a powerful voice you have..." Then, he thought for a moment and added: "Powerful...and awful." *(Laughs and exits.)*

NINA: My father and his wife won't allow me to come here. They say it's too Bohemian…They're afraid I'll become an actress…But I'm drawn here, to the lake, just like a seagull. My heart is so full of you. *(She looks around.)*

TREPLEV: We're alone.

NINA: It feels as if there's someone there…

TREPLEV: No, no one.

They kiss.

NINA: What kind of tree is this?

TREPLEV: Elm.

NINA: Why is it so dark?

TREPLEV: It's evening, everything looks dark. Don't leave early, I beg of you.

NINA: I can't stay.

TREPLEV: What if I come to your house, Nina? I could stand in the garden all night and gaze at your window.

NINA: Don't. The guard will see you. And Trezor doesn't know you yet — he'll bark like mad.

TREPLEV: I love you.

NINA: Shhh…

TREPLEV: *(Hearing footsteps.)* Who's there? Is that you, Yakov?

YAKOV: *(From behind the stage.)* Yes it is, sir.

TREPLEV: Call places. It's time to start. Is the moon rising?

YAKOV: Yes it is, sir.

TREPLEV: Do you have the spirits ready? And the sulphur? When the red eyes appear, there has to be the smell of sulphur. *(To NINA.)* Go — everything's ready. Are you nervous?…

NINA: Yes, very. Your mother — never mind, I'm not afraid of her, but Trigorin's here…I'm absolutely terrified, I'm ashamed to perform in front of him…He's such a great writer…Is he young?

TREPLEV: Yes.

NINA: What wonderful stories he writes!

TREPLEV: *(Coldly.)* I wouldn't know…I haven't read them.

NINA: It's so hard to be in your play…There are no living characters in it.

TREPLEV: Living characters! The point is not to show life as it is, or as it should be, but as we dream it to be!

NINA: But there's so little action in your play, only speeches. And in a play, above all, there must be love…

They both go behind the stage. Enter POLINA ANDREEVNA and DORN.

POLINA ANDREEVNA: It's getting damp out. Go back and put on your galoshes.

DORN: I'm hot.

POLINA ANDREEVNA: You don't take care of yourself! You're so pig-headed. And you're a doctor — you know very well that damp air is bad for you, but no, better I should suffer while you sit out on the terrace all last evening just to spite me...

DORN: *(Singing.)* "Don't say that our youth has been wasted..."

POLINA ANDREEVNA: You were so caught up in conversation with Irina Nikolaevna that you didn't even notice how cold it was. It's obvious you're infatuated with her...

DORN: Polina, I'm fifty-five years old.

POLINA ANDREEVNA: Nonsense, for a man that's not old. You're in excellent shape and still very attractive to women.

DORN: So what do you want me to do?

POLINA ANDREEVNA: You kiss the ground she walks on just because she's an actress! You and everyone else!

DORN: *(Sings.)* "Again, before you, I stand..." Look, just because the world loves artists, and treats them differently than, let's say, merchants — well, that's just the way of the world. Call it — idealism.

POLINA ANDREEVNA: Women are always falling for you and hanging around your neck. Is that Idealism, too?

DORN: *(Shrugs.)* Well, I don't know. I've always gotten along with women. And what they like about me most is that I'm an excellent doctor. Ten, fifteen years ago, remember, I was the only decent obstetrician in the entire province. And then I've always been an honorable man.

POLINA ANDREEVNA: *(Takes his hand.)* My darling!

DORN: Shhh, They're coming.

Enter ARKADINA on SORIN's arm, with TRIGORIN, SHAMRAEV, MEDVEDENKO, and MASHA.

SHAMRAEV: At the Poltava Festival in '73 she gave an amazing performance! Pure delight! A marvelous performance! And whatever happened to the comedian Chadin, Pavel Semyonich Chadin? His Rasplyuyev was immortal, better even than Sadovsky's, I swear to you, my esteemed lady. Where is he now?

ARKADINA: You keep asking me about people from before Noah's Ark. How on earth should I know? *(Sits.)*

SHAMRAEV: *(Sighs.)* Pashka Chadin! They don't make them like that any more. The theatre is dead, Irina Nikolaevna! Once there were mighty oak trees, and now we see only stumps.

DORN: There isn't much brilliant talent around any more, it's true, but your average actor is a lot better than he used to be.

SHAMRAEV: I beg to disagree. But then again, it's always a matter of taste. "De gustibus aut bene, aut nihil."

TREPLEV appears from behind the stage.

ARKADINA: *(To her son.)* My darling son, when does it all begin?

TREPLEV: In a minute. Just be patient, please.

ARKADINA: *(Reciting from* Hamlet.*)*
>   "O Hamlet, speak no more;
>   Thou turn'st mine eyes into my very soul;
>   And there I see such black and grained spots
>   As will not leave their tinct."

TREPLEV:
>   "Nay, but to live
>   In the rank sweat of an enseamed bed
>   Stew'd in corruption, honeying and making love
>   Over the nasty sty…"

A horn sounds from behind the stage.

Ladies and gentlemen, your attention please.

Pause.

Let the play begin. *(Knocks his baton and speaks loudly.)* "O, you venerable, ancient shadows who nightly linger o'er this lake, lull us to sleep, and let us dream of what life will be in two hundred thousand years!"

SORIN: In two hundred thousand years, there will be nothing.

TREPLEV: Good, let them show us that "nothing."

ARKADINA: Yes, let them. We'll sleep.

The curtain rises; a view of the lake is unveiled; the moon is on the horizon, its reflection in the water; NINA ZARECHNAYA sits on a large rock, dressed all in white.

NINA: "Men, lions, eagles, and partridges, horned stags, geese, spiders, the silent fish dwelling deep in the water, starfish, and those invisible to the naked eye — all life, all life, all life, its sad cycle ended, has died away…Thousands of centuries have passed since the earth has borne any living creature, and the poor moon in vain lights up her lantern. No longer do the waking cranes cry out in the meadow, and maybugs are silent in the lime groves. Cold, cold, cold. Empty, empty, empty. Terrible, terrible, terrible.

Pause.

All living creatures have disappeared into dust, eternity has cast them into stone, water, and cloud — but their souls have all melted into one. And I, I am the universal soul…In me lives the soul of Alexander the Great, and Caesar, and Shakespeare, and Napoleon, and the very lowest form of life. In me human consciousness and animal instinct are one, and I remember all, all, all, each and every life I relive again."

The marsh-lights appear.

ARKADINA: *(Whispers.)* Something from the Decadent School.
TREPLEV: *(Pleading, reproachful.)* Mama!
NINA: "I am alone. Once every one hundred years I open my lips to speak. My lonely voice echoes into the void, and no one hears me…And you, too, pale fires, you do not hear me…Born before dawn from the rotting swamp, you drift into daybreak, thoughtlessly, aimlessly, listlessly. Fearing that you will spring to life, the father of all matter, the devil, changes you, moment by moment, atom by atom, as if you were stone and water, and you change and change. One thing, and one alone in this universe, stays eternal, unchanging — and that is the eternal spirit.

Pause.

Like a captive, cast into a deep and empty well, I know not where I am and what awaits me. Only this I know — that in the cruel confrontation with the devil, master of all material matter, I am destined to triumph, and spirit and matter will unite in glorious harmony. Thus begins the reign of the universal will. But this shall come slowly, after endless, endless multiples of millennia, while the moon, and bright Sirius, and the earth itself turn to dust...And until that time, what horror, what horror. . .

Pause; against the background of the lake, two red points of light appear.

My mighty opponent, the devil, approaches. I see his terrible, crimson eyes."
ARKADINA: It smells like sulphur. Is this really necessary?
TREPLEV: Yes.
ARKADINA: *(Laughs.)* Ah, yes, special effects!
TREPLEV: Mama!
NINA: "He longs for human company..."
POLINA: *(To DORN.)* You took off your hat. Put it on, or you'll catch cold.
ARKADINA: The Doctor's taken his hat off to the devil, the father of eternal matter.
TREPLEV: *(In a rage.)* The play's over! That's enough! Curtain!
ARKADINA: Why are you so angry?
TREPLEV: That's enough! Curtain! Can we have the curtain! *(Stamps his foot.)* Curtain!

The curtain falls.

Forgive me! I've forgotten that writing plays and acting on the stage are only for the chosen few. I've trespassed on your territory! I...*(Wants to say more, but instead waves his hand and exits left.)*
ARKADINA: What's the matter with him?
SORIN: Irina, darling, that's not the way to treat a sensitive young man.
ARKADINA: Well, what in the world did I say to him?
SORIN: You offended him.
ARKADINA: He told us beforehand it was all in fun, so that's how I took it, for fun.
SORIN: But still...
ARKADINA: Now it appears that he's written a great masterpiece. I mean, really! Here he went and put on this show and sprayed us all with sulphur, not to entertain us, but to teach us a lesson on how to write plays and how to act on the stage. Really, it's too much. And these constant attacks against me, these diatribes, say whatever you like, I am sick and tired of them. He's a willful, egotistical little boy.

SORIN: He only wanted to please you.

ARKADINA: Is that so? Then why didn't he choose a real play, instead of making us sit through all this decadent delirium. I mean, for the sake of fun, I'll even put up with delirium, but all this pretentiousness about new forms, about a new era for the theatre…As far as I'm concerned, what we got tonight was bad form.

TRIGORIN: Each of us writes what he wants to and what he can.

ARKADINA: Fine, let him write whatever he feels like writing, only spare me, please.

DORN: Ah, Jupiter, thou art angered.

ARKADINA: I'm not Jupiter, I'm a woman. *(Lights up a cigarette.)* And I'm not angry, only it irritates me to see a young man waste his time like that. I didn't mean to hurt his feelings.

MEDVEDENKO: No one has any reason to separate the spirit from matter anyway, since for all we know, the spirit itself may be made up of nothing more than an aggregate of atoms. *(Quickly, to TRIGORIN.)* Now, you know, someone should write a play about the life of our friend the schoolmaster, and produce that. What a hard, hard life!

ARKADINA: Of course it is, but please, let's not talk about plays any more, or about atoms. What a glorious evening! Listen, everyone, is that singing? *(Listens.)* How lovely!

POLINA ANDREEVNA: It's on the other shore.

Pause

ARKADINA: *(To TRIGORIN.)* Sit next to me. Ten, fifteen years ago, on this lake, you could hear music and singing almost every night, it never ceased. Here on this shore there are six country estates. I remember the laughter, the noise, the guns going off, and people falling in love, falling in love…And the leading man in all this, the idol of all six estates was, ladies and gentlemen, I give you *(nods to DORN)* Doctor Yevgeny Sergeich. I mean, he is charming now, but in those days he was irresistible. But now my conscience is starting to bother me. Why did I hurt my poor boy? I'm so upset. *(Loudly.)* Kostya! Son! Kostya!

MASHA: I'll go look for him.

ARKADINA: Please do, darling.

MASHA: *(Goes off left.)* A-oo! Konstantin Gavrilovich…A-oo! *(Exits.)*

NINA: *(Coming out from behind the stage.)* Well, it seems we're not going on any further, so I can come out now. Good evening! *(Kisses ARKADINA and POLINA ANDREEVNA.)*

SORIN: Bravo! Bravo!

ARKADINA: Bravo! Bravo! We were all charmed. With those looks and that wonderful voice, it's a sin to be stuck out here in the country. You've got talent! Do you hear me? You absolutely must go on the stage!

NINA: Oh, that is my dream! *(Sighs.)* But it will never happen.

ARKADINA: Who knows? Now, let me introduce Trigorin, Boris Alekseevich.

NINA: Oh, I'm so delighted…*(Embarrassed.)* I always read your work…

ARKADINA: *(Sitting NINA down beside her.)* Don't be embarrassed, darling. For a celebrity, he's just an ordinary fellow. You see, he's embarrassed, too.

DORN: They can lift the curtain now, can't they? It's eerie like that.

SHAMRAEV: *(In a loud voice.)* Yakov — raise the curtain, will you, fellow?

The curtain goes up.

NINA: *(To TRIGORIN.)* It is a strange play, isn't it?

TRIGORIN: I didn't understand a word of it. But I enjoyed watching it. Your acting is so truthful. And the set was beautiful.

Pause.

There must be a lot of fish in this lake.

NINA: Yes.

TRIGORIN: I love to fish. For me, there is no greater pleasure than to sit on the shore of the lake at day's end, and gaze at the float on the end of the line.

NINA: But I always thought that, for one who has experienced the joy of creativity, no other pleasures exist.

ARKADINA: *(Laughing.)* Don't talk like that. When you flatter him, he wishes he could simply disappear.

SHAMRAEV: I remember once in Moscow at the opera, when the famous Silva sang a low C. Now that night, it just so happened that one of the basses from our local church choir was sitting in the gallery. Imagine our utter amazement when all of a sudden we heard from the gallery: "Bravo, Silva," an entire octave lower…Just like this *(in a low voice):* "Bravo, Silva"…I mean, the entire theatre just froze.

Pause.

DORN: An angel of silence has flown over us.

NINA: Oh, I must go. Good-bye.

ARKADINA: Where are you going? Why so early? We won't let you.

NINA: Papa will be waiting up for me.

ARKADINA: He's something, your father, really...

They kiss.

Ah, well, what can we do. Such a pity to let you go.

NINA: If only you knew, how hard it is for me to leave!

ARKADINA: Someone should take you home, my sweet.

NINA: *(Frightened.)* Oh no, no!

SORIN: *(Imploring.)* Stay!

NINA: I can't, Pyotr Nikolaevich.

SORIN: Stay just one hour longer, that's all. Come now, what can it hurt...

NINA: *(After a moment, in tears.)* I can't. *(Shakes hands and quickly exits.)*

ARKADINA: Pathetic girl, really. They say her late mother left an enormous fortune to her husband, all of it, down to the last kopek, and now this poor girl is left with nothing, because her father promised it all to his second wife. It's shocking.

DORN: Let's do him justice, her dear papa is a first-class scoundrel.

SORIN: *(Rubbing his hands together.)* Come on, everyone, let's go in. It's getting damp out. My legs ache.

ARKADINA: Those legs of yours, they're as stiff as wood. You can hardly walk. Come, ill-fated old man. *(Takes his arm.)*

SHAMRAEV: *(Offers his hand to his wife.)* Madam?

SORIN: That damn dog is barking again, I can hear it. *(To SHAMRAEV.)* Ilya Afanasevich, be a good fellow, tell them to untie her.

SHAMRAEV: I can't, Pyotr Nikolaevich, so sorry. I'm afraid thieves might get into the barn. I've got millet in there. *(Walking alongside of MEDVEDENKO.)* Yes, a whole octave lower: "Bravo, Silva." And not even a soloist, just a lowly member of the church choir.

MEDVEDENKO: And how much salary does a church choir member get paid?

They all exit, except DORN.

DORN: *(Alone.)* I don't know. Maybe I don't understand anything, or maybe I'm crazy, but I really liked that play. There's something about it. When that little girl talked about loneliness, and then, when the red devil eyes appeared, I was so excited, my hands shook. So fresh, so innocent…Here comes the man himself. I want to be complimentary.

TREPLEV: *(Enters.)* No one's here.

DORN: I am.

TREPLEV: Masha's been looking for me all over the grounds. Unbearable creature.

DORN: Konstantin Gavrilovich, I liked your play enormously. Yes, it was a bit strange, and of course I haven't heard the ending yet, but nevertheless it had a tremendous impact on me. You're a talented fellow — you must keep on writing.

TREPLEV squeezes his hand tightly and embraces him impetuously.

Whoa, how sensitive you are. You've got tears in your eyes…What was I saying? Oh, yes. You picked a topic from the realm of abstract ideas. That was right — a work of art must always express some great thought. It's only worthwhile if it's profound. How pale you are!

TREPLEV: Then you're saying I should keep on writing?

DORN: Of course…But write only about what is meaningful, what is eternal. You know, I've lived a very full life, I've lived it well, I'm content, but if ever I had the chance to feel that surge, that inspiration an artist feels when he's creating, why then I would shed my material cloak, with all its earthly trappings, and I'd take to the air, I'd soar.

TREPLEV: Forgive me, but where is Nina?

DORN: And another thing. Work with clarity, with purpose. Know why you're writing, otherwise you'll go down the aesthetic road with no destination, you'll lose your way, and your talent will be your downfall.

TREPLEV: *(Impatiently.)* Where's Nina?

DORN: She went home.

TREPLEV: *(In despair.)* What am I going to do? I want to see her…I must see her…I'm going…

MASHA enters.

DORN: *(To TREPLEV.)* Calm down, my friend.

TREPLEV: No, really, I'm going. I must go.

MASHA: Go home, Konstantin Gavrilovich. Your mama is waiting for you. She's worried.

TREPLEV: Tell her I left. And please, all of you, leave me alone, I beg of you. Leave me alone! Stop following me around!

DORN: Now, now, now, my dear fellow…don't be like that…it's not good for you.

TREPLEV: *(In tears.)* Good-bye, Doctor. Thank you…*(He exits.)*

DORN: *(Sighing.)* Ah, youth, youth!

MASHA: That's what they all say, when there's nothing else left: "Ah, youth, youth…" *(Takes snuff.)*

DORN: *(Grabs the snuff box and flings it into the bushes.)* That's disgusting!

Pause.

I think they've started playing cards up at the house. We'd better go in.

MASHA: Wait!

DORN: What?

MASHA: I want to say something to you. I feel like talking for a minute. *(Upset.)* I don't like my father…but there's a special place in my heart for you. For some reason, I've always felt deep down inside that you're close to me…Help me, please. Help me, or else I'll do something foolish, make a mockery of my life, ruin it…I can't go on…

DORN: What? Help with what?

MASHA: How I'm suffering. No one, no one knows my suffering! *(Lays her head on his chest, quietly.)* I love Konstantin.

DORN: How neurotic you all are! So neurotic! And all this love…Oh, the spells this lake casts! *(Tenderly.)* So, what can I do, my child, tell me? What? What?

CURTAIN

ACT TWO

A lawn for playing croquet. Far upstage right is the house, with a large terrace. Upstage left, the lake is visible, with the sparkling reflection of the sun. Flower gardens. Noontime. It is hot. To the side of the lawn, in the shadow of an old linden tree, ARKADINA, DORN, and MASHA sit on a bench. A book lays open on DORN's knees.

ARKADINA: *(To MASHA.)* Come on, let's stand up.

Both stand.

Side by side. All right, here we are. You're twenty-two, and I'm almost twice your age. Yevgeny Sergeich, which one of us looks younger?

DORN: You, of course.

ARKADINA: You see…and why? Because I'm always working, feeling, I'm in constant motion, always, while you're stuck in once place and never move, you're not alive. And I live by a golden rule — never look into the future. I never think about old age, or death. What will be, will be. You can't escape it.

MASHA: And I feel as if I were born centuries ago. I drag my life around behind me, like a dress with an endless train…And often I don't even feel like living any more. *(Sits.)* Of course, this is all nonsense. Cheer up, snap out of it.

DORN: *(Singing softly.)* "Tell her, my flowers…"

ARKADINA: Then again, my dear, I can be as proper as the English. I'm very well-behaved, as they say, always dressed up and done up 'comme il faut.' And I wouldn't be caught dead going out of the house, even into my own garden, in a housecoat or without my hair done. Ever. No, I've kept in good shape, I've never gotten frumpy, never let myself go, like some women…*(With hands on her hips, walks up and down the lawn.)* Look, light as a bird. I could play a fifteen year old.

DORN: Hmmm, yes. In the meantime, however, why don't I continue. *(Picks up the book.)* We had stopped at the part about the corn dealer and the rats.

ARKADINA: Right, the rats. Go on. *(Sits down.)* Wait a minute, hand it over, I'll read. It's my turn. *(Takes the book and looks for her place.)* And the rats…Here it is…*(Reads.)* "And so, it stands to reason, for society people to nurture novelists and invite them into their homes is as dangerous as it is for a corn merchant to breed rats in his barn. And yet they love to do it. So, when a woman picks a writer whom she wants to captivate, she besieges him with compliments, little kindnesses, indulgences..." Well, maybe that's the way the French do it, but that's certainly not our style, we have no such custom. Here, a woman is usually head over heels in love with her writer first, before she tries to capture him, if you please. You don't have to go far for an example. Take me and Trigorin...

Enter SORIN, leaning on a cane, and beside him, NINA; MEDVEDENKO pushes an empty wheelchair behind them.

SORIN: *(In a gentle tone meant for children.)* So? Are we all happy? Happy at last? *(To his sister.)* Yes, today we are ecstatic! Our father and stepmother have gone off to Tver, and we're free for three whole days!

NINA: *(Sits next to ARKADINA and embraces her.)* I'm so happy! Now I'm all yours!

SORIN: *(Sits in his wheelchair.)* Doesn't she look radiant today!

ARKADINA: She looks lovely, stunning...What a clever girl she is! *(Kisses NINA.)* Let's not praise her too much, it will bring bad luck. Where is Boris Alekseevich?

NINA: He's down by the bathhouse, fishing.

ARKADINA: You'd think he'd get sick of it! *(She goes to read some more.)*

NINA: What are you reading?

ARKADINA: Maupassant. "On the Water," darling. *(She reads a few lines to herself.)* Oh, well, the next part is dull and inaccurate, anyway. *(Closes the book.)* I'm so anxious. Tell me, what's the matter with my son? Why is he so moody and depressed? He spends the entire day by the lake, and I hardly ever lay eyes on him.

MASHA: He's sick at heart. *(To NINA, shyly.)* Please, recite something from his play!

NINA: *(Shrugs her shoulders.)* Do you really want me to? It's so uninteresting.

MASHA: *(Restraining her delight.)* When he reads from his own work, his eyes shine and his face grows pale. He has such a wonderful, mournful voice, and the ways of a poet.

SORIN's snoring can be heard.

DORN: Pleasant dreams.

ARKADINA: Petrusha!

SORIN: Hah?

ARKADINA: Were you asleep?

SORIN: Just a little.

Pause.

ARKADINA: You're not taking any medicine, that's not good, brother dear.

SORIN: I'd be happy to, but my doctor doesn't want to prescribe it.

DORN: Prescriptions, at sixty years of age!

SORIN: Even at sixty, you still want to go on living.

DORN: *(Annoyed.)* So, take some valerian drops.

ARKADINA: I think it's best if he went to a spa somewhere.

DORN: What? Fine. He can go, or he can not go. Whatever.

ARKADINA: And what is that supposed to mean.

DORN: Nothing in particular. It's all very clear, really.

    (Pause.)

MEDVEDENKO: Pyotr Nikolaevich should give up smoking.

SORIN: Nonsense.

DORN: No, it's not. Liquor and tobacco deprive you of your 'self.' Smoke a cigar or drink vodka and you're no longer Pyotr Nikolaevich, you're Pyotr Nikolaevich plus someone else; your true 'self' fades away, and you start seeing yourself in the third person.

SORIN: *(Laughs.)* It's easy for you to say. You've lived your life, but what about me? I've spent twenty-eight years in the department of justice, and still haven't lived, when all's said and done, still haven't really experienced anything, and how I long to live, no doubt about it. You have it all, so what do you care, you can afford to be philosophical, but now it's my turn, I want to live, so I have a sherry and a cigar after dinner, that's all. And that's all.

DORN: You must take life seriously; seeking medical treatment at sixty for a case of self-pity and lost youth, sorry, but that's simply indulgent.

MASHA: *(Stands up.)* It must be time for lunch. *(She walks slowly, limping.)* My leg fell asleep…*(Exits.)*

DORN: She'll go and put away two drinks before lunch.

SORIN: That poor girl has no happiness in life.

DORN: Oh, come on, Your Excellency.

SORIN: You talk like a man who's had everything.

ARKADINA: God, what can be more deadly than this sweet country boredom? It's hot, it's quiet, nobody doing anything, everyone sitting around philosophizing…Good to see you, my friends, nice to hear you talk, but… frankly, I'd much rather be sitting in my hotel room learning a new part!

NINA: *(Thrilled.)* Oh, yes! I know what you mean.

SORIN: Of course it's much better living in town. You sit in your own study, no one gets past the doorman, you have a telephone, plenty of cabs out in the street, that's all…

DORN: *(Singing.)* "Tell her, my flowers…"

SHAMRAEV enters, followed by POLINA ANDREEVNA.

SHAMRAEV: Here they are! And good day to you all! *(Kisses ARKADINA's hand, then NINA's.)* What a pleasure it is to see you in good health. *(To ARKADINA.)* My wife says you're planning to go into town together today, is that right?

ARKADINA: Yes, we are.

SHAMRAEV: Hmmm…Well, that's wonderful, yes, but how are you planning to go, my dear lady? We're hauling rye today, and all our workmen are tied up. And what horses were you thinking of using, may I ask?

ARKADINA: What horses? How on earth should I know?

SORIN: We've got the carriage horses, don't we?

SHAMRAEV: *(Agitated.)* Carriage horses? And where am I going to find a yoke for them? Hm? Where? Tell me? This is unbelievable! Incredible! My esteemed lady! Please, forgive me, I worship your talent, I'd give you ten years of my life, but horses I cannot give you.

ARKADINA: But what if I absolutely must go? Oh, this is extraordinary!

SHAMRAEV: My esteemed lady! You don't understand what's involved in farming!

ARKADINA: *(In a rage.)* It's the same old story. In that case, I'm going to Moscow today. Hire horses for me in the village, or else I'll walk to the station.

SHAMRAEV: *(In a rage.)* In that case, I resign. Go find yourself another manager. *(Exits.)*

ARKADINA: Every summer it's the same thing, every summer I am insulted. I'll never set foot in this place again. *(Exits left, in the direction of the bathhouse; in a minute, she is seen crossing to the house, followed by TRIGORIN with a fishing rod and bucket.)*

SORIN: *(In a rage.)* What insolence! God only knows what is going on here! I am sick of it. Order all the horses immediately!

NINA: *(To POLINA ANDREEVNA.)* Saying no to Irina Nikolaevna, the famous actress! Isn't any wish of hers, even a whim, more important than your farming? It's simply incredible!

POLINA ANDREEVNA: *(In despair.)* But what can I do? Put yourself in my place: What can I do?

SORIN: *(To NINA.)* Let's go after my sister…We'll all beg her to stay. All right? *(Looks in the direction in which SHAMRAEV exited.)* Unbearable man! Tyrant!

NINA: *(Restrains him from getting up.)* Sit, sit…We'll take you in…

She and MEDVEDENKO push the wheelchair.

Oh, how terrible this is!…

SORIN: Yes, yes, it is terrible…But he won't leave, I'll talk to him right away.

They leave; only DORN and POLINA ANDREEVNA remain.

DORN: People are so boring. The truth is, your husband should have been thrown out by his neck, but in the end, you know, that silly old sissy Pyotr Nikolaevich and his sister will offer him an apology! You'll see!

POLINA ANDREEVNA: He sent the carriage horses into the field. And every day there's a misunderstanding like this. If only you knew how it upsets me. It makes me ill; look, I'm trembling…I can't bear his crudeness. *(Imploring.)* Yevgeny, dearest, darling, take me away with you…Our time is running out, we're not young any more. If only at the end of our lives we could stop hiding, stop lying…

Pause.

DORN: I'm fifty-five years old, it's already too late to change my life.

POLINA ANDREEVNA: I know why you're rejecting me, I know there are other women. Just remember, you can't have them all. I understand. I'm sorry I've bothered you, you're tired of me.

NINA appears by the house; she is picking flowers.

DORN: No, I'm not.

POLINA ANDREEVNA: I'm tormented with jealousy. Of course, you're a doctor, you can't avoid women. I understand…

DORN: *(To NINA, who is approaching.)* What's going on?

NINA: Irina Nikolaevna is weeping, and Pyotr Nikolaevich is having an asthma attack.

DORN: *(Stands.)* I'm going to give them both some valerian drops…

NINA: *(Gives him flowers.)* Here you are!

DORN: "Merci bien." *(Goes toward the house.)*

POLINA ANDREEVNA: *(Going with him.)* What lovely flowers! *(Near the house, in a low voice.)* Give me those flowers! Give them to me! *(Takes them, tears them up, and throws them on the ground.)*

Both go into the house.

NINA: *(Alone.)* How strange it is, to see a famous actress cry, and for such a silly reason! And isn't it strange, a celebrated writer, adored by the public, his name in all the papers, his picture sold everywhere, his work translated into foreign languages, — and he spends all day fishing and is thrilled that he's caught two chubb! I always thought that famous people were proud, unapproachable, that they hated crowds, that they used their fame and brilliance to seek vengeance on a world that holds birth and money above all. But no, here they cry, they fish, play cards, laugh, and get angry, like everyone else...

TREPLEV: *(Enters without a hat, with a gun and a seagull he has killed.)* Are you alone here?

NINA: Yes.

TREPLEV places the seagull at her feet.

What does this mean?

TREPLEV: Today I have done something despicable — I have killed this seagull. I lay it at your feet.

NINA: What's the matter with you? *(Picks up the seagull and looks at it.)*

TREPLEV: *(After a pause.)* Soon, in the same way, I shall kill myself.

NINA: I don't know you any more.

TREPLEV: Yes, right, ever since I stopped knowing you. You've changed toward me, your eyes are cold, you're embarrassed by my presence.

NINA: You've become so irritable lately, and I can't understand what you're saying, you talk in symbols. And now this seagull, it must be some kind of symbol too, only, forgive me, I don't understand it. *(Places seagull on the bench.)* I'm too simple to understand you.

TREPLEV: It all started that night, when my play failed so miserably. Women don't forgive failure. I burned it all, all of it, down to the last page. If only you knew, how unhappy I am. You're cold to me, and it's so terrible, so incredible, it's as if I woke up and saw that the lake had suddenly dried up, or drained into the earth. You just said you were too simple to understand me. Oh, what is there to understand?! They hated my play, you despise my inspiration, you already think of me as mediocre, insignificant, like so many others...*(Stamps his foot.)* How well I understand it all, how well! It's like a nail boring into my brain, and curse it — and curse my pride too, it's sucking my life away, sucking it away like a viper...*(Sees TRIGORIN, walking and reading a book.)* Here comes the true literary genius, walking like Hamlet, and with a book, too. *(Mocks him.)* "Words, words, words..." This sun has scarcely shone upon you yet, and already you're smiling, your eyes are melting in his rays. I won't stand in your way. *(Exits quickly.)*

TRIGORIN: *(Writing in a book.)* Takes snuff and drinks vodka...Always wears black. Loved by the schoolmaster...

NINA: Hello, Boris Alekseevich!

TRIGORIN: Hello. Unforeseen circumstances have arisen, and it seems we're leaving today. That means we probably won't see each other again. And what a pity. I don't often get the chance to meet young women, so young and so attractive, and I've completely forgotten, can't even imagine, what it feels like to be eighteen-nineteen years old — that's why all the young girls in my stories don't ring true. I'd give anything to be in your place, just for one hour, to know how you think and what kind of creature you are.

NINA: And I'd love to be in your place.

TRIGORIN: Why?

NINA: To know what it's like to be a famous, gifted writer. What does fame really feel like? And what does that feeling do to you?

TRIGORIN: What does it feel like? Nothing special, really. I've never thought about it. *(After a moment.)* Either you have an exaggerated view of my fame, or else I'm not feeling it, one or the other.

NINA: And when you read about yourself in the papers?

TRIGORIN: When they praise you, it's very pleasant, and when they call you names, then you feel badly for a few days.

NINA: What a wonderful world! If only you knew, how much I envied you! People have different destinies. Some just drag out their dull, dreary existence, all of them the same, all unhappy; others, like you, for example — you're one in a million — you've been given a fascinating, brilliant life, a meaningful life…you're happy…

TRIGORIN: Me? *(Shrugs.)* Hmm…here you are, talking about fame, happiness, about some kind of brilliant, fascinating life, but for me they are just pretty words, forgive me, like candy, which I never indulge in. You're so young and naive.

NINA: But you have a wonderful life!

TRIGORIN: What's so good about it? *(Looks at his watch.)* I have to go and write now. I'm so sorry, I don't have any time…*(Laughs.)* You…how shall I put it…you've stepped on my toes, as they say, and frankly it's gotten to me and I'm a little annoyed. All right, so let's talk about it. Let's talk about my wonderful, brilliant life…Where shall we begin? *(After a moment's thought.)* Let's talk about obsession, when, for example, a man will think night and day about nothing else except the moon. Well, I have had my own moon. Day and night, one persistent thought will overpower me; and I have to write, I have to write, I *have* to…And no sooner do I finish one story, then for some reason I have to write another, and then a third, and after that a fourth…I'll write constantly, as if I'm in a relay race, I can't stop. What's so wonderful and brilliant about that, I ask you? Oh, what a cruel life! Here I am with you, all excited and yet the whole time, I am thinking about the unfinished story that's waiting for me. I'll see that cloud up there, the one that looks like a piano. And I'll think: I've got to put that in a story somewhere, how a cloud was sailing by, a cloud that looked like a grand piano. The smell of heliotrope. Right away I'll make a note of it: sweetish scent, pinkish purple, use it when describing a summer's evening. Every phrase, every word you and I are saying right now, I'll snatch them up as fast as I can and lock them away in my literary closet: Perhaps I'll use them one day! And when I'm through working, I'll run off to the theatre, or go fishing, to rest, to lose myself, — but no, there it is, already casting around in my head like an iron cannonball, a new plot, and already it's pulling me back to my desk, and again I'm racing to write it down, to write, and write. And that's the way it always is, always, I have no peace from myself, and I feel that I'm devouring my own life, that in order to get that sweet honey I give to my nameless, faceless public, I'm gathering the pollen from my own best flowers, then tearing these flowers up, and trampling their roots. Now, really, am I not crazy? Do my nearest and dearest treat me as if I were a sane man, really? "What are you writing now? What new gift will you bestow upon us next?" And so on, and so on, always the same thing over and over again, and I begin to think that all this attention my friends give to me, the praise, the admiration — that it's all a lie, that they're deceiving me, like they would a sick man, and sometimes I'm terrified that what they're really going to do is creep up behind me, grab me, and carry me off to the madhouse, like that poor fellow in Gogol's story. And even in the early years, the best years, when I was starting out, my writing was one continuous torture. A young writer, especially when he hasn't had any luck yet, feels clumsy, awkward, out of place, he's tense, on edge; he's constantly hanging around other writers and artists, unrecognized, unnoticed, afraid to look anyone straight in the eye, like a compulsive gambler who has no money. I could not see my reader, but somehow I imagined him as unfriendly, mistrustful. And I was afraid of my audience, they terrified me, — every time my newest play would open, there they were before me, and I would imagine that everyone with dark hair was hostile, and everyone with fair hair was cold and indifferent. Oh, how terrible! What torture!

NINA: Forgive me, but inspiration and the creative process, don't they give you the moments of greatest happiness?

TRIGORIN: Yes. When I'm writing, it's fine. And when I'm reading the proofs, it's fine…but…it hasn't even come off the press, and already I can't stand it, it's all wrong, it's a mistake, I never should have written it, and I'm irritable, I feel terrible…*(Laughs.)* Meanwhile, the public is reading: "Yes, it's charming, it's witty, but Tolstoy it's not," or "Wonderful, but Turgenev's *Fathers and Sons* is better." And so, to my dying day, it will always be "charming and witty," "charming and witty" — and never anything more, and when I'm dead and gone, all my friends will say, as they file past my grave: "Here lies Trigorin. He was a good writer, but not as good as Turgenev."

NINA: Forgive me, but I can't understand you. You're just spoiled by success.

TRIGORIN: What success? I've never liked myself, and I don't like my own work. Worst of all, I live in some kind of daze and often don't even understand what I'm writing…Look — I love this lake, the trees, the sky, I feel nature, it arouses a great passion in me, an uncontrollable urge to write. But I'm not just a landscape painter, am I, I'm a Russian, I love my native land, the people, I feel that since I am a writer, I am obliged to write about the people, about their suffering, about their future, to address the issues of science, the rights of man, and so on and so on, and so I write about all of it, urgently, and they drive me on and on, angrily, they come at me from all sides, and back and forth I chase, like a fox with the hounds at my heels, and all the while life and science advance onward, ever onward, while I fall behind, far behind, like a peasant chasing after the train he's missed, and in the end I feel that all I know how to write is landscape, and with everything else I am a fraud, a fraud down to the marrow of my bones.

NINA: You're lost in your work, you've neither the time nor the desire to recognize your own importance. Yes, you may be dissatisfied with yourself, but to others you're a great and wonderful man! If I were a writer like you, I would give my entire life to the multitude, knowing that their happiness lay only in reaching my heights, so that then they could draw me in my chariot.

TRIGORIN: Well now, a chariot…Who am I, Agamemnon?

Both smile.

NINA: For the happiness of being a writer or an actress, I would endure rejection of my loved ones, poverty and disillusionment, I'd live in a garret, and eat only black bread, I'd suffer discontent and disappointment in myself, but in return for all this, I shall have fame…real, resounding fame… *(Covers her face with her hands.)* My head is spinning…Oh!…

Voice of ARKADINA from outside the house: "Boris Alekseevich!"

TRIGORIN: I'm being summoned...It must be time to pack. But I don't feel like going. *(Looks around the lake.)* Look! What a paradise this is!...How wonderful!

NINA: Do you see the house and garden on the other shore?

TRIGORIN: Yes.

NINA: That was my late mother's country estate. I was born there. I've spent my whole life on this lake. I know every little island.

TRIGORIN: It's so wonderful here! *(Sees the seagull.)* What's this?

NINA: A seagull. Konstantin Gavrilovich shot it.

TRIGORIN: It's a beautiful bird. Oh, how I don't want to leave. Try to convince Irina Nikolaevna to stay. *(Makes a note in his notebook.)*

NINA: What are you writing?

TRIGORIN: Just making a note...An idea came to me...*(Hides the notebook.)* An idea for a short story: Once upon a time there lived a young girl, on the shore of a lake, a young girl like you; she loved the lake, like a seagull, and she was happy and free, like a seagull. But one day by chance there came a man, who saw her, and, for lack of anything better to do, destroyed her, just like this seagull.

Pause. ARKADINA appears in the window.

ARKADINA: Boris Alekseevich, where are you?

TRIGORIN: Coming! *(As he goes, he looks back at NINA. At the window, to ARKADINA.)* What?

ARKADINA: We're staying.

TRIGORIN goes into the house.

NINA: *(Comes downstage; reflects for a moment.)* A dream!

CURTAIN

ACT THREE

The dining room in SORIN's house. Doors to the right and left. A sideboard. A medicine cabinet. A table in the middle of the room. A trunk and hatboxes; signs of preparation for a departure. TRIGORIN is having lunch. MASHA stands by the table.

MASHA: I'm telling you all this because you're a writer. Use it, if you want. I swear to you: If he had been seriously wounded, I couldn't bear to live one minute longer. But I have courage, you know. I pulled myself together and decided: All right, I'm going to tear this love out of my heart, tear it out by the roots.

TRIGORIN: How?

MASHA: I'm going to get married. To Medvedenko.

TRIGORIN: To the schoolmaster?

MASHA: Yes.

TRIGORIN: I don't see the necessity.

MASHA: To be hopelessly in love, to wait year after year for something is…what…But once I get married, there won't be any time for love, I'll have a whole new set of troubles to drown all the old ones. And anyway, it's a change. Have another one?

TRIGORIN: Won't that be a bit too much?

MASHA: Oh, come on! *(Pours a glass each.)* And stop looking at me like that. Women drink more often than you think. A few drink openly, like I do, but the majority do it in secret. Yes, indeed. And always vodka or brandy. *(Clinks glasses.)* Cheers! You're a nice man, sorry you're leaving. *(Drinks.)*

TRIGORIN: I don't feel much like going.

MASHA: So ask her to stay.

TRIGORIN: No, she won't, not now. Her son has behaved in extremely bad taste. First, he tried to shoot himself, and now, they say, he wants to challenge me to a duel. I mean, what's the point? He sulks, he mocks, he carries on about new forms…But really, there's plenty of room for old forms and new ones — why push each other around?

MASHA: Try jealousy. Sorry, none of my business.

Pause. YAKOV crosses left to right with a suitcase; NINA enters and stops by the window.

My schoolmaster isn't that smart, but he's a good fellow, he's poor, and he's crazy about me. I feel sorry for him. And for his old mother, too. Oh well, let me wish you all the best. Remember me kindly. *(Shakes his hand firmly.)* And thank you for caring about me. Send me your books — oh, and be sure to autograph them. Only don't write: "To Masha, etcetera," just put: "To Marya, who doesn't know where she comes from or why she's living on this earth." Good-bye! *(Exits.)*

NINA: *(Holding out a clenched hand to TRIGORIN.)* Odd or even?

TRIGORIN: Even.

NINA: *(Sighs.)* No, only one pea in this hand. The question is: Will I become an actress or not? If only someone would tell me.

TRIGORIN: No one can.

Pause.

NINA: We're saying good-bye and…perhaps we'll never see each other again. Please, take this momento from me — it's a little medallion. I had your initials engraved on it…and look, on this side, there's the title of your book: *Days and Nights.*

TRIGORIN: How lovely! *(Kisses the medallion.)* What a charming gift!

NINA: Think about me sometimes.

TRIGORIN: I shall. I shall remember how you were on that clear day — do you recall? — a week ago, when you were dressed all in white…We talked…and there on a bench lay a white seagull.

NINA: *(Pensively.)* Yes, a seagull…

Pause.

We can't talk any longer, people are coming…Before you go, give me two minutes more, I beg of you…*(Exits left.)*

At the same time, ARKADINA enters from the right with SORIN, who is wearing a dress coat with a decoration, and then YAKOV, who is preoccupied with the luggage.

ARKADINA: Stay home, you old fool. Are you going to go running around visiting people with that rheumatism of yours? *(To TRIGORIN.)* Who just left? Nina?

TRIGORIN: Yes.

ARKADINA: "Pardon," we've disturbed you. *(Sits.)* Well, we're packed. I'm all worn out.

TRIGORIN: *(Reading the medallion.)* "*Days and Nights,* page 121, lines eleven and twelve."

YAKOV: *(Clearing the table.)* Should I pack up all the fishing rods?

TRIGORIN: Yes, I still need them. But you can give the books away.

YAKOV: Right-o, sir.

TRIGORIN: *(To himself.)* Page 121, lines eleven and twelve. What are those lines? *(To ARKADINA.)* Are any of my notebooks here in the house?

ARKADINA: In my brother's study, in the corner bookcase.

TRIGORIN: Page 121...*(Exits.)*

ARKADINA: So, Petrusha, better stay at home...

SORIN: You're going, and it will be so boring around the house.

ARKADINA: What's going on in town?

SORIN: Nothing in particular, the usual. *(Laughs.)* There'll be a groundbreaking ceremony for the district council building, that sort of thing...I've got to get out for an hour or two, stop laying around, I'm getting stale as an old cigar. I've ordered the horses for one o'clock, we'll go together.

ARKADINA: *(After a pause.)* So, live here, then, but don't get too bored, and don't catch a cold. And keep an eye on my son for me. Take good care of him. Straighten him out.

Pause.

Here I am, going away, and I'll never know why Konstantin tried to shoot himself. Jealousy, that was the main reason, it seems, and the sooner I take Trigorin away from here, the better.

SORIN: How shall I put it — there are other reasons, too, no doubt about it. You have a young, intelligent man, living in the country, in the middle of nowhere, with no money, no position, no future. He has no occupation whatsoever. He's idle — and he's ashamed of it, afraid of it. I'm devoted to him, and he's attached to me, but in the end, he feels out of place, like a boarder, a parasite. It's a question of pride, no doubt about it.

ARKADINA: What grief he gives me! *(Deep in thought.)* You know, maybe he should get a job or something, what do you think...

SORIN: *(Whistles, then, tentatively.)* Maybe the best thing would be for you...to give him a little money. First, he needs to dress decently, that's all. Look at him, he's been wearing the same jacket for three years now, he goes around without an overcoat...*(Laughs.)* And it wouldn't hurt him to get out a little and see the world...Go abroad, whatever...That wouldn't cost much, really.

ARKADINA: Well...Look, a new suit I could manage, but a trip abroad...No, I can't even afford a suit right now. *(Decisively.)* I don't have any money!

SORIN laughs.

No!

SORIN: *(Whistles.)* So, there we are. Forgive me, my dear, don't be angry! I believe you, you're a noble and generous woman.

ARKADINA: *(In tears.)* I don't have any money!

SORIN: If I had it, I'd give it to him, no doubt about it, but I don't, I have nothing, not a kopek. *(Laughs.)* My business manager takes my entire pension and spends it all on farming, cattle raising, beekeeping, and my money seems to disappear into thin air. The bees die, the cattle die, they never give me any horses...

ARKADINA: Well, yes, I do have some money, but, after all, I'm an actress — my wardrobe alone has ruined me.

SORIN: You're so good, my dear...I have the greatest respect for you...Yes...There's something wrong with me again...*(Staggers.)* My head is spinning. *(Holds onto the table.)* I feel faint, that's all.

ARKADINA: *(Frightened.)* Petrusha! *(Tries to hold him up.)* Petrusha, darling... *(Calls out.)* Help me! Help!...

Enter TREPLEV with a bandage on his head, and MEDVEDENKO.

He's going to faint!

SORIN: It's nothing, it's nothing...*(Smiles and drinks water.)* Now it's passed...that's all...

TREPLEV: *(To his mother.)* Don't be frightened, Mama, it's nothing serious. This happens to him all the time. *(To his uncle.)* Uncle, you've got to lie down.

SORIN: All right, just for a bit...But I'm going into town no matter what .. . First I'll lie down and then I'll go into town...no doubt about it...*(Starts to exit, leaning on a cane.)*

MEDVEDENKO: *(Takes him by the arm.)* Here's a riddle: What walks on all fours in the morning, on two feet at midday, and on three feet in the evening...

SORIN: *(Laughing.)* Right. And at night on his back. Thanks very much, I'll manage by myself…

MEDVEDENKO: Why stand on ceremony!…

He and SORIN exit.

ARKADINA: How he frightened me!

TREPLEV: It's not good for him to live in the country. He's miserable. If only you'd show a sudden burst of generosity, Mama, and lend him a thousand rubles or two, then he could live in town all year round.

ARKADINA: I don't have any money. I'm an actress, not a banker.

Pause.

TREPLEV: Mama, change my bandage. You do it so well.

ARKADINA: *(Gets first aid kit and materials from the medicine cabinet.)* The doctor's late.

TREPLEV: He promised to be here at ten, and it's noon already.

ARKADINA: Sit. *(Takes the bandage off his head.)* It looks like a turban on you. Yesterday, a passerby asked at the kitchen door what nationality you were. Now it's almost all healed. Only a tiny bit left to go. *(Kisses his head.)* You're not going to do anything foolish again, when I'm gone?

TREPLEV: No, Mama. It was a moment of insane despair, and I lost control. It won't happen again. *(Kisses her hand.)* You have magic in your hands. Do you remember, a long time ago, you were still working in the state theatre — I was just a little boy, — there was a fight in our courtyard, and a laundress was severely beaten? Do you remember? They found her unconscious…You took care of her, gave her medicine, bathed her children. You really don't remember?

ARKADINA: No. *(Puts on a new bandage.)*

TREPLEV: Two ballerinas lived in the same house we did…They used to come and have coffee with you…

ARKADINA: That I remember.

TREPLEV: They were very devout.

Pause.

These last few days, I've loved you as tenderly and as completely as I did when I was a child. Without you, I have no one. Only why, why do you let this man control you?

ARKADINA: You don't understand him, Konstantin. He's a man of the highest integrity...

TREPLEV: Yes, and when it was announced that I intended to challenge him to a duel, his integrity didn't stop him from playing the coward. He's leaving...better yet, fleeing. It's disgraceful.

ARKADINA: What nonsense! I asked him to leave myself.

TREPLEV: Yes, a man of the highest integrity. Here we are almost quarrelling about him, and meanwhile, he's somewhere in the drawing room or the garden, laughing at us...tutoring Nina, trying to talk her into thinking he's a genius.

ARKADINA: You delight in saying things to upset me. I respect this man and I ask you not to speak ill of him in my presence.

TREPLEV: And I don't respect him. You want me to consider him a genius, too, but forgive me, I can't lie to you, his work makes me sick.

ARKADINA: That's jealousy. People who have no talent, only pretensions, have nothing better to do than put down people who have *real* talent. It must be a consolation for them.

TREPLEV: *(Ironically.)* Talent! *(Angrily.)* I am more talented than the whole lot of you, as far as that goes! *(Rips the bandage from his head.)* You and your little 'élite' have taken possession of art — you ordain that the only real art is what you create yourselves, and the rest you suppress and suffocate. I renounce you all! You and him!

ARKADINA: Decadent!...

TREPLEV: Go back to your precious theatre, and perform in your mediocre, pathetic little plays!

ARKADINA: I have never appeared in a mediocre play! Leave me alone! You couldn't even write one miserable little comic skit! You Kiev bourgeois! Parasite!

TREPLEV: Miser!

ARKADINA: Beggar!

TREPLEV sits and cries softly.

Nonentity! *(Pacing in agitation.)* Don't cry. You mustn't cry...*(She weeps.)* Please don't...*(Kisses him on the forehead, cheeks, head.)* My darling child, forgive me...Forgive your wretched mother. Forgive your unhappy mother.

TREPLEV:*(Embraces her.)* If only you knew! I've lost everything. She doesn't love me, I can't write any more…all my hopes are gone…

ARKADINA: Don't despair…Everything will be all right. He's leaving now, she'll love you again, she will. *(Wipes away his tears.)* Enough. We've already made up.

TREPLEV: *(Kisses her hands.)* Yes, Mama.

ARKADINA: *(Tenderly.)* Now make up with him, too. You don't need a duel…do you?

TREPLEV: All right…Only Mama, I beg of you, don't let me see him. It's more than I could bear…

Enter TRIGORIN.

So…I'm leaving…*(Quickly puts medicine away in the cabinet.)* The doctor can fix the bandage later…

TRIGORIN: *(Looks in the notebook.)* Page 121…lines eleven and twelve…Here it is…*(Reads.)* "If ever you have need of my life, then come and take it."

TREPLEV picks up the bandage from the floor and exits.

ARKADINA: *(Looking at her watch.)* The horses will be arriving soon.

TRIGORIN: *(To himself.)* "If ever you have need of my life, then come and take it."

ARKADINA: You're all packed, I hope?

TRIGORIN: *(Impatiently.)* Yes, yes…*(Deep in thought.)* A cry from a pure heart: Why does it touch me, why does it wring my own heart so…"If ever you have need of my life, then come and take it." *(To ARKADINA.)* Let's stay for just one more day!

ARKADINA shakes her head "no."

Let us stay!

ARKADINA: Darling, I know what's keeping you here. But get a hold of yourself. You're a little intoxicated, sober up.

TRIGORIN: And you, too, be sober, be sensitive and reasonable, I beg of you, look upon all this like a true friend…*(Squeezes her hand.)* You who are capable of sacrifice…Be my friend, set me free…

ARKADINA: *(Tremendously agitated.)* So you're that enamored?

TRIGORIN: I am drawn to her! Perhaps this is just what I need.

ARKADINA: The love of a little provincial girl? Oh, how little you know yourself!

TRIGORIN: Sometimes, you know, you fall under a spell, like I am now, I'm talking to you, and at the same time I'm sleeping and dreaming, dreaming of her...Such sweet, marvelous dreams have taken hold of me...Set me free...

ARKADINA: *(Trembling.)* No, no...I'm just an ordinary woman, you can't talk to me like that...Don't torture me, Boris...I'm terrified...

TRIGORIN: Yes, but if you wanted, you could be an extraordinary woman. A young love, a charming, poetic love, transporting me into a world of dreams, it alone can bring me happiness on this earth. Such a love I've never felt before...I never had time for it when I was young, always haunting publishers' doors, struggling with poverty...Now here it is, this love, it has come at last, and it beckons me...What sense is there to run from it?

ARKADINA: *(With great anger.)* You're out of your mind!

TRIGORIN: So be it.

ARKADINA: You've all conspired to torture me today! *(Weeps.)*

TRIGORIN: *(Holds his head in his hands.)* She doesn't understand! She doesn't want to understand!

ARKADINA: Am I really so old and ugly that you can talk about other women in front of me without any shame? *(Embraces and kisses him.)* Oh, you really have gone mad! My glorious, marvelous man...You are the last page of my life! *(Gets on her knees.)* My joy, my pride, my ecstasy...*(Embraces his knees.)* Leave me, even for one hour, and I won't survive, I'll go out of my mind, my wonderful, magnificent man, my master...

TRIGORIN: Someone might come in. *(Helps her to her feet.)*

ARKADINA: Let them, I'm not ashamed of my love for you. *(Kisses his hand.)* My treasure, my desperate one, so you want to behave like a madman, but I won't let you, I won't...*(Laughs.)* You're mine...You're mine...This forehead is mine, and these eyes are mine, and this wonderful, silky hair is mine, too...You're all mine. You're so talented, so brilliant, the best of all living writers, you're the one hope of Russia...And what sincerity you have, what simplicity, freshness, humor...In one stroke, you can conjure up a character or an entire landscape, your people are so alive. Oh, what a delight it is to read you! You think I'm showering praise on you, flattering you? Go on, look me in the eye...look at me...Do I look like a liar? There, you see, I'm the only one who can truly appreciate you; I'm the only one who tells you the truth, my darling, wonderful man...You'll go with me? Yes? You won't desert me?

TRIGORIN: I have no will of my own...I've never had a will of my own...I'm weak, fragile, always submissive…how could any woman want me? Go on, take me away, kidnap me, do it, but never let me leave your side, not even one step…

ARKADINA: *(To herself.)* Now he's mine. *(Casually, as if nothing has happened.)* Anyway, if you want to, you can stay. I'm going, and you can follow in a week or so. Really, what's the hurry?

TRIGORIN: No, we'll go together.

ARKADINA: Whatever you want. If it's together, then it's together…

Pause. TRIGORIN makes a note in his notebook.

What are you doing?

TRIGORIN: Heard a great expression this morning, "the virgin forest" …Might be useful somewhere. *(Stretches.)* So, we're going? Once again, it's the coaches and the stations, the station restaurants, cutlets and conversations…

SHAMRAEV: *(Enters.)* It is with great regret that I inform you that the horses are ready. It is time, esteemed lady, to go to the station. The train will be arriving at five minutes past two. And, if you will be so kind, Irina Nikolaevna, don't forget to ask: where is the actor Suzdaltsev? Is he alive and well? We used to go out drinking in the old days…His performance in *The Great Mail Robbery* was incomparable…At the time, I remember, he was also appearing in the town of Yelisavetgrad together with the trage-dian Izmailov, another famous actor…What's the hurry, esteemed lady, we still have five minutes. Once they were playing conspirators in a melodra-ma, and when suddenly they were discovered, Izmailov's line was: "We've been caught in a trap," but instead, he said: "We've been caught on a trip"…*(Shouts with laughter.)* A trip!…

While he is speaking, YAKOV is busy with the luggage, a MAID brings ARKADINA her hat, cloak, parasol, gloves; they are all helping ARKADINA to dress. The COOK peeks out from the door stage left, and after waiting a moment, he enters with hesitation. Enter POLINA ANDREEVNA, then SORIN and MEDVEDENKO.

POLINA ANDREEVNA: *(With a basket.)* Here are some plums for your jour-ney…They're nice and sweet. Perhaps you'll feel like a treat…

ARKADINA: You're so kind, Polina Andreevna.

POLINA ANDREEVNA: Good-bye, my dearest. If everything wasn't as it should have been, forgive me. *(Weeps.)*

ARKADINA: *(Embraces her.)* Everything was fine, just fine. There's nothing to cry about, really.

POLINA ANDREEVNA: Our time is running out!

ARKADINA: And what can we do about it!

SORIN: *(Enters from the door stage left, wearing a coat with a cape, a hat, and a cane; he crosses the room.)* Come, my dear sister, it's time to go, let's not be late, after all. I'll wait in the carriage *(Exits.)*

MEDVEDENKO: And I'll walk to the station...to see you off. I'd better get going...*(Exits.)*

ARKADINA: Good-bye, my dear ones...If we're alive and well, we'll see each other again next summer...

The MAID, YAKOV, and the COOK kiss her hand.

Don't forget me. *(Gives the COOK a ruble.)* Here's a ruble, it's for the three of you.

COOK: We humbly thank you, madam. Have a pleasant journey. We're very grateful!

YAKOV: God bless you!

SHAMRAEV: Drop us a line — we'd be delighted! Good-bye, Boris Alekseevich!

ARKADINA: Where's Konstantin? Tell him I'm leaving. I must say good-bye to him. Well, remember me kindly. *(To YAKOV.)* I gave a ruble to the cook. It's for the three of you.

All exit stage right. The stage is empty. Backstage there is a general noise of farewell. The MAID returns to get the basket of plums from the table, and exits again.

TRIGORIN: *(Returning.)* I forgot my walking stick. It's out there on the terrace, somewhere. *(Crosses, and meets NINA as she enters from the door stage left.)* It's you! We were just leaving...

NINA: I had the feeling we'd see each other again. *(Excitedly.)* Boris Alekseevich, I've finally decided, the die is cast, I'm going on the stage. By tomorrow, I'll be gone, I'm leaving my father, forsaking everything, I'm starting a new life...I'm going away, like you...to Moscow. We shall see each other there.

TRIGORIN: *(Looking around.)* Stay at the Slavyansky Bazaar...Let me know as soon as you get there…Grokholsky's house on Molchanovka Street…I must hurry…

Pause.

NINA: One minute more…

TRIGORIN: *(In a low voice.)* You are so beautiful…Oh, what happiness, to think we'll see each other again so soon!

She leans against his chest.

I'm going to see these wonderful eyes again, and this beautiful, tender smile, beautiful beyond words…these gentle features, the image of angelic purity…My darling…

A prolonged kiss.

CURTAIN

————————————————

Between Acts III and IV, two years have passed.

One of the drawing rooms in SORIN's house, which TREPLEV has converted into a study. To the right and left are doors leading to interior rooms. A glass door, upstage center, opens onto the terrace. In addition to the usual drawing room furniture, there is a writing table in the right corner, a Turkish divan by the left door, bookcases filled with books, and books on the window sills and chairs. It is evening. A single shaded lamp is burning. Semidarkness. The wind is heard whistling through the trees and howling in the chimneys. There is the sound of the night watchman passing by.

MEDVEDENKO and MASHA enter.

MASHA: *(Calling out.)* Konstantin Gavrilovich! Konstantin Gavrilovich! *(Looks around.)* No one's here. Every other minute the old man's asking, where's Kostya, where's Kostya…Can't live without him…
MEDVEDENKO: He's afraid of being alone. *(Listens.)* What terrible weather! It's been like this now for almost two whole days.
MASHA: *(Turns up the lamp.)* There are waves on the lake. Huge ones.
MEDVEDENKO: It's dark in the garden. Someone really should have that theatre torn down. It's standing out there, bare and ugly, like a skeleton, the curtain's flapping in the wind. Last night, when I was passing by, I thought I heard someone crying…
MASHA: Really…

Pause.

MEDVEDENKO: Come on, Masha, let's go home!
MASHA: *(Shakes her head "no.")* I'm spending the night here.
MEDVEDENKO: *(Pleading.)* Masha, let's go! The baby must be hungry by now.
MASHA: Nonsense. Matryona will feed him.

Pause.

MEDVEDENKO: It's pitiful. The third night without his mother.
MASHA: How boring you've become. Before, at least, you would philosophize, now it's baby, house, baby, house — that's all I ever hear from you.
MEDVEDENKO: Masha, come on, let's go.
MASHA: Go yourself.

MEDVEDENKO: Your father won't give me any horses.

MASHA: Yes, he will. Ask him, he'll give them to you.

MEDVEDENKO: All right, I will. So that means you'll come home tomorrow, then?

MASHA:*(Takes snuff.)* Yes, yes, tomorrow. You're bothering me…

Enter TREPLEV and POLINA ANDREEVNA. TREPLEV carries pillows and a quilt, and POLINA ANDREEVNA carries the bed linen; they put it on the divan, and then TREPLEV goes to his writing table and sits down.

What's all this for, Mama?

POLINA ANDREEVNA: Pyotr Nikolaevich asked to have a bed made up for him in Kostya's room.

MASHA: Let me do it…*(Makes up the bed.)*

POLINA ANDREEVNA: *(Sighing.)* Old people are such children…*(Goes to the writing table, and, leaning on her elbows, looks at a manuscript.)*

Pause.

MEDVEDENKO: So, I'm leaving. Good-bye, Masha. *(Kisses his wife's hand.)* Good-bye, Mama dear. *(Goes to kiss his mother-in-law's hand.)*

POLINA ANDREEVNA: *(Irritated.)* All right! Go, already. Travel safely.

MEDVEDENKO: Good-bye, Konstantin Gavrilovich.

Silently, TREPLEV gives him his hand; MEDVEDENKO exits.

POLINA ANDREEVNA: *(Looking at the manuscript.)* Who would have believed it, who would have thought that you'd become a real writer, Kostya. And now, thank God, the journals are sending you money. *(Runs her hand through his hair.)* How handsome you've become…Darling Kostya, my dear boy, why don't you be a little kinder to my Mashenka!…

MASHA: *(Making the bed.)* Leave him alone, Mama.

POLINA ANDREEVNA: *(To TREPLEV.)* She's such a sweet girl.

Pause.

All women need, Kostya, is a little tenderness. This I know from experience.

TREPLEV gets up from the writing table and exits silently.

MASHA: You see — he's angry. You had to go and bother him.

POLINA ANDREEVNA: I feel so sorry for you, Mashenka.

MASHA: That helps!

POLINA ANDREEVNA: My heart aches for you. Believe me, I see everything, I understand everything.

MASHA: Oh, it's all ridiculous. Unrequited love — that's only in novels. It's nonsense. You can't just let yourself go, and sit by the seashore, waiting for something, waiting for the weather to change…If you've fallen in love, why then you'll just have to fall out of it. They've promised to transfer my husband to another district. So as soon as we move there, — I'll forget everything…I'll rip it out of my heart by the roots.

Two rooms away, someone plays a melancholy waltz.

POLINA ANDREEVNA: Kostya's playing. That means he's sad.

MASHA: *(Dances a few steps of the waltz, noiselessly.)* Out of sight, out of mind, Mama, that's the main thing. Just let them transfer my Semyon, and then, I swear, in one month I'll have forgotten him. It's all nonsense.

The door stage left opens, DORN and MEDVEDENKO enter, pushing SORIN in a wheelchair.

MEDVEDENKO: I've got six at home now. And with flour at seven kopeks a pound.

DORN: It goes on and on.

MEDVEDENKO: Go ahead, laugh, it's easy for you. You're rolling in money.

DORN: Money? I've practiced medicine for thirty years, my friend, thirty hard years, gave up my life day and night for it, saved up a miserable two thousand, and then spent it all when I went abroad. I don't have a thing left.

MASHA: *(To her husband.)* You mean you haven't gone yet?

MEDVEDENKO: *(Guiltily.)* How can I? When they won't give me any horses!

MASHA: *(With bitter irritation, in a low voice.)* I wish I'd never laid eyes on you!

The wheelchair is placed stage left; POLINA ANDREEVNA, MASHA, and DORN sit alongside it; MEDVEDENKO, dejected, moves aside.

DORN: So much has changed here, though! You've turned the drawing room into a study.

MASHA: Konstantin Gavrilovich is more comfortable working here. He can go out into the garden and think whenever he wants.

Sound of the night watchman passing.

SORIN: Where's my sister?

DORN: She went to the station to meet Trigorin. She'll be back soon.

SORIN: If you thought it necessary to send for my sister, I must be seriously ill. *(After a moment's silence.)* And so it goes, I am seriously ill, and they won't give me any medicine.

DORN: So what would you like? Some valerian drops? Soda? Quinine water?

SORIN: And let the philosophizing begin! Oh, what punishment! *(Nodding toward the divan.)* That's been made up for me?

POLINA ANDREEVNA: Just for you, Pyotr Nikolaevich.

SORIN: Bless you.

DORN: *(Hums.)* "The moon floats through the night sky…"

SORIN: Now, let me give Kostya an idea for a story. The title: *The Man Who Wanted To. 'L'homme qui a voulu.'* Once upon a time, when I was young, I wanted to become a man of letters — and I never did; I wanted to speak beautifully, and I have always spoken abominably *(imitates himself)*: "That's all, and so on, and blah blah blah," my summaries would go on and on till I worked myself into a sweat; I wanted to get married — and I never got married; I always wanted to live in town — and here I am ending my life in the country, that's all.

DORN: You wanted to become a state councillor — and you did.

SORIN: *(Laughs.)* I didn't want that. It happened all by itself.

DORN: Complaining like that after sixty-two good years of living, that's not in very good taste, now is it?

SORIN: What a stubborn man you are! Don't you understand, I want to live!

DORN: That's indulgent. According to the laws of nature, every life must come to an end.

SORIN: Talk all you want, what do you care? You're the man who's had it all, so what difference does it make? But you too will be afraid to die, you'll see.

DORN: Fear of death — that's a natural fear…we must learn to overcome it. Only the religious fear death, and that's because they believe in life eternal and they're afraid for their sins. But first of all, you're not religious, and second of all — what are your sins? Only that you've served in the department of justice for twenty-five years — that's about all.

SORIN: *(Laughs.)* Twenty-eight…

TREPLEV enters and sits on a small stool at SORIN's feet. MASHA doesn't take her eyes off him the entire time.

DORN: We're keeping Konstantin Gavrilovich from his work.
TREPLEV: No, it doesn't matter.

Pause.

MEDVEDENKO: May I ask, Doctor, what is your favorite foreign city?
DORN: Genoa.
TREPLEV: Why Genoa?
DORN: Because of the crowds in the street. They're wonderful. In the evening, when you walk out of your hotel, the streets are teeming with people. You drift through the crowd with no destination, aimlessly, randomly, here and there, you live with it, merge with it in spirit, and soon you begin to believe that a universal soul indeed is possible, like the one Nina Zarechnaya played so long ago in your play. By the way, where is Nina now? Where is she and how is she?
TREPLEV: Fine, as far as I know.
DORN: I heard she was leading a very strange life. What happened?
TREPLEV: That, Doctor, is a long story.
DORN: Give us the short version.

Pause.

TREPLEV: She ran away from home and met up with Trigorin. Did you know that?
DORN: Yes, I knew.
TREPLEV: They had a child. The child died. Trigorin fell out of love with her and returned to his former liaison, as was expected. Not that he ever really left it, no, in his own weak fashion, he somehow contrived to keep both. As far as I can tell, Nina's personal life hasn't been a complete success.
DORN: And her career?
TREPLEV: Worse, I'm afraid. She made her debut at a summer theatre outside Moscow, and then she went away to the provinces. At the time I wouldn't let her out of my sight, and for a while, wherever she went, I would follow her. She played all the big roles, but she overacted badly, gesticulating, ranting and raving. There were moments when she showed some talent —

she played hysteria and the death scenes well — but those were only moments.

DORN: Still, she had talent, didn't she?

TREPLEV: Difficult to say. Probably. I could see her, but she wouldn't see me, her maid wouldn't let me into her hotel room. I understood how she felt and didn't insist.

Pause.

What else can I tell you? When I returned home, I would get letters from her. Warm, intelligent, interesting letters. She didn't complain, but I could tell how deeply unhappy she was; you could feel the pain and anxiety in every line. And her mind was distracted. She would sign her name 'Seagull.' You know, the way the miller said he was a raven in Pushkin's *Rusalka* — so she kept saying in her letters, that she was a seagull. And now she's here.

DORN: What do you mean, here?

TREPLEV: Here in town, she's staying at the inn. She's been here five days now, she's taken a room. I tried to visit her, and so did Marya Ilyinichna, but she won't see anyone. Semyon Semyonovich is convinced that yesterday evening, after dinner, he saw her in the field, about a mile from here.

MEDVEDENKO: Yes, I did. She was walking toward town. I gave her my greetings, and asked her why she hadn't come to visit us. She said she would.

TREPLEV: She won't.

Pause.

Her father and stepmother have disowned her. They have watchmen stationed everywhere so she can't even get near to the estate. *(Goes to the writing table with the doctor.)* How easy it is to be a philosopher on paper, doctor, and how hard in real life!

SORIN: She was a charming girl.

DORN: What did you say?

SORIN: I said, what a charming girl she was. Even state councillor Sorin was a bit in love with her for a little while.

DORN: You old so-and-so.

SHAMRAEV's laughter is heard.

POLINA ANDREEVNA: It sounds as if they've come back from the station.
TREPLEV: Yes, I hear Mama.

Enter ARKADINA and TRIGORIN; behind them, SHAMRAEV.

SHAMRAEV: *(Entering.)* We're all getting older, the elements are aging us, but you, my dear lady, you get younger and younger...so colorful, so full of life...and grace...
ARKADINA: Are you trying to put the evil eye on me again, you tiresome man!
TRIGORIN: *(To SORIN.)* Hello, Pyotr Nikolaevich! What, you're still ill? We can't have that! *(Sees MASHA, delighted.)* Marya Ilyinichna!
MASHA: You recognized me! *(Shakes his hand.)*
TRIGORIN: Are you married?
MASHA: Long ago.
TRIGORIN: Are you happy? *(Greets DORN and MEDVEDENKO, then goes to TREPLEV with uncertainty.)* Irina Nikolaevna said that you've buried the past, and you're no longer angry with me.

TREPLEV holds out his hand.

ARKADINA: *(To her son.)* Boris Alekseevich brought you the journal with your new story.
TREPLEV: *(Taking the book, to TRIGORIN.)* Thank you. That's very kind of you.

They sit.

TRIGORIN: Your admirers send you their regards...There's a lot of talk about you in Petersburg and Moscow, everyone asks about you. They want to know: What's he like, how old is he, does he have dark hair, or light? For some reason, they all think you're an old man. And nobody knows your real name, you're published under a pseudonym. You're as mysterious as the 'Man in the Iron Mask.'
TREPLEV: Are you here for long?
TRIGORIN: No, tomorrow I'm leaving for Moscow. I must. I'm in a rush to finish a piece, and then I've promised something for a collection. You know, it's the same old story.

While they are speaking, ARKADINA and POLINA ANDREEVNA place a card table in the middle of the room and open it. SHAMRAEV lights the candles, and puts the chairs in place. The lotto set is brought from the cupboard.

The weather didn't give me a very warm welcome. There's a cruel wind. Tomorrow morning, if it dies down, I'm going to go fishing on the lake. Oh, and I want to take a look around the garden and that place — do you remember — where your play was performed? I've been thinking about an idea for a story, and I only need to see the setting to refresh my memory.

MASHA: *(To her father.)* Papa, let my husband take a horse! He needs to go home.

SHAMRAEV: *(Imitates her.)* Horse…home…*(Severely.)* They've just come back from the station, you can see for yourself. I can't send them running out again.

MASHA: But surely you've got others…*(Sees that her father is silent, waves her hand.)* I give up…

MEDVEDENKO: Masha, I'll walk home. Really…

POLINA ANDREEVNA: *(Sighing.)* Walking, in such weather…*(Sits at the card table.)* Come on, everyone.

MEDVEDENKO: Really, it's only four miles…Good-bye…*(Kisses his wife's hand.)* Good-bye, Mama dear.

His mother-in-law reluctantly extends her hand to be kissed.

I didn't want to bother anyone, but the baby, you know…*(Bows to everyone.)* Good-bye…*(Exits with a guilty walk.)*

SHAMRAEV: Don't worry, he can walk. He's not a general.

POLINA ANDREEVNA: *(Knocks on the table.)* Everyone, please. Let's not waste time, they'll be calling us to supper soon.

SHAMRAEV, MASHA, and DORN sit at the table.

ARKADINA: *(To TRIGORIN.)* When the long autumn evenings descend upon us, here's where we sit and play lotto. Look, it's the same old lotto set mother used to play with us when we were children. Won't you join us in a hand before supper? *(Sits with TRIGORIN at the table.)* It's a boring game, but once you get used to it, it's not so bad. *(Gives everyone three cards each.)*

TREPLEV: *(Looking through the journal.)* He's read his own story, and hasn't even cut the pages of mine. *(Puts the journal on the writing table, and then goes to the left door; as he passes his mother, he kisses her on the top of her head.)*

ARKADINA: What about you, Kostya?

TREPLEV: Sorry, no thanks, I don't feel like it. I'm going for a walk. *(Exits.)*

ARKADINA: The ante is ten kopeks. Put in for me, Doctor.

DORN: Yes, madam.

MASHA: Everyone anted up? I'll start…Twenty-two!

ARKADINA: Yes.

MASHA: Three!

DORN: Right!

MASHA: Did you cover three? Eight! Twenty-one! Ten!

SHAMRAEV: Not so fast.

ARKADINA: How they loved me in Kharkov, my darlings, my head is still spinning from it!

MASHA: Thirty-four!

Offstage a melancholy waltz is played.

ARKADINA: The students gave me a standing ovation…Three bouquets, two garlands, and this…*(Takes off her brooch and throws it on the table.)*

SHAMRAEV: How about that…

MASHA: Fifty!…

DORN: Fifty what?

ARKADINA: I wore an amazing outfit…Whatever they may say about me, I know how to dress.

POLINA ANDREEVNA: Kostya's playing. He's sad, poor fellow.

SHAMRAEV: They've been hard on him in the newspapers

MASHA: Seventy-seven!

ARKADINA: Why pay attention.

TRIGORIN: He hasn't had any luck. Somehow he still hasn't found his own voice. There's something strange and vague about his writing, at times it's almost delirious. And not one single living character.

MASHA: Eleven!

ARKADINA: *(Glancing at SORIN.)* Petrusha, are you bored?

Pause.

He's asleep.

DORN: Our esteemed state councillor's asleep.

MASHA: Seven! Ninety!

TRIGORIN: If I lived on an estate like this, by a lake, I wonder if I'd ever have been a writer. I'd give up this obsession, and do nothing but fish.

MASHA: Twenty-eight!

TRIGORIN: I'd catch ruff or perch — what bliss!

DORN: Now I believe in Konstantin Gavrilovich. There's something there! Something there! He thinks in images, his stories are vivid, striking, and they move me deeply. It's a pity, though, that he doesn't have a clear message. He makes an impression, that's all, and you can't go far on impression alone. Irina Nikolaevna, are you pleased you have a writer for a son?

ARKADINA: Can you imagine, I haven't read any of his work yet. There just isn't enough time.

MASHA: Twenty-six!

TREPLEV enters quietly and goes to his writing table.

SHAMRAEV: *(To TRIGORIN.)* We still have something of yours here, Boris Alekseevich.

TRIGORIN: What's that?

SHAMRAEV: You remember once, Konstantin Gavrilovich shot a seagull, and you told me to have it mounted.

TRIGORIN: I don't remember. *(Thinks for a moment.)* I don't remember.

MASHA: Sixty-six! One!

TREPLEV: *(Flings open the window, listens.)* How dark it is! I don't know why I feel so uneasy.

ARKADINA: Kostya, shut the window, there's a draft.

TREPLEV shuts the window.

MASHA: Eighty-eight!

TRIGORIN: Ladies and gentlemen, game!

ARKADINA: *(Joyfully.)* Bravo! Bravo!

SHAMRAEV: Bravo!

ARKADINA: This man has all the luck, always. *(Gets up.)* Now let's go have a bite to eat. Our celebrity hasn't had his supper yet. We'll continue playing afterwards. *(To her son.)* Kostya, leave your manuscripts, come and eat.

TREPLEV: I don't feel like it, Mama, I'm not hungry.

ARKADINA: Suit yourself. *(Wakens SORIN.)* Petrusha, time for supper! *(Takes SORIN by the hand.)* I'll tell you all about the fuss they made over me in Kharkhov...

POLINA ANDREEVNA puts out the candles on the table, then she and

DORN push the wheelchair. They all exit by the door stage left; TREPLEV is left alone on stage at the writing table.

TREPLEV: *(Preparing to write, reviews what he has already written.)* Forms. For so long I've been going on and on about the need for new forms. And now, little by little, I'm falling into the same old rut myself. *(Reads.)* "The poster on the fence proclaimed it...a pale face, framed by dark hair"..."proclaimed," "framed"...It's so trite. *(Crosses it out.)* I'll start with the part where the hero is awakened by the sound of the rain, and strike all the rest. All this about a moonlit night is drawn-out and pretentious. Now Trigorin has technique, it's easy for him...He's got a "broken bottle neck gleaming on the bank," a "mill wheel casting a somber shadow"   and presto — there's his moonlit night right there. And what do I have — "the shimmering light," and "the soft twinkling of the stars," and "the distant sounds of the piano receding into the quiet, fragrant air"...I mean, it's unbearable!

Pause.

Yes, more and more I've come to see...it's not about forms — old forms, new forms — it's about writing, not bound by any forms at all, just writing, freely, from the soul.

Someone raps on the window near the writing table.

What's that? *(Looks out the window.)* I can't see anything...*(Opens the glass door and looks out into the garden.)* Someone's running down the steps. *(Calls out.)* Who's there? *(Exits; he can be heard walking rapidly along the terrace; a moment later, he returns with NINA.)* Nina! Nina!

Nina lays her head on his chest and sobs with restraint.

(Deeply moved.) Nina! Nina! It's you...it's you...I knew it — all day long my soul has been in anguish. *(Takes off her hat and cape.)* Oh, my darling, my beloved — she's come! Let's not cry, please, let's not!
NINA: Someone's here.
TREPLEV: No, no one.
NINA: Lock the doors, someone will come in.
TREPLEV: No one will come in.
NINA: Irina Nikolaevna is here, I know it. Please lock the doors...

TREPLEV: *(Locks the right door with a key, and then crosses to the left.)* There's no lock on this one. I'll put a chair against it. *(Puts armchair against the door.)* Don't worry, no one will come in.

NINA: *(Gazes at him intently.)* Let me look at you. *(Looks around.)* It's so warm in here, so lovely…This used to be the living room. Have I changed a lot?

TREPLEV: Yes…You're thinner, and your eyes are bigger, much bigger. Nina, it's so strange to be seeing you. Why didn't you ever let me visit you? Why didn't you come sooner? I know you've been here almost a week already… Every day I've been coming over, time and time again, I stand outside your window like a beggar.

NINA: I was afraid you'd hate me. Every night I have the same dream — you look at me and you don't recognize me. If only you knew! From the moment I arrived I've been coming here…to walk by the lake. I've gone past your house so many times, but I couldn't bring myself to come in. Come, let's sit down.

They sit.

Let's just sit and talk, and talk. It's so lovely here, isn't it, so warm, so safe…Oh! Do you hear it? The wind? There's a line in Turgenev that goes: "Lucky is he who, on nights like these, has a roof over his head, a warm place to sit." I'm a seagull…No, that's not it. *(Rubs her forehead.)* What was I saying? Oh, yes… Turgenev…"And God watches over all homeless wanderers…" Never mind. *(Sobs.)*

TREPLEV: Nina, not again…Nina!

NINA: Never mind, really, it feels much better, it does…I haven't cried in two years. Late last night, I went out in the garden, to see if our theatre were still there. And it is — it's there, it's been there all this time! I burst out crying for the first time in two years, and a weight, such a weight lifted from my soul. You see, I'm not crying any more! *(Takes his hand.)* So, you've become a writer after all…You're a writer, and I'm an actress…We're drawn into the vortex, both of us…I used to be so happy, blissful, like a child — I'd wake up every morning and burst out singing. I loved you, I dreamed of fame…and now? Tomorrow morning early it's off to Yelets, third class…with the peasants, and then in Yelets, it's the businessmen, with their little "invitations." What a miserable life!

TREPLEV: Why Yelets?

NINA: I've taken an engagement there for the winter season. It's time for me to go.

TREPLEV: Nina. I've cursed you, hated you, torn your letters and photographs to pieces, but every minute I knew my soul was bound to you forever. To stop loving you is not within my power, Nina. From the moment I lost you, and after that, even when my work started to be published, my life has been unbearable — I suffer so much…It's as if my youth had suddenly been stripped away from me, and I feel I've been living endless years upon this earth. I call out your name, I kiss the ground you walk on — wherever I look, I see your face before me, your tender smile, that smile which illuminated the most precious years of my life…

NINA: *(Dismayed.)* Why are you talking like this, why?

TREPLEV: I'm alone, with no love to warm me, I'm cold, it's like living in a grave, and no matter what I write, no matter what, it's flat, stale, lifeless. Stay here, Nina, I beg of you, or else let me go away with you.

NINA quickly puts on her hat and cape.

Nina, why? For God's sake, Nina…*(Watches her put her things on.)*

Pause.

NINA: My horses are waiting at the gate. Don't bother to come out, I can find my own way…*(In tears.)* Give me some water.

TREPLEV: *(Gives her water.)* Where are you going now?

NINA: Into town.

Pause.

Is Irina Nikolaevna here?

TREPLEV: Yes…Thursday, my uncle took ill. We cabled her to come.

NINA: Why do you say you kiss the ground I walk on? I ought to be killed. *(Leans against the table.)* I'm so exhausted. If only I could rest, just rest. *(Lifts her head.)* I'm a seagull!…No, that's not it. I'm an actress. Yes, that's right! *(She hears ARKADINA and TRIGORIN's laughter, listens, then runs to the left door and looks through the keyhole.)* So, he is here, too…*(Turns to TREPLEV.)* Ah well…what does it matter…Yes…He never believed in the theatre, you know, he always laughed at my dreams, and little by little I stopped believing and lost faith, too…And then there were the pressures of love, the jealousy, the constant worry over my little one…I became — I don't know — mediocre, pitiful, my acting made no sense any more…I didn't know what to do with my hands, how to stand on stage, how to control my own voice. You have no idea how it feels, to know you're acting badly. I'm a seagull. No that's not it…Do you remember, when you shot that seagull? "One day, by chance, there came a man who saw her and, for lack of anything better to do, destroyed her"…An idea for a short story…No, that's not it…*(Rubs her forehead.)* What was I saying?… Oh yes, I was talking about the stage. No, I'm not like that any more…I'm a true actress now, and I perform with joy, with ecstasy, I'm intoxicated on the stage, and I feel beautiful. And now, while I've been staying here, I've been walking, walking and thinking, thinking and feeling, how my spirit is growing stronger every day…And now I know, I understand, Kostya, that in our work — it's all the same, whether we perform or we write — the main thing is not the glory, not the glitter, no, not any of those things I dreamed of, it's having the strength to endure. The strength to bear your cross, to have faith. I have faith, and it's not so painful for me any more, and when I think about my calling, I'm not so afraid of life. I'm not.

TREPLEV: *(Sadly.)* You've found your way, you know where you're going, while I'm still floundering in a sea of dreams and images, not knowing what or whom they are for. I don't believe in anything, and I don't know what my calling is.

NINA: *(Listening.)* Shh…I'm going. Good-bye. When I become a famous actress, come and see me. Promise? But now…*(Squeezes his hand.)* It's late — I can hardly stand…I'm so exhausted, so hungry…

TREPLEV: Stay, let me give you some supper…

NINA: No, no…don't bother, I'll find my way out…My horses are near…So, she brought him with her. Well, what does it matter. When you see Trigorin, tell him nothing…I love him. I love him even more than ever…An idea for a short story…I love him, I love him passionately, I love him to distraction. How glorious it was then, wasn't it, Kostya! Do you remember? What a life! A clear, warm, joyful, pure life, and what feelings — feelings like delicate, lovely flowers…Do you remember?…*(Recites.)* "Men, lions, eagles and partridges, horned stags, geese, spiders, the silent fish dwelling deep in the waters, starfish, and creatures invisible to the naked eye — all life, all life, all life, its sad cycle ended, has died away. Thousands of centuries have passed since the earth has borne any living creature, and the poor moon in vain lights up her lantern. No longer do the waking cranes cry out in the meadow, and maybugs are silent in the lime groves."

Embraces TREPLEV impetuously and runs out through the glass door.

TREPLEV: *(After a pause.)* I hope no one sees her in the garden and tells Mama. It might upset Mama…*(For the next two minutes, in silence, he tears up all his manuscripts and throws them under the writing table; then he unlocks the right door and exits.)*

DORN: *(Trying to open the door stage left.)* That's strange…The door's locked, somehow…*(Enters and puts the armchair in its place.)* It's like an obstacle course in here.

Enter ARKADINA, POLINA ANDREEVNA, behind them, YAKOV carrying bottles, and MASHA, then SHAMRAEV and TRIGORIN.

ARKADINA: Put the red wine and the beer for Boris Alekseevich here on the table. We'll have something to drink while we're playing. Let's be seated, everyone.

POLINA ANDREEVNA: *(To YAKOV.)* And bring the tea in, right away. *(Lights the candles, sits at the card table.)*

SHAMRAEV: *(Takes TRIGORIN over to the cupboard.)* Here's the thing I was talking about just now…*(Takes a mounted seagull out of the cupboard.)* As requested.

TRIGORIN: *(Looks at the seagull.)* I don't remember! *(Thinks for a moment.)* I don't remember!

To the right, offstage, a shot; all are startled.

ARKADINA: *(Frightened.)* What was that?

DORN: Nothing, something exploded in my medicine bag, most likely. Don't worry. *(He exits through the door stage right, and after a few moments, returns.)* That was it. A bottle of ether exploded. *(Hums.)* "Again, before you I stand, enchanted…"

ARKADINA: *(Sitting at the table.)* Oh, I was so frightened. It reminded me of the time…*(Covers her face with her hands.)* For a moment, everything went dark…

DORN: *(Looking through a magazine, to TRIGORIN.)* Two months ago an article was published here…a letter from America, and I wanted to ask you, by the way…*(puts an arm around TRIGORIN and leads him downstage)* since I was so interested in this issue…*(In a low voice, under his breath.)* Get Irina Nikolaevna out of here. The fact is, Konstantin Gavrilovich has just shot himself…

CURTAIN

Premiere
October 17, 1896

UNCLE VANYA

Scenes from Country Life
in Four Acts

The premiere of this new translation was produced by the Philadelphia Festival Theatre for New Plays, Annenberg Center, opening night, January 16, 1994; Scenic Designer, Philip A. Graneto; Lighting Designer, Jerold R. Forsyth; Costume Designer, Janus Stefanowicz; Sound Designer, Conny M. Lockwood; Properties Master, Janice Munser; Musical Director, John S. Lionarons; Production Dramaturg, Michael Hollinger; Casting, Hilary Missan; Stage Manager, Paul Lockwood; directed by Carol Rocamora.

CAST (in order of appearance)

Marina	Katharine Minchatt
Astrov, Mikhail Lvovich	Timothy Wheeler
Voynitsky, Ivan Petrovich	Tom Teti
Serebryakov, Aleksandr Vladimirovich	Louis Lippa
Telegin, Ilya Ilyich	Rick Stoppleworth
Sofya Aleksandrovna	Julia Gibson
Yelena Andreevna	Lisbeth Bartlett
Voynitskaya, Maria Vasilyevna	Sheila Bader
Workman, Musician	John S. Lionarons
Musician	Jay Ansill
Night Watchmen	John S. Lionarons
	Jeffrey L. Reim

CAST OF CHARACTERS

SEREBRYAKOV, Aleksandr Vladimirovich, a retired professor

YELENA ANDREEVNA, his wife, aged twenty-seven

SOFYA ALEKSANDROVNA (SONYA), his daughter from a first marriage

VOYNITSKAYA, Maria Vasilyevna, widow of a privy councillor, mother of the professor's first wife

VOYNITSKY, Ivan Petrovich, her son

ASTROV, Mikhail Lvovich, a doctor

TELEGIN, Ilya Ilyich, an impoverished landowner

MARINA, an old nurse

A WORKMAN

The action takes place on SEREBRYAKOV's country estate.

Uncle Vanya

ACT ONE

The garden. Part of the house and terrace are visible. On the pathway, under an old poplar tree, is a table, set for tea. There are benches and chairs; on one of the benches lies a guitar. Not far from the table, there is a swing. — It is between two and three o'clock in the afternoon, and overcast.

MARINA, a plump, slow-moving little old lady, sits by the samovar, knitting a stocking, and ASTROV paces nearby.

MARINA: *(Pours a glass of tea.)* Drink up, dearie.

ASTROV: *(Reluctantly takes the glass.)* I don't feel like it.

MARINA: How about a little vodka, then?

ASTROV: No. I don't drink vodka every day. Anyway, it's too hot.

Pause.

So, nanny, how far back do we go, you and I?

MARINA: *(Reflecting.)* How far back? Lord, let me think...you came out here to our part of the world...when was it?...Vera Petrovna was still alive, Sonechkina's mother. Her last two winters you came to us...remember? So, let me see, that must be, what, eleven years ago. *(After a moment.)* Or even more, maybe, who knows...

ASTROV: Have I changed a lot since that time?

MARINA: Yes, a lot. You were young then, young and handsome...And now, you've gotten old. And you're not so good-looking any more. All that vodka, it doesn't help, you know.

ASTROV: Yes...Ten years, and I've become someone else. And why? I'm overworked, nanny. On my feet from morning till night, not a moment's peace, and then in bed at night I lie under the covers, terrified that they're coming to drag me out on a call. In all the time I've known you, not a single day of rest, not one. How could I not age? Tell me. Yes, this life is boring, stupid, squalid…And it drags you down, this life, it does. You live, surrounded by strange people, no, really, each and every one of them, truly strange; and two or three years go by, and little by little, without knowing it, you've become strange yourself! It's inevitable! *(Fiddles with his moustache.)* Look at this huge moustache I've grown…ridiculous, isn't it! I've become an eccentric, nanny…I mean, thank God, I'm not stupid yet, no, that I'm not, my brain's still intact, but my feelings have grown numb, somehow…I want nothing, need nothing, love no one…Except you, nanny, you I love. *(Kisses the top of her head.)* I had a nanny once, just like you.

MARINA: Perhaps you'd like something to eat?

ASTROV: No. Third week of Lent, I went to Malitskoe for the epidemic… Typhus…In the huts, on the floor, wall-to-wall bodies…Mud, stench, filth…calves on the floor, lying right there, alongside the sick…Pigs, too… I worked all day long, never sat down, never ate a morsel of food, and no sooner do I get home, not a moment's rest — they bring the switchman over from the railroad yard; I lay him out on the table, you know, for surgery, and he up and dies on me under chloroform. Just like that. Right on the spot. And that's when my feelings come alive again, just when I don't need them…and my conscience starts to torment me, as if I'd killed him myself, on purpose…I sat down, right then and there, I closed my eyes — just like this, and I thought: those who will live after us, one hundred – two hundred years from now, those for whom we show the way, will they remember us kindly? Will they? No, nanny, they won't!

MARINA: People won't, but God will.

ASTROV: Thanks, nanny. Well said.

VOYNITSKY (VANYA) enters.

VANYA: *(Enters from the house; he has had a nap after lunch and looks rumpled; sits on the bench and adjusts his dapper tie.)*
Yes…

Pause.

Yes…

ASTROV: Had a good nap?

VANYA: Yes…Very. *(Yawns.)* Since the advent of our professor and his blushing bride, life has been complete chaos…I sleep at the wrong time, eat all kinds of rich nonsense for lunch and dinner, drink wine…unhealthy, that's what it is! Before, there was not a moment to spare, how Sonya and I would work, bless our hearts, and now, Sonya toils away all alone, while I sleep, eat, drink…it's not right!

MARINA: *(Shakes her head.)* It's the new way! The professor gets up at eleven, and meanwhile the samovar's been boiling all morning, everybody's waiting for him. Before they came, we used to have our midday meal at one, like normal people, and now we eat at seven. Then the professor's up all night reading and writing, and suddenly at two in the morning the bell rings…What in the world…? Tea, he wants! And it's "Wake up everybody, get the samovar started"…The new way!

ASTROV: And how long will they be staying?

VANYA: *(Whistles.)* One hundred years. The professor has decided to settle here for good.

MARINA: And that's how it is nowadays. The samovar's been going for two hours already, and they went for a walk.

VANYA: They're coming, they're coming…Don't get upset.

Voices are heard; SEREBRYAKOV, YELENA ANDREEVNA, SONYA, and TELEGIN enter from the garden, returning from their walk.

SEREBRYAKOV: Splendid, splendid…Glorious views.

TELEGIN: Remarkable, your excellency.

SONYA: And tomorrow, we'll take a walk in the forests, Papa. All right?

VANYA: Ladies and gentlemen, tea is served!

SEREBRYAKOV: My dear friends, be so kind as to bring the tea to my study, would you? I still have some catching up to do today.

SONYA: You'll love the forests, I know you will…

YELENA ANDREEVNA, SEREBRYAKOV, and SONYA go into the house; TELEGIN goes to the table and sits down next to MARINA.

VANYA: It's hot out, it's stifling, and our esteemed scholar sports an overcoat and galoshes, complete with umbrella and gloves.

ASTROV: Takes care of himself, doesn't he?

VANYA: And how marvelous she is! Simply marvelous! I've never seen a more beautiful woman in my entire life.

TELEGIN: When I drive through the field, Marina Timofeevna, when I walk through the shady garden, when I look at this tea table, I experience such indescribable bliss! The weather is lovely, the little birds sing, we live in peace and harmony, — what more could we want? *(Takes a glass.)* I'm deeply grateful to you.

VANYA: *(Dreamily.)* Those eyes…A magnificent woman.

ASTROV: So tell me something, Ivan Petrovich.

VANYA: *(Listlessly.)* What's there to tell?

ASTROV: Anything new, at least?

VANYA: Nothing's new. It's all old. I'm the same as I was, thank you very much, only worse, I've gotten lazy, I don't do a thing, except grumble, like an old goat. My dear 'Maman,' the old crow, still babbles on and on all the time about women's emancipation; she's got one foot in the grave, and the other in her beloved library, searching for the dawn of a new life.

ASTROV: And the professor?

VANYA: And the professor, as always, from dawn till deepest night, sits in his study and writes. And writes.

> "With strained mind, with furrowed brow,
> Our sacred odes we write,
> Yet hear we not a word of praise,
> Although we wish we might."

The poor, poor paper! Better he should write his autobiography! Now what a sublime subject that would be! A retired professor, listen to this, a dried up old stick, a scholarly old trout…Rheumatism, gout, migraines, liver jaundiced with jealousy and envy…Lives on the estate of his first wife, this old trout does, lives here against his will, mind you, because living in town is far more than he can possibly afford. Forever complains about his misfortunes, although, truth be told, he is a very very fortunate man, oh yes, abnormally so. *(Irritably.)* You can't imagine how fortunate! The son of a simple sexton, a seminarian, and he goes and gets himself a doctoral degree, a faculty chair, a title of your excellency, a senator for a father-in-law, and so on, and so on, and so on, blah, blah, blah. But never mind, forget about all that. Now, here comes the good part. This is a man who for twenty-five years precisely has been reading and writing about art, while understanding absolutely nothing about art. For twenty-five years he regurgitates someone else's theories on realism, naturalism, and all other kinds of ridiculous nonsense; for twenty-five years he reads and writes about things that intelligent people have already known for a long, long time, and stupid people find boring anyway; in other words, for twenty-five years he's been pouring from one empty vessel into another. And all the while behold, what self-importance! What grandiosity! He is retired, and not one living, breathing soul has ever even heard of him, he's an utter unknown; in other words, for twenty-five years he's been occupying someone else's place. Yet, behold: how he parades around, like a demi-god!

ASTROV: Sounds like you're jealous.

VANYA: Of course, I'm jealous! And what success with women! Don Juan himself never knew such success! His first wife, my sister, a lovely, gentle creature, pure as that blue sky up above, noble, warm-hearted, with far more admirers than he ever had students, — loved him as only the purest of angels above can love others as pure and perfect as themselves. My mother, his mother-in-law, worships him till this day, till this very day he inspires in her a kind of religious awe. His second wife, a beauty, a fine woman — you just saw her, — married him when he was already an old man, gave up her youth for him, her beauty, her freedom, her radiance. What for? Why? Tell me.

ASTROV: Is she faithful to the professor?

VANYA: Unfortunately, yes.

ASTROV: Why unfortunately?

VANYA: Because this fidelity is false from start to finish. It has rhyme, but no reason. To be unfaithful to an old husband whom you can't stand any more — that's immoral; to suffocate the youth and vitality living and breathing inside you — that's not?

TELEGIN: *(Whining.)* Vanya, I don't like it, when you talk that way. Now, really… He who betrays his wife, or husband, he is an unfaithful soul, one who is capable of betraying his own country.

VANYA: *(Annoyed.)* Oh dry up, Waffles!

TELEGIN: Permit me to continue, Vanya. My own wife ran away from me the day after our wedding with her lover, because of my unattractive appearance. Yet since that time I have never broken my vow to her. I have loved her to this very day and have remained faithful to her, I've helped her however I can, I've even given up my own property for the education of the children she brought into this world with her lover. My happiness I have lost, but I've kept my pride. And she? Her youth has long since gone, her beauty has faded according to nature's laws, her lover has died…What does she have left?

Enter SONYA and YELENA ANDREEVNA; a moment later, enter MARIA VASILYEVNA with a book; she sits and reads; tea is served to her, and she drinks, oblivious.

SONYA: *(Hurriedly, to the nurse.)* Nanny, some peasants have come. Go talk to them, I'll pour the tea…*(Pours the tea.)*

MARINA exits. YELENA ANDREEVNA takes her cup and drinks, sitting on the swing.

ASTROV: *(To YELENA ANDREEVNA.)* You know, I came all the way out here just to see your husband. You wrote he was quite ill, rheumatism, and something else, I don't remember, but as it turns out, he's perfectly fine.

YELENA ANDREEVNA: Yesterday evening he was depressed, he complained of pain in his legs, but today, he's all right…

ASTROV: And meanwhile, I galloped like mad over twenty miles just to get here…Well, never mind, it's not the first time. So, I'll stay with you till tomorrow…at least I'll get a good night's sleep, "quantum satis."

SONYA: Wonderful! You hardly ever spend the night with us! I suppose you haven't eaten yet?

ASTROV: No, I haven't.

SONYA: Then why not have dinner with us. We eat at seven now. *(Drinks.)* The tea's cold!

TELEGIN: The temperature of the samovar has been reduced significantly.

YELENA ANDREEVNA: Never mind, Ivan Ivanich, we'll drink it cold.

TELEGIN: Forgive me, madam…I am not Ivan Ivanich, I am Ilya Ilyich, madam…Ilya Ilyich Telegin, or, as some call me because of my pock-marked face, Waffles. I served as Sonechka's godfather some time ago, and his excellency, your spouse, knows me quite well. I live with you now, madam, here, on this estate…If you would care to notice, I dine with you each day.

SONYA: Ilya Ilyich is our deputy, our right-hand man. *(Tenderly.)* Come, god-father dear, I'll pour you another cup of tea.

MARIA VASILYEVNA: Ah!

SONYA: What's the matter, grandmother?

MARIA VASILYEVNA: I forgot to tell Aleksandr…it slipped my mind…today I received a letter from Kharkov, from Pavel Alekseevich…He sent his newest pamphlet…

ASTROV: Is it interesting?

MARIA VASILYEVNA: Interesting, but also somewhat strange. Imagine, he refutes what he advocated only seven years ago. It's shocking!

VANYA: Nothing is shocking. Drink your tea, maman.

MARIA VASILYEVNA: But I want to talk.

VANYA: But we've been talking for fifty years, talking and talking, and reading pamphlets. It's time to stop.

MARIA VASILYEVNA: For some reason you find it unpleasant to listen, when I talk. Forgive me, Jean, but in the past year you've changed so much, I hardly recognize you at all…You used to be a person of clear convictions, an enlightened individual…

VANYA: Ah, yes! I was an enlightened individual, an individual who has enlightened no one…

Pause.

I was an enlightened individual…What a cruel joke! I am now forty-seven years old. Up until last year, I tried so desperately, as you did, I deluded myself with this pedantry of yours, my eyes were blinded, so that I could not see life as it truly is, — and I thought I was doing 'good.' And now, if only you knew! I don't sleep at night with frustration, with rage, that I've wasted my time so foolishly, that I could have had everything that my old age is now denying me!

SONYA: Uncle Vanya, this is boring!

MARIA VASILYEVNA: *(To her son.)* You're blaming everything on your former convictions…They're not to blame, you are. You've forgotten that convictions themselves are nothing but words on paper. You should have done something!

VANYA: Done something! Not everyone is clever enough to be a perpetual writing machine, like your Herr Professor, the "perpetuum mobile."

MARIA VASILYEVNA: And what is that supposed to mean?

SONYA: Grandmother! Uncle Vanya! I beg of you.

VANYA: I'll be quiet. I'll be quiet, and I apologize.

Pause.

YELENA ANDREEVNA: What lovely weather today…not too hot…

Pause.

VANYA: Lovely weather to hang oneself…

TELEGIN tunes the guitar. MARINA walks by the house and calls for the chickens.

MARINA: Chick, chick, chick...

SONYA: Nanny, why did the peasants come?

MARINA: Same old thing, on and on about the wilderness. Chick, chick, chick...

SONYA: Which one are you looking for?

MARINA: The speckly one, she's gone off with her chicks...Crows might get them...*(Exits.)*

TELEGIN plays a polka; all listen in silence; a WORKMAN enters.

WORKMAN: Is the doctor here? *(To ASTROV.)* Excuse me, please, Mikhail Lvovich, they've come for you.

ASTROV: Where from?

WORKMAN: The factory.

ASTROV: *(Annoyed.)* I thank you. Well, then, time to go...*(Looks for his cap.)* Annoying, damn it...

SONYA: It's a pity, really...Come back for dinner after the factory.

ASTROV: No, it will be too late. What's the use...*(To the WORKMAN.)* Look, be a good man, would you, bring me a glass of vodka...may as well...

WORKMAN exits.

What's the use...*(Finds the cap.)* There's a character in some Ostrovsky play, a fellow with a lot of moustache and only a little finesse...That's me. So, my respects, ladies and gentlemen...*(To YELENA ANDREEVNA.)* If you'd like to drop by some time, you and Sofya Aleksandrovna, it would be a pleasure. I have a small estate, it's not much, eighty acres or so, but if it interests you, there's a fine garden and nursery, the kind you won't find for hundreds of miles. And right next to my estate is the forest district...The forester there's an old fellow, he's always sick, so, in essence, I manage the place.

YELENA ANDREEVNA: I've heard them say how much you love the forests. Of course, you must do a great deal of good, but doesn't it interfere with your true calling? You're a doctor, aren't you?

ASTROV: Only God knows what our true calling is.

YELENA ANDREEVNA: And is it interesting?

ASTROV: Yes, it is interesting work.

VANYA: *(With irony.)* Very!

YELENA ANDREEVNA: *(To ASTROV.)* You're still a young man, you look…how old…thirty-six, thirty-seven…and I wonder…it can't possibly be as interesting as you say it is. Miles and miles of forests. Monotonous, I would think.

SONYA: No, it's terribly interesting. Every day, Mikhail Lvovich plants new trees, he's already received a bronze medal and a diploma for his work. His cause is the conservation of the old forests. Just listen to him, and you'll agree with him completely. He says that the forests grace the earth, that they teach man to appreciate beauty and inspire in him a kind of majesty. The forests temper the more severe climate. In countries where the climate is milder, less energy is expended on the struggle with nature, and there you find a gentler, warmer temperament; there the people are beautiful, free-spirited, light hearted, their speech is refined, their movements are graceful. Learning and art flourish, their philosophy of life isn't so pessimistic, their attitudes toward women are endowed with refinement, gentility…

VANYA: *(Laughing.)* Bravo, bravo!…All this is very lovely indeed, but not very convincing, *(to ASTROV)* therefore allow me, my dear friend, to continue to stock my stove with kindling and build my barn with wood.

ASTROV: You can heat your stove with peat, and your barn you can build with stone. All right, go on, chop down your firewood if you must, but why destroy the forests completely? The Russian forests are falling under the stroke of the axe, billions of trees are being destroyed, wildlife and birds are deserting their dwellings, rivers are drying up, our wonderful countryside is disappearing forever, and all because one lazy man doesn't have sense enough to bend down and pick up fuel from the earth. *(To YELENA ANDREEVNA.)* It's the truth, isn't it, dear lady? You have to be a senseless barbarian to burn this beauty in your stove, to destroy that which we can't create. Man is endowed with reason, creativity, and strength to increase that which has been given to him, but up until now, he hasn't created, he's destroyed. The forests are fewer and fewer, rivers are drying up, wildlife is becoming extinct, the climate is spoiled, and each and every day the earth is growing poorer and uglier. *(To VANYA.)* I see how you look at me — with irony, you're not taking a thing I'm saying seriously, and…and, as a matter of fact, perhaps it is strange, but when I walk through the countryside, past the forests which I've rescued from devastation, when I hear the sounds of the young forests planted by my very own hands, I realize that the forces of nature are somehow within my power, and that if in a thousand years people will find happiness, then in some small way I shall be responsible for it. When I plant a birch tree, and then watch it grow and turn green and sway in the wind, my soul fills with pride, and I…*(Sees the WORKMAN, who has brought a small glass of vodka on a tray.)* However…*(drinks)* time to go. It all probably sounds very strange, in the end. I bid you all farewell! *(Goes toward the house.)*

SONYA: *(Takes his arm and walks with him.)* When will you come back to see us?

ASTROV: I don't know…

SONYA: In a month?…

ASTROV and SONYA go into the house; MARIA VASILYEVNA and TELE-GIN remain at the table; YELENA ANDREEVNA and VANYA walk to the terrace.

YELENA ANDREEVNA: Ivan Petrovich, you've behaved abominably again. Was it really necessary to irritate Maria Vasilyevna with all that talk about 'perpetuum mobile'? And today after lunch you quarreled with Aleksandr again. How petty it all is!

VANYA: And what if I hate him?

YELENA ANDREEVNA: Why hate him, he's like everyone else. And no worse than you.

VANYA: If only you could see your expression, your movements…What an idle creature you are! Too idle to live!

YELENA ANDREEVNA: Yes, idle…and bored! Everyone finds fault with my husband, everyone looks at me with such pity: Poor woman, what an old husband she has! This compassion — oh, how well I understand it! It's just as Astrov said: You're all recklessly destroying the forests, and soon there will be nothing left on earth. Just in the same way you're recklessly destroying human beings, and soon thanks to you there will be no purity, no devotion, no fidelity left on earth. Why can't you look at a woman who doesn't belong to you without wanting her? Why? Because, — he's right, this doctor, — you're all possessed by the demon of destruction. You don't care about forests, about wildlife, about women, not even about each other.

VANYA: I don't like this philosophizing!

Pause.

YELENA ANDREEVNA: That doctor has a tired, sensitive face. An interesting face. Sonya's attracted to him, it's obvious…she's in love with him, and I understand her. He's been here three times already since I've come, but I'm shy, I haven't talked to him properly, haven't treated him kindly. He must think I'm awful. That's probably why we're such good friends, you and I, Ivan Petrovich, because we're both such awful, boring people! That's right, boring! Don't look at me that way, I don't like it.

UNCLE VANYA: How else can I look at you, if I love you! You're my happiness, my life, my youth! I know my chances that you'll return my love are nil, nonexistent, but I need nothing, if only you'll let me look at you, listen to your voice…

YELENA ANDREEVNA: Be quiet, they'll hear you!

Goes into the house.

VANYA: *(Following her.)* Let me speak of my love, don't drive me away, it alone can bring me the greatest happiness…

YELENA ANDREEVNA: This is torture…

Both go into the house.

TELEGIN strikes a chord and plays a polka; MARIA VASILYEVNA notes something in the margins of the pamphlet.

CURTAIN

ACT TWO

The dining room in SEREBRYAKOV's house. Night. The knocking of the night watchman can be heard in the garden.

SEREBRYAKOV sits in the armchair before an open window, dozing; YELENA ANDREEVNA sits next to him, also dozing.

SEREBRYAKOV: *(Stirring.)* Who's there? Is that you, Sonya?

YELENA ANDREEVNA: It's me.

SEREBRYAKOV: You, Lenochka…the pain is unbearable!

YELENA ANDREEVNA: Your blanket fell on the floor. *(Covers his feet.)* I'll close the window, Aleksandr.

SEREBRYAKOV: No, it's stifling in here…I just dozed off, and dreamed that my left leg belonged to someone else. I woke up in excruciating pain. No, this is not gout, this is more like rheumatism. What time is it?

YELENA ANDREEVNA: Twenty minutes past twelve.

Pause.

SEREBRYAKOV: In the morning, go find me a copy of Batyushkov in the library. I think we've got one here.

YELENA ANDREEVNA: What?

SEREBRYAKOV: Go find me a copy of Batyushkov in the morning. I remember we had one somewhere. Why is it so difficult for me to breathe?

YELENA ANDREEVNA: You're exhausted. It's the second night you haven't slept.

SEREBRYAKOV: They say Turgenev developed angina pectoris from his gout. The same thing will happen to me, I'm afraid. Abominable, detestable old age. Curse it. Ever since I've become old, I find myself repulsive. Yes, and all of you must find me repulsive, too.

YELENA ANDREEVNA: The way you speak of your old age, you make it sound as if it's our fault.

SEREBRYAKOV: And you, most of all, you find me repulsive.

YELENA ANDREEVNA walks away and sits in the corner.

Of course, you're right. I'm not a fool, I understand. You're young, healthy, beautiful, you want to live, and I'm an old man, a corpse, almost. You see? I understand, don't I? And, how stupid it is, of course, that I'm still alive. But just wait, soon I'll liberate you all. This won't drag on much longer.

YELENA ANDREEVNA: I can't stand it any more…For God's sake, please be quiet.

SEREBRYAKOV: As it turns out, thanks to me, everyone's exhausted, everyone's miserable, everyone's youth has been wasted, only I am content and enjoying life. Yes, of course!

YELENA ANDREEVNA: Be quiet! You're torturing me!

SEREBRYAKOV: I torture everyone. Of course.

YELENA ANDREEVNA: *(In tears.)* This is unbearable. Tell me, what do you want from me?

SEREBRYAKOV: Nothing.

YELENA ANDREEVNA: Then be quiet. I beg of you.

SEREBRYAKOV: It's strange, isn't it, Ivan Petrovich can talk his head off, or that old idiot, Maria Vasilyevna, — and never mind, everyone listens, but no sooner do I utter one word, and everyone gets depressed. Even my voice is repulsive. All right, let's face it, I'm repulsive, I'm selfish, I'm a tyrant, but, really, don't I have a right to be selfish in my old age? Really, don't I deserve it? No, really, I ask you, don't I have the right to a tranquil old age, to the tender loving care of others?

YELENA ANDREEVNA: No one is disputing your rights.

The window rattles from the wind.

The wind is rising, I'll close the window. *(Closes it.)* Any moment, it will rain. No one is disputing your rights.

House, in the garden, the watchman knocks, and sings a song.

SEREBRYAKOV: All my life, I have served scholarship, I've had my study, my lecture hall, the company of distinguished colleagues — and now, all of a sudden, I find myself in this crypt, every day I see these stupid people, hear their worthless babble…I want to live, I love success, I love fame, society, — and here, it's like living in exile. Every minute mourning for the past, slavishly following the successes of others, dreading death…I can't bear it! I haven't the strength! And here, they won't even forgive me for being old!

YELENA ANDREEVNA: Wait, have patience: In five or six years I'll be old, too.

Enter SONYA.

SONYA: Papa, you sent for Dr. Astrov yourself, and when he came, you refused to see him. It's not right. To put someone out for no reason...

SEREBRYAKOV: What do I need your Astrov for? He knows as much about medicine as I do about astronomy.

SONYA: You can't summon an entire medical faculty here for your gout.

SEREBRYAKOV: I'm not going to waste time talking to that fanatic.

SONYA: Do whatever you want. *(Sits.)* I don't care.

SEREBRYAKOV: What time is it now?

YELENA ANDREEVNA: Almost one.

SEREBRYAKOV: It's stifling...Sonya, bring me my drops from the table!

SONYA: In a minute. *(Hands him the drops.)*

SEREBRYAKOV: *(Irritated.)* Ach, not these! You can't ask for anything around here!

SONYA: Please, don't play games with me. Others may like it, but I don't, spare me, please! I don't enjoy it. And I haven't got the time, I have to get up early tomorrow, there's haying to be done...

Enter VANYA in a dressing gown with a candle.

VANYA: There's a storm rising.

Lightning.

So-o-o, I see! Hélène and Sonya, go to bed, I have come to relieve you of your posts!

SEREBRYAKOV: *(Frightened.)* No, no! Don't leave me alone with him! No. He'll talk me to death!

VANYA: But you must give them their rest! They haven't slept for two nights.

SEREBRYAKOV: All right, let them go to bed, but you go, too. I beg of you. I beseech you. For the sake of our former friendship, don't argue. We'll talk about it later.

VANYA: *(With a grin.)* For the sake of our former friendship...our former...

SONYA: Be quiet, Uncle Vanya.

SEREBRYAKOV: *(To his wife.)* My darling, don't leave me with him. He'll talk me to death.

VANYA: This is getting ridiculous.

Enter MARINA with a candle.

SONYA: You should be in bed, nanny. It's late already.

MARINA: The samovar's still on. So how can we go to bed?

SEREBRYAKOV: No one's sleeping, they're all exhausted, only I am enjoying myself.

MARINA: *(Goes to SEREBRYAKOV, tenderly.)* What is it, dearie? Don't feel so well? My old legs ache too, yes, they do. *(Adjusts the blanket.)* You've been sick for such a long time now, haven't you. Vera Petrovna, may her soul rest in peace, Sonechkina's mother, wouldn't sleep for nights, bless her heart, how she suffered over you…how she loved you…

Pause.

Old people are like children, they just want someone to feel sorry for them, but no one does, now do they? *(Kisses SEREBRYAKOV on the shoulder.)* Come on, dearie, let's go to bed…Come on, love…I'll make you some limeleaf tea, warm your old legs, pray a little to God for you…

SEREBRYAKOV: *(Moved.)* Let's go, Marina.

MARINA: My old legs ache too, yes, they do! *(Leads him out, together with SONYA.)* Vera Petrovna, bless her heart, how she suffered over you, how she cried…You were such a little girl then, Sonyushka, such a silly little girl…Come on, dearie, come on…

SEREBRYAKOV, SONYA, and MARINA exit.

YELENA ANDREEVNA: He's worn me out. I can hardly stand up.

VANYA: He's worn you out, I've worn myself out. It's the third night I haven't slept.

YELENA ANDREEVNA: Something is wrong in this house. Your mother hates everything except her pamphlets and the professor; the professor is in a wretched mood, he doesn't trust me, he's afraid of you; Sonya is angry with her father, and with me, she hasn't spoken to me for two weeks; you hate my husband, you openly despise your own mother; I'm irritable, I've burst into tears twenty times today…Something is wrong in this house.

VANYA: Let's stop philosophizing!

YELENA ANDREEVNA: Ivan Petrovich, you are an educated, intelligent man, you of all people should understand that the world will be destroyed not by crime and not by fire, but by hatred and hostility and these petty little squabbles…Your life's work should be not to find fault, but to make peace.

VANYA: First let me make peace with myself! My darling…*(Attempts to kiss her hand.)*

YELENA ANDREEVNA: Leave me alone! *(Takes her hand away.)* Go away!

VANYA: Soon the rain will pass, and everything in nature is refreshed and revived, everything breathes anew. I alone am not refreshed by the storm. Day and night, one thought haunts me, like an apparition, the thought that my life is lost, beyond hope. There is no past, it has been wasted on nonsense, and the present is terrifying in its absurdity. And there you have it — my life and my love: What can I do with them, what will become of them? My love is lost, like a ray of sunlight disappearing into a dungeon, and I am lost.

YELENA ANDREEVNA: When you speak to me of love, I simply grow numb, I don't know what to say. Forgive me, there's nothing I can say to you. *(Wants to leave.)* Good night.

VANYA: *(Blocks her way.)* And if only you knew how I suffer from the thought that, right here in the same house, another life is lost along with mine — yours! What are you waiting for? What cursed philosophy forbids you? Face it, face it…

YELENA ANDREEVNA: *(Gazes intently at him.)* Ivan Petrovich, you are drunk!

VANYA: It's possible, possible…

YELENA ANDREEVNA: Where is the doctor?

VANYA: Here…he's staying with me tonight. It's possible, possible…Anything is possible!

YELENA ANDREEVNA: And you've been drinking tonight? Why?

VANYA: At least I feel alive…Don't stop me, Hélène.

YELENA ANDREEVNA: You never used to drink, and you never used to talk so much…Go to bed! You bore me.

VANYA: *(Bends down to kiss her hand.)* My darling…my marvelous one!

YELENA ANDREEVNA: *(Annoyed.)* Leave me alone. This is disgusting, really. *(She leaves.)*

VANYA: *(Alone.)* She's gone…

Pause.

Ten years ago it was, when I met her, at my poor late sister's…She was seventeen, I was thirty-seven…Why couldn't I have fallen in love with her then, why couldn't I have proposed to her? It would have been possible, oh yes! And now, she would be my wife…Yes…Now we would both be awakened by the storm; she would be frightened by the thunder, and I would hold her in my arms and whisper: "Don't be afraid, I am here." Oh, marvelous thoughts, how lovely, look, I'm laughing...but, my God, how these thoughts get muddled up in my head...Why am I old? Why doesn't she understand me? All her talk, her idle moralizing, her absurd, idle views on the destruction of the world — I despise it all, deeply.

Pause.

Oh, how I have been betrayed! I adored this professor, this wretched old gout bag, I toiled for him like an ox! Sonya and I, we squeezed the last drop from this estate; like kulaks we sold oil, peas, cheeses, went hungry ourselves, just to scrape together every last miserable kopek and then send thousands to him. I worshipped him and his scholarship, I lived and breathed for him! Every word he wrote, every phrase he uttered, to me was a stroke of genius...My God, and now? Now he's retired, and now we see the sum total of his life: not one single page of his work will live after him, he's a complete unknown, he doesn't exist! A soap bubble! And I am betrayed...I see it — foolishly betrayed...

Enter ASTROV in a frockcoat, without a waistcoat and tie; he is slightly drunk; TELEGIN follows, with a guitar.

ASTROV: Play!
TELEGIN: But everyone's asleep, girl.
ASTROV: Play!

TELEGIN strums quietly.

(To VANYA.) Are you alone? No ladies here? *(Arms akimbo, sings softly.)* "Dance, my stove, dance, my shed, where will the master lay his head..." The storm woke me up. Quite a downpour. What time is it?
VANYA: Who cares.
ASTROV: I thought I heard Yelena Andreevna's voice.
VANYA: She was just here.
ASTROV: A gorgeous woman. *(Looks at the phial bottle on the table.)* Medicine. What prescriptions don't we have here! From Kharkov, from Moscow, from Tula...All these towns must be sick to death of his gout. Is he ill, or is he faking it?
VANYA: He's ill...

Pause.

ASTROV: And why are we so depressed today? Feeling sorry for the professor, are we?

VANYA: Leave me alone.

ASTROV: Or, maybe we're in love with the professor's wife?

VANYA: She's my friend.

ASTROV: Already?

VANYA: What does "already" mean?

ASTROV: A woman is a man's friend only in the following order: first an acquaintance, then a lover, then a friend.

VANYA: A vulgar philosophy.

ASTROV: What? Yes...I must confess — I have become vulgar. Look at me, I'm drunk, too. Usually I get drunk like this once a month. When I'm in this state, I become arrogant to the extreme...outrageous, even! There's nothing I can't do! I undertake the most difficult operations and perform them brilliantly; I design the most visionary plans for the future...I'm not strange any more now — I believe I bring enormous benefit to mankind...enormous! And I have a philosophy all my very own now, and you, my little friends, you're all insects to me...microbes! *(To TELEGIN.)* Waffles, play!

TELEGIN: Dear friend, I'd be happy to play my heart out for you, but don't you understand — everyone's asleep!

ASTROV: Play!

TELEGIN plays softly.

ASTROV: Time for a drink. Let's see, I think there's some cognac left. And then, come dawn, we'll go to my place. "Right-o?" I have this assistant who never says "all right" but "right-o." A real rogue. So, "right-o"? *(Sees SONYA entering.)* Excuse me, I don't have a tie on. *(Exits quickly.)*

TELEGIN follows him.

SONYA: So, Uncle Vanya, you've been drinking with the doctor again. Two fine-feathered friends...That may be all well and good for him, but why do you do it? At your age, it doesn't suit you.

VANYA: What does age have to do with it? When you have no real life, you live an illusion. It's better than nothing.

SONYA: Our hay has been cut, it's raining every day, everything's rotting away, and you're talking about illusions. You've let the whole estate go…I work alone, I have no more strength left…*(Frightened.)* Uncle, you've got tears in your eyes!

VANYA: What tears? It's nothing…nonsense…You looked at me just now, the way your poor dear mother used to. My darling…*(Eagerly kisses her hands and face.)* My sister…my darling sister…where is she now? If only she knew! Oh, if only she knew!

SONYA: What? Uncle, knew what?

VANYA: How painful, how futile…Never mind…later…never mind…I'm going… *(Exits.)*

SONYA: *(Knocks on the door.)* Mikhail Lvovich! Are you asleep? May I have a word with you?

ASTROV: *(Behind the door.)* Just a moment! *(A few moments later he enters; he is now in a waistcoat and tie.)* What may I do for you?

SONYA: You can drink, go ahead, if it doesn't disgust you, but, I beg of you, don't let my uncle do it. It's bad for him.

ASTROV: Very well. We shall drink no more.

Pause.

I'm going home immediately. Done, decided. By the time they harness the horses, it will be dawn.

SONYA: It's raining. Wait until morning.

ASTROV: The storm's passing, we'll just catch the edge of it. I'm going. And, please, don't call me out here again to see your father. I tell him — gout, he says — rheumatism; I tell him to lie down, he sits up. And today, he wouldn't talk to me at all.

SONYA: He's spoiled. *(Looks in the buffet.)* Would you like a little something to eat?

ASTROV: All right.

SONYA: I love to nibble at night. There's something to eat in the buffet, I think. They say that he had great success with women in his time, and all his lady friends spoiled him. Here, have some cheese.

They both stand at the buffet and eat.

ASTROV: I haven't had a thing to eat all day…I've only been drinking. Your father has a difficult personality. *(Takes a bottle from the buffet.)* May I?

(Pours a glass.) There's no one here, we can speak frankly. You know, I don't think I could survive one month in your house, I'd suffocate in this atmosphere…There's your father with his books and his gout, Uncle Vanya with his depression, your grandmother, and, finally, your stepmother…

SONYA: What about my stepmother?

ASTROV: They say, everything about a person should be beautiful: face and dress, mind and soul. She is beautiful, no question, but…really, what does she do, other than eat, sleep, move about, and bewitch us all with her beauty? Nothing. She has absolutely no responsibilities, everyone else waits on her…Isn't that right? And an idle life cannot be a pure one.

Pause.

But, perhaps, I judge her too harshly, I don't know. I'm dissatisfied with life, just like your Uncle Vanya, and we've become grumblers, both of us.

SONYA: You're unhappy with life?

ASTROV: In general, I love life, but our life, our narrow-minded, provincial Russian life, I can't bear it, I despise it to the depths of my soul. As for my own personal life, well, God only knows, there's nothing there, absolutely nothing. You know, when you walk through the forest in the darkness of the night and there's a small light shining somewhere in the distance, then you don't feel the fatigue, or the darkness, or the sharp branches beating against your face…I work harder than anyone else in this district, you know that, fate flogs me on, it never stops, at times I suffer unbearably, but there is no light in the distance for me. I have nothing to look forward to, I don't like people…It's been a long time since I've loved anyone…

SONYA: No one?

ASTROV: No one. Oh, I feel some tenderness toward your nurse — for old time's sake. But that's about all. The peasants are a dull, backward lot, they live a squalid life, and you can't get along with the intelligentsia. They wear you out. All of them, our dear acquaintances, they're superficial, shallow, they don't see farther than their own noses — to put it simply, they're stupid. And the more intelligent, the more promising ones among them, they're high-strung, tormented, self-absorbed…They complain, criticize, spread vicious slander about each other, they go sneaking around, spiting each other, sizing each other up, saying: "Oh, this one's a psychopath!" or "That one's a hypocrite!" And when they can't figure out what label to paste on my forehead, then they say: "This man is strange, strange!" I love the forests — that's strange; I don't eat meat — that's strange, too. Tell me, what compassion do they have for nature and for people, what genuine, pure, spontaneous empathy are they capable of expressing...None, none whatsoever! *(Goes to take a drink.)*

SONYA: *(Stops him.)* No, please, I beg of you, don't drink any more.

ASTROV: Why not?

SONYA: It doesn't suit you! You're refined, you have such a gentle voice...and more...you're like no one I've ever known, — you're beautiful. Why do you want to be like ordinary people, who drink and play cards? Oh, don't do it, I beg of you! You always say that people don't create, that they only destroy what God gave them. Why then, why are you destroying yourself? You must not do it, you must not, please, I beg of you.

ASTROV: *(Holds out his hand to her.)* I shall drink no more.

SONYA. Give me your word.

ASTROV: Word of honor.

SONYA: *(Squeezes his hand tightly.)* Thank you!

ASTROV: Basta! I'm sobered up. You see, I'm completely sober already, and so I shall stay for the rest of my days. *(Looks at his watch.)* And so, we move on. As I was saying: My time is up, it's too late for me...I've lived too long, worked too hard, indulged too much, my feelings have grown numb, and it seems I can't get close to anyone any more. I love no one, and...I won't fall in love again. There's only one thing that can still excite me. Beauty. I can't resist it. And, I suppose, that if your Yelena Andreevna felt like it, she could turn my head in a day...But that's not love, you know, that's not true feeling...*(Covers his eyes with his hands and shudders.)*

SONYA: What's the matter?

ASTROV: Yes...During Lent, I had a patient die under chloroform.

SONYA: It's time to forget.

Pause.

Tell me, Mikhail Lvovich...If I had a friend or a younger sister, and if you knew that she...well, let's suppose that she were in love with you, how would you respond?

ASTROV: *(Shrugs his shoulders.)* I don't know. I wouldn't, probably. I'd let her know that I couldn't fall in love with her...and that, anyway, I have other things on my mind. Whatever, and now, if I'm going to go, it's time. I'll say good-bye, my dear, or else we'll still be talking come morning. *(Shakes her hand.)* I'll go out through the drawing room, if you don't mind, or else I'm afraid your dear uncle might detain me. *(Exits.)*

SONYA: *(Alone.)* He said nothing, to me, nothing…His heart and soul are still hidden from me, so then why do I feel so happy? *(Laughs with happiness.)* I said to him: You're refined, you're noble, you have such a gentle voice…Was that the wrong thing to say? His voice trembles, caresses…I can still hear it echo in the air. But when I spoke to him of a younger sister, he didn't understand…*(Wrings her hands.)* Oh, how awful it is, that I am not beautiful! How awful! And I know I'm not beautiful, I know it, I know it…Last Sunday, when we were coming out of church, I heard them talking about me, and one woman said: "She's good, she's kind, what a pity it is that she's so plain…" Plain…

Enter YELENA ANDREEVNA.

YELENA ANDREEVNA: *(Opens a window.)* The storm has past. What lovely fresh air!

Pause.

Where is the doctor?
SONYA: Gone.

Pause.

YELENA ANDREEVNA: Sofi!
SONYA: What?
YELENA ANDREEVNA: How much longer will you go on being angry with me? We haven't done each other any harm. Why should we be enemies? Enough…
SONYA: Oh yes, I've wanted to, myself…*(Embraces her.)* Let's not be angry any more.
YELENA ANDREEVNA: Good. Let's not.

They are both moved.

SONYA: Has Papa gone to bed?
YELENA ANDREEVNA: No, he's still sitting in the drawing room…We don't speak for weeks at a time, God only knows why…*(Notices that the buffet is open.)* What's this?
SONYA: Mikhail Lvovich was having some supper.

YELENA ANDREEVNA: And there's wine…Let's drink to our friendship — 'brüderschaft.'

SONYA: Yes, let's.

YELENA ANDREEVNA: From one glass…*(Pours.)* It's better like this. So, now — friends?

SONYA: Friends.

They drink and kiss each other.

I've wanted to make up for so long, but, I don't know, somehow, I was ashamed…*(Weeps.)*

YELENA ANDREEVNA: Why are you crying?

SONYA: It's nothing, I can't help it.

YELENA ANDREEVNA: Don't cry, don't…*(Weeps.)* Silly girl, now I'm crying, too…

Pause.

You're angry with me, because you think I married your father for money…If you want me to, I'll swear to you — I married him for love. I was attracted by his intellect and his fame. My love wasn't genuine, it wasn't real, but, believe me, I thought it was at the time. I'm not to blame. And yet ever since our wedding day, you've never stopped punishing me with those shrewd, suspicious eyes.

SONYA: Peace, peace! Let's forget…

YELENA ANDREEVNA: You mustn't look like that — it doesn't suit you. You must trust in people, or else life is not worth living.

Pause.

SONYA: Tell me the truth, as a friend…Are you happy?

YELENA ANDREEVNA: No.

SONYA: I knew it. One more question. Be honest with me, — wouldn't you rather have a young husband?

YELENA ANDREEVNA: What a child you are, still. Of course, I would! *(Laughs.)* So, now, ask me anything, go ahead, ask…

SONYA: Do you like the doctor?

YELENA ANDREEVNA: Yes, very much.

SONYA: *(Laughs.)* I look foolish now…don't I? He's gone, and I can still hear his voice, his footsteps, I look through the dark window, — and there is his face before me. Let me tell you…No, I can't, I can't say it aloud, I'm ashamed. Come to my room, we'll talk there. You think I'm foolish, don't you? Say it…Tell me something about him…

YELENA ANDREEVNA: What?

SONYA: He's so brilliant…He is capable of anything, anything…He cares for the sick, he plants forests…

YELENA ANDREEVNA: It's not about forestry and medicine…Darling, don't you understand, it's about genius! And do you know what genius is? Courage, freedom of mind, breadth of vision…He can plant a tree, and in that moment see it a thousand years from now, he can imagine a future happiness for mankind. Such people are rare, they must be loved…Yes, he drinks, and sometimes he's a bit rough, — but so what, what harm is there in that? A talented person cannot remain pure in Russia. Imagine what a life this doctor has! Impassable mud on the roads, frosts, blizzards, enormous distances, a brutal, savage population, poverty, disease all around — it's hard for a man working and struggling in such conditions day after day after day to reach forty pure and sober…*(Kisses her.)* I wish you every happiness with all my heart, you deserve it…*(Stands.)* But I'm only a minor character, aren't I, and a useless one…In music, in my husband's house, in all my love affairs, — everywhere, really, all I've ever played is a minor role. As a matter of fact, Sonya, come to think of it, I am very, very unhappy! *(Paces, agitated.)* There's no happiness for me on this earth. None! Why are you laughing?

SONYA: *(Laughs, covering her face.)* I'm so happy…so happy!

YELENA ANDREEVNA: I feel like playing now…I want to play something.

SONYA: Yes, play. *(Embraces her.)* I can't sleep…. Play!

YELENA ANDREEVNA: Wait. Your father isn't asleep. When he's ill, music annoys him. Go ask. If he doesn't mind, I'll play. Hurry.

SONYA: I will. *(Leaves.)*

The watchman knocks in the garden.

YELENA ANDREEVNA: It's been such a long time since I've played the piano. I'll play and cry, cry like a fool. *(At the window.)* Is that you knocking, Yefim?

Voice of the watchman: "Yes!"

YELENA ANDREEVNA: Don't knock, the master's not well.

Voice of watchman: "Right-o…we're leaving!" (Whistles.) "Here, Zhuchka, here, Boy! Zhuchka!"

Pause.

SONYA: *(Returning.)* No!

CURTAIN

Act Three

The living room in SEREBRYAKOV's house. There are three doors: to the right, left and center. Daytime.

VANYA, and SONYA are seated, and YELENA ANDREEVNA is pacing, thinking about something.

VANYA: The Herr Professor has kindly requested that we gather together in this very living room at precisely one o'clock today. *(Looks at his watch.)* It is now a quarter to. He has something to communicate to the world at large.

YELENA ANDREEVNA: Some business matter, probably.

VANYA: He has no business — none of any kind. He writes rubbish, he grumbles, he envies people, that's about it.

SONYA: *(In a reproachful tone.)* Uncle!

VANYA: I know, I know, sorry, sorry. *(Points to YELENA ANDREEVNA.)* Just look at her: roaming about, reeling with idleness. How very, very adorable!

YELENA ANDREEVNA: You drone on and on, every day, on and on — it gets on my nerves, I'm sick of it! *(With anguish.)* I'm dying of boredom, I don't know what to do with myself.

SONYA: *(Shrugs her shoulders.)* Not enough to do? There's plenty to do, if you wanted to.

YELENA ANDREEVNA: Such as?

SONYA: Help with the estate, teach, care for the sick. Still not enough? You know, when you and Papa weren't here, Uncle Vanya and I used to go to the market ourselves to trade flour.

YELENA ANDREEVNA: I couldn't possibly. Besides, it doesn't interest me. It's only in romantic novels that you teach and take care of the peasants, how can you expect me to go running out all of a sudden and start teaching and healing people?

SONYA: And I don't understand why you just don't try it, try teaching. Be patient, you'll get used to it. *(Embraces her.)* Don't be bored, darling. *(Laughs.)* You're bored, you're restless, and your boredom and idleness are infectious. Look: Uncle Vanya does nothing but follow you around like a shadow, I neglect my work and come running to you all the time, just to talk. I've grown lazy, I can't bear it! And Doctor Mikhail Lvovich hardly ever used to come here, once a month perhaps, we had to beg him, and now he comes every day, he's neglected his forests and his practice. You're a witch, you must be!

VANYA: Why languish away. *(Quickly.)* Come, my darling, my treasure, be smart! You've got mermaid's blood coursing through your veins, go, swim like a mermaid! Let yourself go for once in your life, fall head-over-heels in love with another water-sprite — dive headlong into the deep, while Herr Professor and the rest of us stand waving helplessly on the shore!

YELENA ANDREEVNA: *(With anger.)* Leave me alone! This is cruel! *(Tries to leave.)*

VANYA: *(Preventing her.)* Wait, wait, my joy, my ecstasy, forgive me...I apologize. *(Kisses her hand.)* Peace.

YELENA ANDREEVNA: An angel wouldn't have the patience, really.

VANYA: As a gesture of peace and harmony I shall bring you a bouquet of roses: Just this morning I picked them for you...Autumn roses — lovely, melancholy roses...*(Exits.)*

SONYA: Autumn roses — lovely, melancholy roses...

Both look out the window.

YELENA ANDREEVNA: It's September already. How shall we live through the winter here!

Pause.

Where is the doctor?

SONYA: In Uncle Vanya's room. Writing something. I'm glad that Uncle Vanya left. I have to talk to you.

YELENA ANDREEVNA: What about?

SONYA: What about? *(Puts her head on YELENA's breast.)*

YELENA ANDREEVNA: Don't, don't...*(Smoothes her hair.)* Please, don't.

SONYA: I'm not beautiful.

YELENA ANDREEVNA: You have such pretty hair.

SONYA: No! *(Turns, to look at herself in the mirror.)* No! When a woman is not beautiful, they always tell her: "What pretty eyes you have, what pretty hair"...I have loved him for six years now, loved him more than my own mother; every moment I hear his voice, feel the touch of his hand...I'm always watching the door, waiting, hoping he'll come any minute...And look how I run to you all the time, just to talk about him! He comes here every day now, but he doesn't look at me, doesn't even see me...What suffering! I have no hope, none, none at all! *(In despair.)* Oh, God, give me strength...I have prayed all night...Sometimes I'll go right up to him, start talking and talking, look

him straight in the eye,…I have no pride, no strength to control myself…
Yesterday, I couldn't bear it any longer, I confessed to Uncle Vanya that I
loved him…All the servants know I love him. Everyone knows.

YELENA ANDREEVNA: And he?

SONYA: No. He doesn't even notice me.

YELENA ANDREEVNA: *(Deep in thought.)* He's a strange man…Do you
know what? Let me talk to him. Carefully, I'll hint at it…

Pause.

Really, how much longer can we live in uncertainty…Let me do it!

SONYA nods her head affirmatively.

Good. Either he loves you or he doesn't — that won't be hard to find out.
Don't be embarrassed, darling, and don't worry — I'll question him so
carefully, he won't even notice it. We have only to find out: yes or no?

Pause.

If it's no, then he won't come here any more. Right?

SONYA nods her head affirmatively.

It's easier if you don't see him. Really. We can't put it off any longer, we'll
question him right away. He agreed to show me some of his drawings…Go
tell him I wish to see him.

SONYA: *(Tremendously agitated.)* Will you tell me the whole truth?

YELENA ANDREEVNA: Yes, of course. And I think that the truth, whatever it
may be, will not be as terrible as the uncertainty…Leave it to me, darling.

SONYA: Yes, yes…I'll say that you want to see his drawings…*(Goes and stops
by the door.)* No, not knowing is better…At least there's hope…

YELENA ANDREEVNA: What did you say?

SONYA: Nothing. *(Exits.)*

YELENA ANDREEVNA: *(Alone.)* Nothing is worse, than knowing another's
secret and not being able to help. *(Deep in thought.)* Obviously he's not in
love with her, — but then why not marry her? She's not beautiful, but for
a country doctor, at his age, she'd make a wonderful wife. She's intelligent,
kind, pure…No, that's not it, that's not it…

Pause.

I understand this poor girl. Amidst desperate boredom, where instead of people you have dull grey shadows wandering about, talking in trivialities, who only know how to eat, drink, sleep, — from time to time he comes upon the scene, so unlike the others, handsome, interesting, fascinating, a bright moon rising in the darkness…To fall under the spell of such a man, to forget…It seems I'm a little fascinated myself. Yes, I'm bored when he's not around, and look how I smile, when I think of him…That Uncle Vanya says I've got mermaid's blood in my veins. "Let yourself go for once in your life…" Well? Perhaps that's just what I need…To fly away free as a bird from all of you, from your sleepy faces, your talk, to forget you ever existed on this earth…But I'm such a coward, I'm shy…my conscience torments me…Look, he comes here every single day, I know why he's here, and I feel so guilty, I'm ready to fall on my knees before Sonya, to beg her forgiveness, to burst into tears…

ASTROV: *(Enters with map.)* Good afternoon! *(Shakes her hand.)* You wanted to see my drawings?

YELENA ANDREEVNA: Yesterday, you promised to show me your work…Are you free now?

ASTROV: Oh, of course. *(Spreads map on the card table and fastens it with pins.)* Where were you born?

YELENA ANDREEVNA: *(Helping him.)* In Petersburg.

ASTROV: And where did you go to school?

YELENA ANDREEVNA: At the music conservatory.

ASTROV: You probably won't find this very interesting.

YELENA ANDREEVNA: Why not? It's true, I don't know that much about the countryside, but I've read a lot about it.

ASTROV: Here, in this house, I have my very own table…In Ivan Petrovich's study. When I'm worn out completely, to the point of exhaustion, I throw everything aside and come running out here, just to amuse myself with all this for an hour or two…Ivan Petrovich and Sofya Aleksandrovna click away on the abacus, doing their accounts, and I sit beside them at my table, daubing away, and it's warm, it's peaceful, you can hear the crickets chirping…But I don't permit myself such pleasure very often, once a month, perhaps…*(Points to the map.)* Look here, now. A map of our district, as it appeared fifty years ago. The dark and light green colors represent the forests; they covered one-half of the entire area. Where you see the red crisscrosses on the green, that's where elk and wild goats once lived…I've indicated both flora and fauna here. On this lake, there were swans, geese, wild duck, birds of every shape and size, multitudes of them, as the old people say, more than the eye could see, clouds of them flying overhead...Besides the villages and hamlets, look — scattered here and there, all sorts of settlements, farmsteads, secluded monasteries, watermills...Cattle and horses were found in abundance, too. They're represented by the blue. Take this tiny area, for example, where the blue is especially dense: In that area alone you could find herd after herd of them, and an average of three horses in every peasant homestead.

Pause.

Now let's look further down. The district as it was twenty-five years ago. Now, you see, only one-third of the area is forested. There are no wild goats left, some elk remain. The green and blue areas are paler and paler. And so on and so on. Now we come to the third part: a map of our district today. You can still see the green in some places, here and there, but not through-out, look how sparse it is; the elk have disappeared, so have the swans, and the wood grouse...As for the former settlements, farmsteads, monasteries, watermills, not even a trace. In general, it's a picture of gradual and unques-tionable degeneration, which in all probability will take another ten – fifteen years to complete its cycle. You might say that this is the work of cultural influences, that the old life must naturally give way to the new. Yes, I understand, as long as in place of the destruction of the forests we lay high-ways and railroads, as long as we build factories, mills, schools — then the population will become healthier, richer, more enlightened, but of course nothing of the kind has happened! In our district, we have the same swamps and mosquitos, the same impassable roads, poverty, typhus, diph-theria, fires...And so, we must face a degeneration caused by an insur-mountable struggle for existence: a degeneration caused by stagnation, by ignorance, by a total lack of consciousness, when a cold, sick, hungry man, in order to save whatever is left of his life, to save his children, instinctively, unconsciously grasps at anything to satisfy that hunger, to keep himself warm, — and thus destroys everything, with no thought for tomorrow... Yes, almost everything is destroyed, and nothing is created to take its place. *(Coldly.)* I can see by your face that you don't find this interesting.
YELENA ANDREEVNA: No, it's just...I understand so little of this...
ASTROV: What's there to understand, it just doesn't interest you.
YELENA ANDREEVNA: Frankly speaking, my mind isn't on this. Forgive

me. I have to…question you briefly, and I'm embarrassed, I don't know how to begin.

ASTROV: Question me?

YELENA ANDREEVNA: Yes, question you, but…it's quite innocent, really. Let's sit down, shall we!

They sit.

It's a matter concerning a young individual. We'll talk straightforwardly, like mature, honest people, like friends. We'll talk about it, and then we'll forget everything that was said. All right?

ASTROV: All right.

YELENA ANDREEVNA: The matter concerns my stepdaughter, Sonya. Do you like her?

ASTROV: Yes, I respect her…

YELENA ANDREEVA: Do you like her as a woman?

ASTROV: *(Not right away.)* No.

YELENA ANDREEVNA: Just two or three words more — and I'm done. You've noticed nothing?

ASTROV: Nothing.

YELENA ANDREEVNA: *(Takes his hand.)* You don't love her, I see it in your eyes…She is suffering…Understand this…and stop coming here.

ASTROV: *(Stands.)* My time is up…There's no time for…*(Shrugs his shoulders.)* When could I, anyway…*(He is embarrassed.)*

YELENA ANDREEVNA: Oh! What an awkward conversation! I'm so upset, I feel I've been dragging a ton of weight. Well, thank God, it's over. Let's forget about it, we never spoke at all, and…and you'll go away, won't you. You're a sensitive man, you understand…

Pause.

I'm blushing all over.

ASTROV: If you'd told me this a month or two ago, perhaps, then, I might have given it some thought, but now…*(Shrugs his shoulders.)* And if she's suffering, then of course…There's only one thing I don't understand: Why was this little interrogation necessary? *(Looks her in the eye and shakes his finger at her.)* What a cunning creature you are!

YELENA ANDREEVNA: What is that supposed to mean?

ASTROV: *(Laughing.)* How very cunning! All right, let's suppose Sonya's suffering, let's assume that, but why this little interrogation of yours? *(Prevents her from speaking, excited.)* Please, don't look so surprised, you know very well why I come here every day…Why and for whom I come, oh, you know very well. My beautiful little beast of prey, come on, don't look at me that way, I'm an old hand at this…

YELENA ANDREEVNA: *(Bewildered.)* Beast of…? I don't know what you're talking about.

ASTROV: A lovely, silky little weasel…You need your victims! Here I've done nothing for a whole month, let everything go, I've sought you out greedily — and how you love it, you love it, terribly…So now what? I'm caught, you know it, with or without your little interrogation. *(Folds his arms and bows his head.)* I submit. Here I am, devour me!

YELENA ANDREEVNA: You've gone mad!

ASTROV: *(Laughs through his teeth.)* You…shy…

YELENA ANDREEVNA: Oh, I'm a far better person than you think I am! Far better! I swear to you! *(Tries to go.)*

ASTROV: *(Blocks her way.)* I'm going away today, I won't come here any more, but…*(Takes her hand, glances around.)* Where shall we meet? Tell me quickly: where? Someone might come in, tell me quickly…*(Passionately.)* What a ravishing, exquisite woman…One kiss…Just let me kiss your fragrant hair…

YELENA ANDREEVNA: I swear to you…

ASTROV: Why swear? There's no need to swear. No need to say another word…Oh, how beautiful you are! What hands! *(Kisses her hands.)*

YELENA ANDREEVNA: Enough, now…go away…*(Takes her hands away.)* You're forgetting yourself.

ASTROV: Tell me, tell me now, where can we meet tomorrow? *(Takes her by the waist.)* Don't you see, it's inevitable, we must see each other. *(Kisses her.)*

Just then, VANYA enters with a bouquet of roses and stops at the door.

YELENA ANDREEVNA: *(Not seeing VANYA.)* Spare me…leave me alone… *(Lays her head on ASTROV'S chest.)* No! *(Tries to go.)*

ASTROV: *(Holding her by the waist.)* Come to the forest tomorrow…two o'clock…. Yes? Yes? Will you?

YELENA ANDREEVNA: *(Sees VANYA.)* Let me go! *(Upset and embarrassed, goes to the window.)* This is terrible.

VANYA: *(Puts the bouquet on the chair; upset, he wipes his face and around his collar with a handkerchief.)* Never mind…really…never mind…

ASTROV: *(Obscurely.)* Today, my esteemed Ivan Petrovich, the weather is not bad, not bad at all. Overcast this morning, looked as if it might rain, but it's sunny now. To tell the truth, autumn has turned out to be just fine...no problem with the winter crops. *(Rolls up the map in a tube.)* The only thing is: The days have gotten shorter...*(Exits.)*

YELENA ANDREEVNA: *(Goes quickly to VANYA.)* You must try, you must do everything in your power, so my husband and I can leave here today! Do you hear me! Today!

VANYA: *(Wiping his face.)* What? Oh, yes...of course...I...Hélène, I saw everything, everything...

YELENA ANDREEVNA: *(Agitated.)* Do you hear me? I must get away from here today!

Enter SEREBRYAKOV, SONYA, TELEGIN, and MARINA.

TELEGIN: You know, your excellency, I haven't been all that well myself. I've been feeling miserable for two days now. My head, it's a bit...you know...

SEREBRYAKOV: Where is everybody? I don't like this house. It's like a maze. Twenty-six enormous rooms, everybody's scattered all over the place, you can't find anyone. *(Rings.)* Ask Maria Vasilyevna and Yelena Andreevna to come in!

YELENA ANDREEVNA: I'm here.

SEREBRYAKOV: Ladies and gentlemen, please be seated.

SONYA: *(Goes up to YELENA ANDREEVNA, impatiently.)* What did he say?

YELENA ANDREEVNA: Later.

SONYA: You're trembling? Are you upset? *(A searching look.)* I understand.... He said he wouldn't come here any more...Am I right?

Pause.

Tell me: Am I right?

YELENA ANDREEVNA affirmatively nods her head.

SEREBRYAKOV: *(To TELEGIN.)* One can accustom oneself to ill health, come what may, but I simply cannot bear the ways of country life. I have the feeling that I've fallen off the earth onto some other planet. Sit down, please, ladies and gentlemen. Sonya!

Pause.

She doesn't hear me. *(To MARINA.)* You too, nanny, sit.

The NURSE sits and knits a stocking.

Ladies and gentlemen, please. Hang your ears on the hook of attention, as
they say. *(Laughs.)*
VANYA: *(Upset.)* Perhaps, then, I'm not needed? May I go?
SEREBRYAKOV: No, you're needed here most of all.
VANYA: And what is it you wish of me?
SEREBRYAKOV: What...But why are you so angry?

Pause.

If I've offended you in any way, then please, forgive me.
VANYA: Spare me that tone. Let's get down to business...what do you want?

Enter MARIA VASILYEVNA.

SEREBRYAKOV: And here is Maman. Ladies and gentlemen, I shall begin.

Pause.

I have invited you here, ladies and gentlemen, to announce that the inspector general is coming. However, all joking aside. This is a serious matter.
Ladies and gentlemen, I have gathered you here, to request your aid and
advice, and knowing your infinite kindness, I hope that I shall have them
both. I am a scholarly man, a man of letters, and have always been a
stranger to the practical affairs of life. Without the guidance of knowl-
edgeable people, I cannot manage, and I look to you, Ivan Petrovich, as
well as you, Ilya Ilyich, you, Maman...The fact is, that "manet omnes una
nox," that is to say, we are all in the hands of God. I am old, and ill, and
for that reason, I find it an opportune time to settle the affairs pertaining
to my property, insofar as they concern my family. My life is already over,
I am not concerned with myself, but I have a young wife, and an unmar-
ried daughter.

Pause.

To continue living in the country will no longer be possible for me. We were not meant to live in the country. To live in town, however, on the allowance we receive from this estate, is also not possible. Let us assume, then, that we sell the forest, that would be an extraordinary measure, one we could not take every year. Such measures must be found, therefore, as would guarantee us a steady, more or less fixed yearly income. I have thought of one such measure, and I have the honor of presenting it to you for your consideration. Details aside, I shall pose it to you in general outline form. Our estate yields a profit, on the average, of no more than two percent. I propose to sell it. If the money we earn is converted into interest-bearing securities, then we shall receive from four to five percent, and, I believe, that there will even be a surplus of several thousand, which will allow us to buy a small dacha in Finland.

VANYA: Wait a minute…I believe my hearing has failed me. Repeat what you just said.

SEREBRYAKOV: The money will be converted into interest-bearing securities and from the surplus, whatever is left, we can buy a dacha in Finland.

VANYA: Not Finland…What you said before that.

SEREBRYAKOV: I propose to sell the estate.

VANYA: That's it. You sell the estate, wonderful, a fabulous idea…And what do you propose to do with me, my old mother, and Sonya here?

SEREBRYAKOV: That we can discuss in due time. There's no rush.

VANYA: Wait a minute. Evidently, up until now I haven't had a drop of common sense. Up until now I had the stupidity to assume that this estate belongs to Sonya. My late father bought the estate as a dowry for my sister. Up until now I have been so naive, imagine, it was my understanding we were not living under Turkish law, and I thought that the estate had passed down from my sister to Sonya.

SEREBRYAKOV: Yes, the estate belongs to Sonya. Who is disputing that? Without Sonya's consent I could not, in effect, sell it. It's for her very sake that I'm proposing to do so.

VANYA: This is unbelievable, unbelievable! Either I'm going out of my mind, or…or else…

MARIA VASILYEVNA: Jean, don't contradict Alexandre. Trust me, he knows better than we do what's right and what's wrong.

VANYA: No… give me some water. *(Drinks water.)* Say whatever you like, whatever you like!

SEREBRYAKOV: I don't understand what you're getting so excited about. I didn't say that my plan was ideal. If everyone finds it unsuitable, I won't insist on it.

Pause.

TELEGIN: *(Confused.)* Your excellency, I have not only the utmost reverence for learning, but I have a kindred feeling for it as well. My brother Grigory Ilyich's wife's brother, perhaps it's possible that you might know him, Konstantin Trofimovich Lakedemonov, has a master's degree…

VANYA: Wait a minute, Waffles, we're discussing business…Save it for later…*(To SEREBRYAKOV.)* Go ahead, ask him. This estate was bought from his uncle.

SEREBRYAKOV: Ach, why should I ask him? For what purpose?

VANYA: This estate was bought for 95,000 at the time. My father only paid 70,000, that left a mortgage of 25,000. Now, you listen…This estate could not have been bought, had I not forfeited my inheritance on behalf of sister, whom I dearly loved. Moreover, I worked for ten years, like an ox, and payed off the entire mortgage…

SEREBRYAKOV: I regret to have started this conversation.

VANYA: This estate is free of debt and disorder thanks only to my own personal efforts. And now that I'm old, they want to throw me out by the neck!

SEREBRYAKOV: I don't understand what you're getting at.

VANYA: For twenty-five years I've managed this estate; I've worked, I've sent you money, like the most conscientious caretaker, and all this time not once did you ever thank me. The whole time — when I was young and even now — I have received a salary of five hundred rubles a year, — a pathetic pittance! — and it didn't even dawn on you to increase it, not once, not even by a single ruble!

SEREBRAYKOV: Ivan Petrovich, how was I to know, really? I'm not a practical man, I know nothing of these matters. You could have raised it yourself as much as you liked.

VANYA: Why didn't I just steal it! Why don't you all despise me for the fact that I didn't just steal it! It would have been just, and I wouldn't be a pauper today!

MARIA VASILYEVNA: *(Severely.)* Jean!

TELEGIN: *(Agitated.)* Vanya, dear friend, please don't, please…I'm trembling…Why ruin good relations? *(Kisses him.)* Please don't.

VANYA: For twenty-five years, I've sat here with my mother, buried like a mole within these four walls…All our thoughts and feelings were for you alone. All day long we'd talk about you, about your works, we were so proud of you, we spoke your name with reverence; we wasted our nights reading journals and books which now I deeply despise!

TELEGIN: Please don't, Vanya, please don't...I can't bear it...

SEREBRYAKOV: *(Irate.)* I don't understand, what do you want?

VANYA: You were a being of a supreme order, we recited your articles by heart...But now my eyes are open! I see everything! You write about art, but you understand nothing about art! All your works, which I adored, aren't worth a lousy half a kopek! You fooled us!

SEREBRYAKOV: Ladies and gentlemen! Please! Calm him down once and for all! I am leaving!

YELENA ANDREEVNA: Ivan Petrovich, I command you to be quiet! Do you hear me?

VANYA: I will not be quiet! *(Blocks SEREBRYAKOV's way.)* Wait a minute, I'm not finished yet! You have ruined my life! I haven't lived, I have not lived! Thanks to you, I have destroyed, wasted the best years of my life. You are my worst enemy!

TELEGIN: I can't bear it...I can't.... I'm leaving. *(Leaves in great distress.)*

SEREBRYAKOV: What do you want from me? And what right do you have to speak to me in that tone of voice! You nonentity! If the estate is yours, go ahead, take it, I have no need for it.

YELENA ANDREEVNA: I am leaving this hell at once! *(Shouts.)* I can't stand it any more!

VANYA: I've wasted my life! I am talented, brilliant, courageous...If I had lived a life, I might have been a Schopenhauer, a Dostoevsky...What am I saying? I'm raving! I'm going out of my mind...Matushka, I'm in despair! Matushka!

MARIA VASILYEVNA: *(Severely.)* Listen to Alexandre!

SONYA: *(Gets on her knees before nurse and clings to her.)* Nanny! Nanny!

VANYA: Matushka! What can I do? Never mind, don't say it! I know myself what I must do! *(To SEREBRYAKOV.)* You will remember me! *(Exits by the center door.)*

MARIA VASILYEVNA follows after him.

SEREBRYAKOV: Ladies and gentlemen, will someone tell me what is happening here? Take this madman away from me! I cannot stay under the same roof with him! He lives there *(points to the center door)*, right next to me, almost...Let him move to the village, to a separate wing, or else I'll move out myself, but I cannot remain in the same house with him...

YELENA ANDREEVNA: *(To her husband.)* We're leaving here today! It must be arranged immediately.

SEREBRYAKOV: Insignificant man!

SONYA: *(On her knees, to her father, upset, in tears.)* Have mercy, Papa! Uncle Vanya and I are so unhappy! *(Controlling her despair.)* You must have mercy! Remember, when you were younger, every night Uncle Vanya and Grandmother translated your books for you, copied your articles...night after night after night! Uncle Vanya and I worked without rest, we were afraid to spend one single kopek on ourselves, everything we sent to you...We've earned our keep! I'm not saying it right, I know I'm not, but try to understand us, Papa. You must have mercy!

YELENA ANDREEVNA: *(Agitated, to her husband.)* Aleksandr, for God's sake, talk to him, I beg of you.

SEREBRYAKOV: Very well, I shall talk to him...I don't blame him for anything, I'm not angry, but don't you agree, his behavior is strange, to say the least. All right, I'll go to him. *(Exits through the center door.)*

YELENA ANDREEVNA: Be a little gentler with him, calm him down...*(Exits after him.)*

SONYA: *(Clinging to the NURSE.)* Nanny! Nanny!

MARINA: It's nothing, child. Just the geese — they cackle —and they stop...they cackle — and they stop...

SONYA: Nanny!

MARINA: *(Pats her on the head.)* You're trembling, you're freezing cold! There, there, my orphan, God is kind. A little limeleaf tea, or raspberry, perhaps, this too will pass...Don't grieve, my little orphan...*(Looks at the center door, with feeling.)* Raising a fuss like that, those geese, shame on them!

Offstage, a shot; YELENA ANDREEVNA is heard screaming; SONYA shudders.

Curse you!

SEREBRYAKOV: *(Runs in, staggering with fright.)* Stop him! Stop him! He's out of his mind!

YELENA ANDREEVNA and VANYA struggle in the doorway.

YELENA ANDREEVNA: *(Trying to take the pistol away from him.)* Give it to me! I said, give it to me!

VANYA: Leave me alone, Hélène! Leave me alone! *(Wrestles free, runs in, looks for SEREBRYAKOV.)* Where is he? Ah, there he is! *(Shoots at him.)* Bang!

Pause.

Didn't hit him? Missed again?! *(In a rage.)* Ah, damn, damn…damn it all…

(Strikes the floor with the gun and collapses on a chair in exhaustion.)

SEREBRYAKOV is stunned; YELENA ANDREEVNA leans against the wall, in a faint.

YELENA ANDREEVNA: Take me away from here! Take me away, kill me, anything…I can't stay here, I can't!
VANYA: *(In despair.)* Oh, what am I doing! What am I doing?
SONYA: *(Softly.)* Nanny! Nanny!

CURTAIN

ACT FOUR

VANYA's room, which serves both as his bedroom and as the office for the estate. By the window, a large table with ledger books and various papers, a bureau, cupboards, scales. A smaller table for ASTROV; on it, drawing materials and paints; beside it, a portfolio. A cage with a starling. On the wall, a map of Africa, of no apparent use to anyone here. A huge sofa, covered with oilcloth. To the left, — a door, leading to another room; to the right, a door to the porch; at the door to the right, a mat has been placed to prevent the peasants from muddying the floor. — A fall evening. It is still.

TELEGIN and MARINA sit opposite each other and wind wool for stockings.

TELEGIN: Better hurry, Marina Timofeevna, they'll be ready to say good-bye soon. They've already ordered the horses.

MARINA: *(Tries to wind faster.)* Only a little bit left.

TELEGIN: They're going to Kharkov. To live there.

MARINA: Better this way.

TELEGIN: They were frightened...Yelena Andreevna said: "Not one more hour," she said, "I don't want to live here one more hour...we're leaving, that's what we're doing...We're going to live in Kharkov," she said, "we'll get settled and then we'll send for our things..." Without any luggage they're leaving. Well, Maria Timofeevna, it wasn't meant for them to live here. It wasn't meant to be...It was preordained.

MARINA: Better this way. All that noise, shooting each other — shame on them!

TELEGIN: Yes, a tableau worthy of the brush of Aivazovsky.

MARINA: Wouldn't want to lay eyes on it.

Pause.

So, we'll live again, like we used to, in the old way. Morning tea at eight o'clock, midday meal at one o'clock — sit down to supper in the evening: nice and orderly, like normal people...a Christian life. *(With a sigh.)* It's been a while since I've tasted noodles, old sinner that I am.

TELEGIN: Yes, they haven't made us noodles in such a long time.

Pause.

Such a long, long time...This morning, Maria Timofeevna, I was walking in the village, and a shopkeeper yelled after me: "Hey you, freeloader!" How terrible it made me feel!

MARINA: Don't pay it any mind, dear. We're all freeloaders of God. You, and Sonya, and Ivan Petrovich, — no one will sit around idle any more, all of us, we'll toil away! All of us...Where's Sonya?

TELEGIN: In the garden. She and the doctor, they're looking everywhere for Ivan Petrovich. They're afraid he'll do himself harm.

MARINA: Where is his pistol?

TELEGIN: *(In a whisper.)* I hid it in the cellar!

MARINA: *(With a laugh.)* You devil!

VANYA and ASTROV enter from outside.

VANYA: Leave me alone. *(To MARINA and TELEGIN.)* Get out of here, leave me alone, even for an hour. I can't bear all this surveillance.

TELEGIN: Right away, Vanya. *(Leaves on tiptoe.)*

MARINA: And the gander goes: go-go-go! *(Gathers up her wool and exits.)*

VANYA: Leave me alone.

ASTROV: With the greatest of pleasure, I should have left here long ago, but, I repeat, I am not leaving, until you return what you have taken from me.

VANYA: I took nothing from you.

ASTROV: I mean it — don't keep me waiting. I should have been gone a long time ago.

VANYA: I took nothing from you.

Both sit.

ASTROV: Really? All right, I'll wait a bit longer, and then, forgive me, we'll have to use force. We'll tie you up and search you. I'm saying this in dead seriousness.

VANYA: Whatever.

Pause.

Such a fool: to shoot twice and miss both times! I shall never forgive myself!

ASTROV: If you felt like shooting so badly, you should have aimed for your own head.

VANYA: *(Shrugs his shoulders.)* Strange. I have attempted murder, and they haven't arrested me yet, haven't put me on trial. They must think I'm mad. *(A malicious smile.)* I am mad, and they are not — they who, in the guise of a professor, a sorcerer of scholarship, hide their mediocrity, their stupidity, their cold-blooded callousness. And no, they are not mad either, they who marry old men and then before everyone's eyes betray them. I saw, I saw how you embraced her!

ASTROV: Yes, sir, I did, I embraced her. So there. *(Thumbs his nose.)*

VANYA: *(Looks at the door.)* No, it's the world that's mad, if it keeps all of you in it!

ASTROV: What a stupid thing to say.

VANYA: So what, I'm mad, I'm out of my mind, I can say whatever I like.

ASTROV: An old trick. You're not mad, you're just an eccentric. A laughing stock. I used to think eccentrics weren't normal, but now I'm of the opinion that the normal condition of man is to be eccentric. You are completely normal.

VANYA: *(Covers his face with his hands.)* I'm so ashamed! If only you knew, how ashamed I am! No pain, no agony, nothing, can compare to this feeling of shame. *(With anguish.)* It's unbearable! *(Bends over the table.)* What can I do? What can I do?

ASTROV: Nothing.

VANYA: Give me something! Oh, my God…I am forty-seven years old; say I live to sixty, that means I still have thirteen years left. An eternity! How can I live through thirteen more years? What will I do, how will I fill them? Oh, think of it…*(squeezes ASTROV's hand, urgently)* think of how it might be to live the rest of your life in some new way. To wake up one calm, clear morning and feel that your life has started anew, that all the past has been forgotten, scattered, like smoke. *(Weeps.)* To start a new life…Prescribe it for me, how to start again…with what…

ASTROV: *(Annoyed.)* What are you talking about! What new life! Our situation, yours and mine, is hopeless.

VANYA: It is?

ASTROV: I am convinced of it.

VANYA: Give me something…*(Points to his heart.)* It hurts so.

ASTROV: *(Shouts angrily.)* Stop it! *(Softens.)* Those who will live after us in one hundred, two hundred years, who will despise us because we've lived our lives so stupidly, so unspeakably — perhaps they will find their way to happiness, but you and I…We have only one hope and here it is: the hope that, while we are sleeping in our graves, we are visited by dreams, perhaps even pleasant ones. *(Sighs.)* Yes, my friend. Once upon a time in this district there lived two decent, honest, intelligent men, only two: you and I. But ten years or so of this contemptible country life, this philistine life, it has dragged us down; it has poisoned our blood with its putrid fumes, and we have become vulgar, like everyone else. *(Briskly.)* But look now, you've done it again, charmed me with all this talk, talk, talk. Give me back what you took from me.

VANYA: I took nothing from you.

ASTROV: You took a bottle of morphine from my medical bag.

Pause.

Listen, if you're really that intent on doing it, go off in the woods and shoot yourself there. If you don't give me back that morphine, there will be talk, speculation, people will think I gave it to you...It's bad enough that I'll have to perform your autopsy...You think that will be interesting?

Enter SONYA.

VANYA: Leave me alone!

ASTROV: *(To SONYA.)* Sofya Aleksandrovna, your uncle stole a bottle of morphine from my bag and won't give it back. Tell him...that it's not wise, in the end. And besides, I've run out of time. I must be on my way.

SONYA: Uncle Vanya, you took morphine?

Pause.

ASTROV: He did. I'm sure of it.

SONYA: Give it back! Why are you trying to frighten us? *(Tenderly.)* Give it back, Uncle Vanya. I may be just as unhappy as you, but I don't despair. I endure, and I shall endure, until my life is over...And so shall you.

Pause.

Give it back! *(Kisses his hands.)* Good, kind, darling uncle, give it back! *(Weeps.)* You are so good, take pity on us and give it back. Have patience, Uncle Vanya, have patience!

VANYA: *(Takes the bottle from the table and gives it to ASTROV.)* Go on, take it! *(To SONYA.)* But we must get back to work as soon as possible, we must do something, I can't bear it...I can't...

SONYA: Yes, yes, work. As soon as they're off, we'll get to work…*(Nervously sorting through the papers on the table.)* We've neglected everything.

ASTROV: *(Puts the bottle in the bag and fastens the strap.)* Now I can be on my way.

YELENA ANDREEVNA: *(Enters.)* Ivan Petrovich, are you here? We're leaving now…Go to Aleksandr, he wants to say something to you.

SONYA: Go, Uncle Vanya. *(Takes VANYA by the hand.)* Let's go. You and Papa must make peace. It's absolutely essential.

SONYA and VANYA exit.

YELENA ANDREEVNA: I'm leaving. *(Gives ASTROV her hand.)* Good-bye.

ASTROV: Already?

YELENA ANDREEVNA: The horses are waiting.

ASTROV: Good-bye.

YELENA ANDREEVNA: Today you promised me you'd go away from here.

ASTROV: I remember. I'm leaving right now.

Pause.

Were you frightened? *(Takes her hand.)* Was it really so terrible?

YELENA ANDREEVNA: Yes.

ASTROV: Why not stay! Yes? Tomorrow, in the forest…

YELENA ANDREEVNA: No…It's already settled…That's why I have the courage to face you — we're leaving, it's settled, once and for all…One thing I ask you: Think more highly of me, please. I would like you to respect me.

ASTROV: Oh! *(Gesture of impatience.)* Stay, I beg of you. Face it, you don't have a thing to do on this earth, no purpose in life whatsoever, nothing at all to occupy you, sooner or later you will have to give into your feelings, — it's inevitable. And far better be it not in Kharkov or Kursk or some place like that, but here, in the lap of nature…At least here, it's poetic, the autumn is lovely…here we have forests, dilapidated old estates right out of Turgenev…

YELENA ANDREEVNA: How absurd you are…I'm angry with you, but nevertheless…I shall remember you with pleasure. You're an unusual man…unique. We'll never see each other again, so why hide it! I was attracted to you, in a way…Come, let's shake hands and part friends. Remember me kindly.

ASTROV: *(Shakes her hand.)* Yes, go…You know, you seem like a good, sincere person, really you do, and yet there is something very strange about you.

You came out here, and all of us who were busy working, puttering around, creating things, we had to drop everything we were doing and spend all summer taking care of you and your gouty old husband. Both of you — you and he — infected us all with your idleness. My head was turned, I didn't do a thing for a whole month, and meanwhile people were getting sick, and in my forests, peasants were letting their cattle graze right where I'd planted my new, young trees...And thus, wherever you and your husband go, you bring destruction...everywhere...I'm only joking, of course, but nevertheless.... it's strange, and I'm convinced of it, had you stayed, the devastation would have been overwhelming. I would have been lost, and things wouldn't have turned out well for you, either. So, go. "Finita la commedia!"

YELENA ANDREEVNA. *(Takes a pencil from his table and quickly hides it.)* I'm taking this pencil as a remembrance.

ASTROV: Strange, isn't it...We met, and suddenly for some reason...we'll never see each other again. That's the way it is on this earth...Before somebody comes, before Uncle Vanya enters with a bouquet, allow me...to kiss you...a farewell kiss...Will you? *(Kisses her cheek.)* There...that's lovely.

YELENA ANDREEVNA: I wish you the very best. *(Looks around.)* Whatever happens, for once in my life! *(Embraces him impetuously, then at once they quickly move apart.)* I must go.

ASTROV: Go, quickly. If the horses are ready, you'd better be off.

YELENA ANDREEVNA: They're coming, I think.

They both listen.

ASTROV: Finita!

Enter SEREBRYAKOV, VANYA, MARIA VASILYEVNA with a book, TELEGIN, and SONYA.

SEREBRYAKOV: *(To VANYA.)* So, let bygones be bygones. After what has happened, I have suffered greatly in these past few hours, and have given the matter considerable thought; so much so that I believe I could write an entire treatise for the benefit of posterity on how we must live our lives. I willingly accept your apology, and by the same token I apologize to you. Good-bye! *(Kisses VANYA three times.)*

VANYA: You'll receive exactly what you've been receiving before. Everything will be as it was.

YELENA ANDREEVNA embraces SONYA.

SEREBRYAKOV: *(Kisses MARIA VASILYENVA's hand.)* Maman...

MARIA VASILYEVNA: Alexandre, have your photograph taken and send it to me. You know how much you mean to me.

TELEGIN: Good-bye, your excellency! Don't forget us!

SEREBRYAKOV: *(Kisses his daughter.)* Good-bye...Good-bye, everyone! *(Gives his hand to ASTROV.)* Thank you for the pleasant company...I respect your way of life, your enthusiasms, your passions, but permit an old man to give you some parting advice: Ladies and gentlemen, we must do something! We must do something! *(A general bow.)* Good luck! *(Exits.)*

MARIA VASILYEVNA and SONYA go after him.

VANYA: *(Fervently kisses YELENA ANDREEVNA's hand.)* Good-bye...Forgive me...We shall never see each other again.

YELENA ANDREEVNA: *(Moved.)* Good-bye, my dearest. *(Kisses him on the head and exits.)*

ASTROV: *(To TELEGIN.)* Tell them, Waffles, to bring my horses around, too, will you?

TELEGIN: Yes indeed, dear friend. *(Exits.)*

Only ASTROV and VANYA are left.

ASTROV: *(Takes his paints from the table and puts them in his suitcase.)* You're not going to see them off?

VANYA: Let them go, I...I can't. It hurts too much. I must start doing something right away...Work, work! *(Rustles through the papers on the table.)*

Pause; bells are heard.

ASTROV: They've gone. The professor's glad, no doubt! Nothing in the world could bring him back here.

MARINA: *(Enters.)* They've gone. *(Sits in the armchair and knits a stocking.)*

SONYA: *(Enters.)* They've gone. *(Wipes her eyes.)* They'll travel safely, God willing. *(To VANYA.)* So, Uncle Vanya, let's do something.

VANYA: Work, work...

SONYA: It's been a long time, such a long time, since we sat at this table together. *(Lights the lamp on the table.)* There doesn't seem to be any ink...*(Takes inkwell, goes to cupboard and pours ink into it.)* I'm so sad that they've gone.

MARIA VASILYEVNA: *(Enters slowly.)* They've gone! *(Sits and becomes absorbed in reading.)*

SONYA: *(Sits at the table and glances through the ledger book.)* Let's do the accounts first, Uncle Vanya. We've neglected them terribly. Today someone sent for a copy of his bill again. So, write…You do one, I'll do the next…

VANYA: *(Writes.)* "Invoice…to Mr…"

Both write in silence.

MARINA: *(Yawns.)* Ready for bed…

ASTROV: Silence. Pens scratch. Crickets chirp. It's warm, it's cozy…I don't want to leave this place.

The harness bells are heard.

They're bringing my horses around…And so, it's good-bye to you, my friends, good-bye to my table, and — I'm off! *(Puts the maps in the portfolio case.)*

MARINA: So what's your hurry? Sit a little.

ASTROV: I can't.

VANYA: *(Writes.)* "And an outstanding balance of two rubles seventy-five kopeks…"

WORKMAN enters.

WORKMAN. Mikhail Lvovich, the horses are ready.

ASTROV: I heard. *(Gives him his medical bag, suitcase, and portfolio case.)* Here, take these. Careful with the portfolio.

WORKMAN: Right-o, sir. *(Exits.)*

ASTROV: And so, ladies and gentlemen…*(Goes to say good-bye.)*

SONYA: When will we see you again?

ASTROV: Not before summer, probably. Doubtful during the winter…If something happens, of course, let me know — I'll come. *(Shakes hands.)* Thank you for your hospitality, for your kindness…for everything. *(Goes to NURSE and kisses her on the top of the head.)* Good-bye, old woman.

MARINA: So, you're going without tea?

ASTROV: I don't want any, nanny.

MARINA: How about a little vodka, then?

ASTROV: *(Tentatively.)* All right…

MARINA exits.

(After a pause.) My trace horse has started to limp. Yesterday I noticed it again, when Petrushka was watering him.

VANYA: You've got to reshoe him.

ASTROV: I'll have to stop at the blacksmith's in Rozhdestvennoe. Can't let it go. *(Goes over to the map of Africa and looks at it.)* Imagine how hot it must be in Africa now — terrible!

VANYA: Yes, probably.

MARINA: *(Returns with a tray, on which there is a glass of vodka and a small piece of bread.)* Drink up.

ASTROV drinks the vodka.

To your good health, dearie. *(Bows low.)* You should have a little bread with it.

ASTROV: No, I'm fine...So, that's it, then! *(To MARINA.)* Don't bother to see me out, nanny. No need.

He leaves. SONYA follows him with a candle; MARINA sits in her armchair.

VANYA: *(Writes.)* " The second of February, vegetable oil, twenty pounds...the sixteenth of February, again, vegetable oil, twenty pounds...Buckwheat..."

Pause.

Harness bells are heard.

MARINA: He's gone.

SONYA: *(Returning, places the candle on the table.)* He's gone

VANYA: *(First calculates on the abacus and then makes a note.)* And a total of...fifty...twenty-five...

SONYA sits and writes.

MARINA: *(Yawns.)* Lord, o lord...

TELEGIN enters on tiptoe, sits by the door, and quietly strums the guitar.

VANYA: *(To SONYA, stroking her hair.)* My child, it hurts so much! Oh, if only you knew, how much!

SONYA: What can we do, we must live!

Pause.

We shall live, Uncle Vanya. We shall live through the endless, endless row of days, the long evenings, we shall patiently bear the ordeals that fate has in store for us; we shall toil for others now and in our old age, we shall know no rest, and when our hour comes, we shall die humbly, and there beyond the grave we shall say that we've suffered, that we've wept, that life was bitter, and God will take pity on us, and you and I, uncle, darling uncle, we shall see a radiant life, a beautiful, blissful life, we shall rejoice, and we shall look back on our present unhappiness with tenderness, with a smile — and we shall rest. I believe it, Uncle Vanya, I believe it fervently, passionately...*(Gets on her knees before him and puts her head in his hands; in a tired voice.)* We shall rest!

TELEGIN plays softly on the guitar.

We shall rest! We shall hear the angels, we shall see the heavens sparkling with diamonds, we shall see all the evil on earth, all our suffering bathed in a mercy which fills all the world, and our life shall be peaceful, gentle, sweet, like a caress. I have faith, I have faith...*(Wipes his tears with her handkerchief.)* Poor, poor Uncle Vanya, you are crying...*(Through tears.)* You have known no joy in your life, but wait, Uncle Vanya, wait...We shall rest...*(Embraces him.)* We shall rest!

WATCHMAN knocks.

TELEGIN quietly strums, MARIA VASILYEVNA makes notes in the margin of the brochure; MARINA knits a stocking.

We shall rest!

CURTAIN SLOWLY FALLS

Date of Publication
1897

Moscow Premiere
October 26, 1899

THE THREE SISTERS

A Drama in Four Acts

The premiere of this new translation was produced by the Philadelphia Festival Theatre for New Plays, Annenberg Center, opening night, January 14, 1996. Scenic Designer: David P. Gordon; Lighting Designer, Jerold R. Forsyth; Costume Designer: Janus Stefanowicz; Sound Designer: Eileen Tague; Properties Designer: Christine Sysko; Musical Director: John S. Lionarons; Choreographer: Andrea Paskman; Casting: Hilary Missan, Jennifer Childs; Stage Manager: Maribeth Hunter; directed by Carol Rocamora.

CAST (in order of appearance)

Olga	Susan Wilder
Masha	Janis Dardaris
Irina	Megan Bellwoar
Tusenbach, Nikolai Lvovich	Greg Wood
Chebutykin, Ivan Romanovich	Louis Lippa
Solyony, Vasily Vasilyevich	Peter de Laurier
Anfisa	Moira Rankin
Ferapont	Fred Shaffmaster
Vershinin, Aleksandr Ignatyevich	Michael Butler
Prozorov, Andrey Sergeevich	Eric Hissom
Kulygin, Fyodor Ilyich	Ezra Barnes
Natalya Ivanovna	Lisbeth Bartlett
Fedotik	Mark Hallen
Rode	Jeff Bleam
Musicians	John S. Lionarons
	Alex Siniavsky
Maid	Brooke Woodruff

CAST OF CHARACTERS

PROZOROV, Andrey Sergeevich

NATALYA IVANOVNA, his fiancée, later his wife

OLGA, his sister

MASHA, his sister

IRINA, his sister

KULYGIN, Fyodor Ilyich, a teacher at the high school, Masha's husband

VERSHININ, Aleksandr Ignatyevich, a lieutenant-colonel, battery commander

TUSENBACH, Baron Nikolai Lvovich, a lieutenant

SOLYONY, Vasily Vasilyevich, a captain

CHEBUTYKIN, Ivan Romanovich, a military doctor

FEDOTIK, Aleksey Petrovich, a second lieutenant

RODE, Vladimir Karlovich, a second lieutenant

FERAPONT, an old watchman from the local district council

ANFISA, an old nurse, aged eighty

The action takes place in the principal town of one of the provinces.

The Three Sisters

ACT ONE

The Prozorov house. A drawing room with columns, beyond which a large hall can be seen. Noontime; outside, it is sunny and bright. In the hall, a table is being set for lunch. OLGA, in a blue uniform worn by teachers of the girls' high school, paces back and forth, correcting student notebooks; MASHA, in a black dress, her hat in her lap, sits and reads a book; IRINA, in a white dress, stands lost in thought.

OLGA: Father died a year ago, yes, one year ago today, the fifth of May, your nameday, Irina. It was so cold, we had snow then, remember? I thought I'd never live through it all, you lay there in a faint, like the dead. And yet, here we are, a year has passed, our spirits are lighter, we remember it with ease, look, you're all in white, you're radiant, your sweet face is beaming...

The clock strikes noon.

The clock struck too, then, in just the same way.

Pause.

I remember, as they carried Father away, there was music playing, they gave a military salute at his grave. He was a general, commander of the brigade, and yet so few people came. But it was raining, then. Raining hard, and snowing, too.

IRINA: Why look back!

Behind the columns, in the hall, Baron TUSENBACH, CHEBUTYKIN, and SOLYONY appear at the table.

OLGA: How warm it is today, you can open the windows wide, and the birch trees aren't even in bloom! Eleven years ago we moved here from Moscow, Father led the brigade, I remember it well, it was early in May, just like today, and Moscow was all in bloom, it was warm, and bathed in sunlight. Eleven years have passed, and yet I remember it all, as if we'd left only yesterday. My God! Today I woke up, I saw the morning, flooded in sunlight and springtime, and such joy stirred in my soul, how I longed to go home, yes, passionately!

CHEBUTYKIN: Not on your life!

TUSENBACH: Don't be ridiculous!

MASHA, lost in her book, whistles a song softly.

OLGA: Don't whistle, Masha. Really, how can you!

Pause.

Every day I teach at the high school, every day I give lessons from morning till night, and how my head aches, it aches constantly, and I think, why, I'm already growing old. No, really, these past four years at school, I feel, slowly but surely, day by day, drop by drop, my youth and my strength draining from me. And yet one dream remains, growing stronger and stronger…

IRINA: To go to Moscow. To sell the house, to end our life here, and — to Moscow…

OLGA: Yes! As soon as possible, to Moscow.

CHEBUTYKIN and TUSENBACH laugh.

IRINA: Our brother will probably be a professor, he couldn't live here, anyway. So that leaves poor Masha…

OLGA: Masha will spend the whole summer in Moscow, every year…

MASHA whistles a song, softly.

IRINA: It will all come true, somehow, God willing. *(Looks out the window.)* The weather is glorious today. I don't know why my heart is so light! This morning I remembered: Today is my nameday, and suddenly I was filled with such joy, I remembered when I was young, when Mama was still alive! Such marvelous, marvelous thoughts, how they thrilled me!

OLGA: You're radiant today, you're more beautiful than ever. And Masha's beautiful, too. Andrey might have been handsome, only he's put on too much weight, it doesn't become him. As for me, I've grown old, look how thin I am, from scolding the girls at school all day, I suppose. Never mind, today I'm free, I'm home, and my head doesn't ache, I feel so much younger than yesterday. I'm only twenty-eight years old...Ah, well, it's all in God's hands, and yet, you know, I often think, if I were to marry and stay at home all day, life would be so much better.

Pause.

How I would love my husband. I would.

TUSENBACH: *(To SOLYONY.)* You're talking nonsense, I'm tired of listening to you. *(Entering the drawing room.)* Oh, yes, I forgot to tell you. Today, you're to receive a visit from our new battery commander, Vershinin. *(Sits at the piano.)*

OLGA: Oh, really! I'm so glad.

IRINA: Is he very old?

TUSENBACH: Not really. Forty, forty-five, at the most. *(Plays softly.)* Seems like a nice fellow, too. He's nobody's fool, that's for sure. Only he talks a lot.

IRINA: Is he attractive?

TUSENBACH: Oh, I don't know, he's not bad, I suppose, the only thing is, he's married, he's got a wife, a mother-in-law, and two little girls. Second marriage, too. Everywhere he goes, he talks about his wife and his two little girls. You'll see, when he gets here. His wife's a bit crazy, you know, she's got these two long braids, she's quite pretentious, talks philosophy all the time, attempts suicide every other day, it seems, just to get even with her husband. I'd have given up long ago, but, no, not he, he suffers and complains about it, that's all.

SOLYONY: *(Enters the drawing room from the hall with CHEBUTYKIN.)* With one hand I can lift only fifty pounds...with two, however, I can lift one hundred and eighty, over two hundred pounds, even...By this, I conclude that two men aren't twice, but three times as strong as one man, even more...

CHEBUTYKIN: *(Reading the newspaper as he walks.)* For loss of hair, take eight point five grams of naphthaline, dissolve in a half bottle of alcohol...apply daily...*(Makes a note of it in a little book.)* Let's make a note of that, shall we!

(To SOLYONY.) Now, where was I, ah, yes, you place the cork in the bottle, insert a small glass tube…That's it, and then you take a pinch, that's right, just a pinch of your everyday aluminum sulphate…

IRINA: Ivan Romanich, dear Ivan Romanich!

CHEBUTYKIN: What is it, my child, my joy?

IRINA: Tell me, why am I so happy today? It's as if I were sailing, with a deep blue sky above me and great white birds soaring overhead. Why do I feel this way? Why?

CHEBUTYKIN: *(Kisses both her hands, tenderly.)* My beautiful white bird…

IRINA When I woke up this morning, I got up, I bathed, and suddenly it seemed that everything on earth was now clear to me, and I knew how I must live. Darling Ivan Romanich, I understand everything now. A man must work, he must work by the sweat of his brow, whoever he may be, and this and this alone is his reason for being, his happiness, his ecstasy. How noble it is to be a humble workman, who rises at break of dawn and smashes stones by the roadside, or a shepherd, or a schoolmaster, who teaches little children, or an engine driver on the railroad…Merciful God, let alone a human being, better to be an ox, better to be a humble horse, even, if only to work, better that than a young lady, who gets up at noon each day, who drinks coffee in bed, who takes two hours to get dressed… Oh, how awful it is! The way one thirsts for water on a sweltering day, so do I thirst for work. And if I don't rise early each day and work, then deny me thy friendship, Ivan Romanich.

CHEBUTYKIN: *(Tenderly.)* I deny, I deny…

OLGA: Father taught us to get up at seven every morning. Now Irina wakes at seven, and lies in bed until nine, at least, thinking. She takes life seriously, you know! *(Bursts out laughing.)*

IRINA: You're used to treating me like a child, you find it strange, that I take life seriously. But I'm twenty years old!

TUSENBACH: A longing for work, oh dear God, how well I understand it! I have never worked a day in my life. I was born in Petersburg, cold and idle Petersburg, into a family which never had a care in the world. I remember, when I'd arrive home from military school, a valet would pull off my boots, I was so spoiled at the time, but my mother worshipped me and was amazed when others felt otherwise. I was protected from work. And yet how could I be protected, how can anyone be! For the time has come when great thunderclouds are gathering over us, a strong, healthy storm is brewing, drawing nearer and nearer, and soon it shall blow away idleness, indifference, prejudice against work, and putrefying boredom. I shall work, and in twenty-five – thirty years or so, every man shall work. Each and every man!

CHEBUTYKIN: I shall not work.

TUSENBACH: You don't count.

SOLYONY: In twenty-five years, you won't be alive, thank God. In two or three years you'll die of apoplexy, or else I'll lose my patience and put a bullet through your brain, my angel. *(Takes a flask of scent from his pocket and sprinkles himself on the chest and hands.)*

CHEBUTYKIN: *(Laughing.)* As a matter of fact, I've never done a stroke of work in my life. When I graduated from the university, I never lifted a finger, never even opened a book, all I've ever read is the newspaper...*(Takes another newspaper out of his pocket.)* Here we are...I know from the newspaper, for example, that there once was a man named Dobrolyubov, and what he wrote — I haven't the slightest idea...God only knows...

A knocking is heard on the floor from the level below.

There, I'm being summoned from below, someone's here to see me. One moment, please...coming...*(Hurries out, combing his beard.)*

IRINA: He's up to something.

TUSENBACH: Right. He tried to keep a straight face, but it's so obvious, he'll be back in a moment with a present for you.

IRINA: How awful!

OLGA: Yes, it's terrible. He's always making such a fool of himself.

MASHA:"In a cove by the sea a green oak stands,
    A golden chain wound round...
    A golden chain wound round..."
(Rises, humming softly.)

OLGA: You're sad today, Masha.

MASHA, still humming, puts on her hat.

Where are you going?

MASHA: Home.

IRINA: How odd...

TUSENBACH: Leaving a name day party!

MASHA: It doesn't matter...I'll be back in the evening. Good-bye, my sweet...*(Kisses IRINA.)*...Once more, I wish you health and happiness. Long ago, when father was alive, we'd have thirty or forty officers at our name day parties, every single time, they were wild and gay, and today, we're lucky if we have a man and a half, and it's as quiet as the desert…I'm leaving…I'm in a rotten mood today, I'm feeling wretched, don't pay the slightest attention to me. *(Laughing through her tears.)* We'll talk later, but for now, farewell, my darling, I've got to get out of here.

IRINA: *(Disappointed.)* How can you…

OLGA: *(In tears.)* I understand you, Masha.

SOLYONY: Give a man philosophy,

He'll do no worse than sophistry,

But give a woman even breath,

And she will talk you all to death.

MASHA: And what is that supposed to mean, you perfectly terrible man?

SOLYONY: Nothing.

"He scarce had time to cry 'beware'

When he was taken by the bear."

Pause.

MASHA: *(To Olga, angrily.)* Stop weeping!

Enter ANFISA and FERAPONT, carrying a large cake.

ANFISA: This way, dearie. Come on in, it's all right, your feet are clean. *(To IRINA.)* From the district council, from Protopopov, Mikhail Ivanich…A cake.

IRINA: Thank you. Please, tell him thank you! *(Takes the cake.)*

FERAPONT: How's that?

IRINA: *(Louder.)* Please, tell him thank you.

OLGA: Nanny, give him some cake. Go on, Ferapont, they'll give you a piece of cake.

FERAPONT: How's that?

ANFISA: Come, Ferapont Spiridonich. Come, dearie…*(Exits with FERAPONT.)*

MASHA: I don't like that Protopopov, Mikhail Potapich, or Ivanich, or whatever his name is. You shouldn't have invited him.

IRINA: I didn't.

MASHA: Good.

Enter CHEBUTYKIN, followed by a soldier's orderly, carrying a silver samovar; a buzz of amazement and disapproval.

OLGA: *(Covers her face with her hands.)* A samovar! How perfectly awful! *(She exits to the table in the hall.)*

IRINA: Dear Ivan Romanich, what are you doing!

TUSENBACH: *(Laughing.)* What did I tell you!

MASHA: Ivan Romanich, have you no shame!

CHEBUTYKIN: My darlings, my treasures, you are all I have, to me you are the most precious creatures on the face of this earth. Soon, I shall be sixty, I am an old man, a lonely, insignificant old man...Without my love for you, I am worthless, and were it not for you, I should have forsaken this world long ago...*(To IRINA.)* My darling, my child, I have known you since the day you were born...I held you in my arms...how I loved your dear mama...

IRINA: But why such expensive gifts!

CHEBUTYKIN: *(In tears, angrily.)* What do you mean...expensive gifts! *(To the orderly.)* Take the samovar away...*(Mocking.)* Expensive gifts...

The orderly carries the samovar into the hall.

ANFISA: *(Crossing through the drawing room.)* The mysterious colonel is here, dearies! He's already taken off his coat, children, he's on his way in. Arinushka, you be nice to him, now, be polite...*(Exiting.)* And it's way past lunchtime, already...Lord, lord...

TUSENBACH: That must be Vershinin.

Enter VERSHININ.

Lieutenant-Colonel Vershinin!

VERSHININ: *(To MASHA and IRINA.)* Allow me to introduce myself: Vershinin. I'm so glad to be here, at long last. My, oh, my, how you've changed!

IRINA: Do sit down, please. We're delighted.

VERSHININ: *(Cheerfully.)* Yes, so glad, so glad! But, wait, aren't there three of you, three sisters? Yes, I remember, three little girls. I don't remember your faces, but your father, Colonel Prozorov, had three little girls, that I remember clearly, I saw you with my very own eyes. How time flies! Ah, yes, how time flies!

TUSENBACH: Aleksandr Ignatyevich is from Moscow.

IRINA: From Moscow? You're from Moscow?

VERSHININ: Yes, indeed, I am. Your late father was a battery commander there, and I was an officer in the same brigade. *(To MASHA.)* Now your face, I think, is somewhat familiar.

MASHA: I don't remember you at all!

IRINA: Olya! Olya! *(Calls out into the hall.)* Olya! Come quickly!

OLGA comes into the living room from the hall.

It seems Lieutenant-Colonel Vershinin is from Moscow!

VERSHININ: You must be Olga Sergeevna, the eldest…And you're Maria…And you're Irina, the youngest…

OLGA: You're from Moscow?

VERSHININ: Yes. I studied in Moscow, I enlisted in Moscow, I served there for a long, long time, then, at last, I was given my own company here — I've moved out here, as you can see. I don't remember you distinctly, I only remember there were three of you, three sisters. Your father is forever preserved in my memory, I can close my eyes and see him before me, as if he were still alive. I used to visit you in Moscow, you know…

OLGA: You know, I thought I remembered everyone, and now…

VERSHININ: My name is Aleksandr Ignatyevich…

IRINA: Aleksandr Ignatyevich, you're from Moscow…what a surprise!

OLGA: You know we're moving back there, of course.

IRINA: We hope to be there by autumn. It's our native town, we were born there…On Old Basmannaya Street…

They both laugh with joy.

MASHA: What a surprise to see someone from home. *(Quickly.)* Yes, now I remember! Olya, do you remember, they used to talk about "the lovesick major." You were a lieutenant then, you were in love with some-body-or-other, and everyone teased you and called you "the major" for some reason…

VERSHININ: *(Laughs.)* Yes, yes…"The lovesick major," that's right…

MASHA: All you had was a moustache then…Oh, and now, you look so much older! *(In tears.)* Much, much older!

VERSHININ: Yes, when they called me "the lovesick major," I was still young, I was in love. But not any more.

OLGA: And yet, you don't have a single gray hair. You may not be young any more, but still, you're not old yet.

VERSHININ: Well, I'm almost forty-three. How long ago did you leave Moscow?

IRINA: Eleven years. What is it, Masha you're crying, silly…*(In tears.)* Now I'm crying, too…

MASHA: I am not. And what street did you live on?

VERSHININ: On Old Basmannaya Street.

OLGA: So did we…

VERSHININ: I lived on Nemetskaya Street for a while. From there I could walk to the Red Barracks. There's a gloomy bridge you cross along the way, with the haunting sound of the water rushing below. When you're alone, it makes you feel so sad.

Pause.

But here, what a broad and beautiful river you have! A majestic river!

OLGA: Well, yes, only it's so cold here. Cold, and there are mosquitos…

VERSHININ: What do you mean! Here you have the beauty of the pure Russian climate. The forest, the river…and you have the birch trees. Lovely little birches, I love them more than any other tree. It's paradise living here. Only it's strange, isn't it, the railroad station is thirteen miles away…And no one knows why.

SOLYONY: Ah, but I know why.

Everyone looks at him.

Because if the railroad station were nearby, why then it wouldn't be far away, whereas if it were far away, why then it wouldn't be nearby.

An awkward silence.

TUSENBACH: He's a joker, our Vasily Vasilyich.

OLGA: Yes, yes, now I remember you. Now I remember.

VERSHININ: I knew your dear mother.

CHEBUTYKIN: How lovely she was, God rest her soul.

IRINA: Mama is buried in Moscow.

OLGA: In the Novo-Devichy Cemetery…

MASHA: Imagine, I've already started to forget her face. So, too, in the same way, shall we be forgotten. They will not remember us. They will forget us.

VERSHININ: Yes. They will forget us. And such is our fate, there is nothing we can do about it. That which seems so serious, so significant, so important to us now — the time will come when it will be forgotten, when it will seem so unimportant.

Pause.

And isn't it interesting, we have absolutely no way of knowing now, just what will be thought of as significant and great, and what will be thought of as pitiful and absurd. The discoveries of Copernicus, or, let us say, Columbus, even, were they not at first considered useless and ludicrous, while the scribblings of charlatans were taken for the truth? And it may happen, the time may come, when our current era, with which we're so content, will seem strange, awkward, foolish, impure, possibly even immoral…

TUSENBACH: Who knows? It's also possible that they will call our era great, and we shall be remembered with respect. I mean, after all, we don't live in an age of torture, or execution, or invasion, but still, what suffering there is!

SOLYONY: *(Lightly.)* Tsip, tsip, tsip…
    Don't give the baron chickenfeed,
    Just feed him some philosophy.

TUSENBACH: Vasily Vasilyich, I beg of you, leave me alone…*(Sits in another place.)* This is getting boring.

SOLYONY: *(Lightly.)* Tsip, tsip, tsip…

TUSENBACH:*(To VERSHININ.)* The suffering we see in our day and age — yes, it is great! — it does, however, signify society's great moral progress…

VERSHININ: Yes, yes, of course.

CHEBUTYKIN: You just said, Baron, that they will call ours the great era, the towering era, but what about the people living in it…aren't they rather small…*(Stands.)* Look at how small I am, for example. It's obvious you're trying to console me, when you tell me how great my life is.

Offstage, a violin is playing.

MASHA: That's our brother Andrey playing.

IRINA: He's the scholar of the family. He's going to be a professor, no doubt. Papa was in the military, but his son has chosen a scholarly career.

MASHA: It was Papa's wish.

OLGA: We've been teasing him today. It's seems he's fallen in love.

IRINA: With one of the local girls. She'll be over today, most probably.

MASHA: God, how she dresses! It's not only ugly or unstylish, it's just plain pathetic. I mean, a bizarre, bright yellowish skirt with a vulgar little fringe, and a red blouse? And those shiny, shiny cheeks, I mean, really! Andrey's not in love, God forbid, after all he's got some taste, no, he's only fooling, he's pretending to be in love just to torture us. Yesterday, I heard she's going to marry Protopopov, the chairman of the district council. Good, let her…*(At the side door.)* Andrey, come here, darling! Just for a moment!

ANDREY enters.

OLGA: This is my brother, Andrey Sergeich.
VERSHININ: Vershinin.
ANDREY: Prozorov. *(Wipes his perspiring brow.)* Are you our local battery commander?
OLGA: Can you imagine, Aleksandr Ignatyevich is from Moscow.
ANDREY: Really? Well, congratulations, now my dear sisters won't give you a moment's peace.
VERSHININ: I've already succeeded in boring your sisters.
IRINA: Look at the pretty picture frame Andrey gave me today! *(She shows him the frame.)* He made it himself.
VERSHININ: *(Looking at the frame, not knowing quite what to say.)* Yes…it's really quite…
IRINA: And that picture frame, the one on the piano, he made that one, too!

ANDREY waves his hand and walks off

OLGA: He's the scholar of the family, and he plays the violin, and he can make all kinds of things, he's a — what do you call it — a jack-of-all-trades. Andrey, where are you going! He has a habit of running away like that. Come back here!

MASHA and IRINA take him by the arm and lead him around, laughing.

MASHA: Come on, come on!
ANDREY: Leave me alone, please.
MASHA: That's funny! We used to call Aleksandr Ignatyevich the "lovesick major," and he didn't mind it at all!
VERSHININ: Not in the slightest!
MASHA: Now why don't I call you: the "lovesick violinist!"
IRINA: Or the "lovesick professor!"…

OLGA: He's in love! Andryusha's in love!

IRINA: *(Applauding.)* Bravo, bravo! Encore! Andryushka's in lo—ve!

CHEBUTYKIN: *(Coming up behind ANDREY and puts both arms around his waist, singing.)* "We're put on earth for love and love alone!" *(He chortles with laughter, holding the newspaper all the while in his hand.)*

ANDREY: Enough, enough…*(Wipes his face.)* I haven't slept all night and I'm feeling a bit out of sorts, as they say. I read till four this morning, then I tried to go to sleep, but nothing happened. I thought about this and that, and meanwhile, dawn comes early here, the sun climbs right through my bedroom window. This summer, while I'm still living here, I'd like to do a translation of an English book.

VERSHININ: Can you read English?

ANDREY: Yes. My father, may his soul rest in peace, tyrannized us with education. Funny, isn't it, I suppose, but the truth of it is that since his death I started gaining weight, and in a year's time I've grown positively fat; it's as if my body were rebelling from all that oppression. Thanks to my father, my sisters and I know French, German, and English, and Irina even knows Italian. But at what cost!

MASHA: In this town, knowing three languages is a useless luxury. No, not even a luxury, more like a useless appendage, a sixth finger. We know too much!

VERSHININ: Imagine that! *(Laughs.)* To know too much! I don't think there is, or ever will be, a town so dull and dismal, that it has no need for educated, cultivated people. Let us suppose, among the one hundred thousand inhabitants of this town, for example, this obviously backward and vulgar town, that there exist only three people like you. Of course, it stands to reason, you can't penetrate the ignorance and the darkness which surround you; in the course of your lifetime, little by little, you will fade into the throng of thousands, your lives will be submerged and suppressed, and yet you will not vanish, you will not disappear without a trace; others after you will appear, just like you, perhaps six, at first, then twelve, and so on and so on, until, finally, at long last, you will become the majority. In two hundred, three hundred years, life on earth will become unimaginably beautiful, astonishingly so. Man needs such a life, and if it is not his to have now, then he must anticipate it, wait, dream, prepare for it, he must see and know more than his father and grandfathers before him. *(Laughs.)* And you complain that you know too much.

MASHA: *(Takes off her hat.)* I'm staying for lunch.

IRINA: *(With a sigh.)* Really, someone ought to write all that down…

ANDREY has gone; he's slipped away, unnoticed.

TUSENBACH: In many years, you say, life on earth will be astonishingly beautiful. That may well be true. But, to take part in that life now, distant though it may be, we must prepare for it, we must work...

VERSHININ: *(Stands.)* Yes. Just look at all the flowers you have! *(Glances around.)* What a marvelous place. How I envy you! I've spent my whole life in close quarters, with two chairs, a sofa, and a stove that's always smoking. Never in my life have I had flowers like these...ever...*(Rubs his hands together.)* Ah, well, never mind!

TUSENBACH: Yes, we must work. I know what you're thinking: There he goes again, the German, he's getting maudlin. Well, I'm not. On my word of honor, I'm a Russian, I don't speak a word of German. My father is orthodox...

Pause.

VERSHININ: *(Walks about the stage.)* Often I think to myself: What if we could begin our lives anew, but this time knowingly, consciously? What if the first life, the one we've lived already, were just, as they say, a rough draft, and the second one, the real one! Then each and every one of us, I think, would try, above all, not to repeat himself, but would instead create another life, another set of circumstances, another place, like this, a place filled with flowers, flooded with light...I have a wife and two little girls, and besides, my wife is not well, and so on and so on, yes, but if only I could begin my life all over again, I would never marry...Never, ever!

Enter KULYGIN, in a coat worn by members of the teaching profession.

KULYGIN: *(Goes up to IRINA.)* Sister dearest, permit me to congratulate you on the occasion of your nameday and wish you, in all sincerity, from the bottom of my heart, good health, and everything else one might wish a girl your age. And, moreover, permit me to present to you, as a gift, this little book. *(Gives her a small book.)* The history of our high school these past fifty years, written by me. A mere trifle of a book, born of having nothing better to do, but read it anyway. Greetings, ladies and gentlemen! *(To VERSHININ.)* Kulygin, teacher at the local high school. Civil servant of the seventh rank. *(To IRINA.)* In this little book, you will find a list of all the students ever to have graduated from our high school for the past fifty years. "Feci, quod potui, faciant meliora potentes." *(Kisses MASHA.)*

IRINA: But you already gave me the exact same book for Easter.

KULYGIN: *(Laughs.)* No, really! Well, in that case, give it back, or, better yet, give it to the colonel. Here you are, colonel, take it. Read it some day to ward off boredom.

VERSHININ: I thank you kindly. *(Prepares to leave.)* I'm extremely delighted to have met you...

OLGA: You're going? Oh, no!

IRINA: You'll stay and have lunch with us. Please.

OLGA: I beseech you!

VERSHININ: *(Bows.)* It seems I've turned up right in the middle of a name-day party. Forgive me, please, I didn't know, I haven't even congratulated you yet...*(Exits with OLGA into the hall.)*

KULYGIN: Today, ladies and gentlemen, is Sunday, the Sabbath, the day of rest, we shall rest, we shall celebrate, each in accordance to his age and rank. The rugs must be taken up for the summer and put away till wintertime...Use Persian powder or naphthaline...The Romans were hale and hearty, they knew how to work, they knew how to rest, they had "mens sana in corpore sano." They lived their lives according to a certain prescribed pattern or form. The headmaster of our school always says: The main thing in life is its form...That which loses its form, destroys itself — so, too, is it true of our everyday life. *(Puts his arm around MASHA's waist, laughing.)* Masha loves me. My wife loves me. The curtains, too, along with the rugs... Today, I am happy, I'm in an excellent mood. Masha, at four o'clock this afternoon we're invited to the home of our headmaster. He is planning a little outing for the faculty and their families.

MASHA: I'm not going.

KULYGIN: *(Chagrined.)* Darling Masha, why not?

MASHA: Can we talk about this later...*(Angrily.)* Fine, I'll go, only leave me alone, please, I beg of you...*(Walks away.)*

KULYGIN: And so, we'll spend the evening at the headmaster's. His own poor health notwithstanding, this is a man who tries, above all, to be hospitable. An outstanding, enlightened individual. A splendid individual. Yesterday, after the faculty meeting, he said to me: "I'm tired, Fyodor Ilyich! So tired!" *(Looks at the wall clock and compares it to his watch.)* Your clock is seven minutes fast. "Yes," he said, "so tired!"

Offstage, a violin is playing.

OLGA: Ladies and gentlemen, please be seated, luncheon is served! We're having meat pie!

KULYGIN: Ach, my Olga, my darling, darling Olga! Yesterday I worked from dawn until eleven o'clock at night, how weary I was, and today, today, I am happy. *(Exits to the table in the hall.)* My darling...

CHEBUTYKIN: *(Puts the newspaper in his pocket, combs his hair.)* Meat pie? Magnificent!

MASHA: *(To CHEBUTYKIN, severely.)* Now look, you: nothing to drink today. Do you hear me? It's bad for you.

CHEBUTYKIN: What are you talking about! That's all in the past. It's been two years since I've done any drinking. *(Impatiently.)* And anyway, my dear, what does it matter!

MASHA: Never mind, don't you dare drink! Don't you dare. *(Angrily, but so that her husband doesn't hear.)* Another endless evening at the headmaster's...to hell with it.

TUSENBACH: I wouldn't go, if I were you...It's as simple as that.

CHEBUTYKIN: Don't go, my sweet.

MASHA: Right, don't go....This cursed life, it's unbearable...*(Goes into the hall.)*

CHEBUTYKIN: *(Follows her.)* Now, now!

SOLYONY: *(Crosses into the hall.)* Tsip, tsip, tsip...

TUSENBACH: Stop it, Vasily Vasilyich! That's enough!

SOLYONY: Tsip, tsip, tsip....

KULYGIN: *(Merrily.)* To your good health, colonel! I am an educator, and here, I am at home. I am Masha's husband...She's so lovable, my Masha, so lovable...

VERSHININ: I'll have some of that dark vodka...*(Drinks.)* To your good health! *(To Olga.)* It's so good to be here!...

Only IRINA and TUSENBACH are left in the drawing room.

IRINA: Masha's in a bad mood today. She was married at eighteen, to her, he was the most intelligent man on earth. But now it's different. He's the kindest, but not the most intelligent.

OLGA: *(Impatiently.)* Andrey, come, already!

ANDREY: *(Offstage.)* Coming! *(Enters, and goes to the table.)*

TUSENBACH: Tell me what you're thinking.

IRINA: All right. I don't like your Solyony, I'm afraid of him. He says the strangest things...

TUSENBACH: He's a strange man. I feel sorry for him, he gets on my nerves, too, but I feel sorry for him more. Do you know, I think he's shy…When we're alone, just the two of us, he can be so warm and witty, but when we're in the company of others, he's a bully and a show-off. Wait, don't go, they're all sitting down. Just let me be near you for a while. Tell me what you're thinking.

Pause.

You're twenty years old, I'm not quite thirty yet. How many years we have before us, endless rows of days and days, filled with my love for you…

IRINA: Nikolai Lvovich, don't speak to me of love.

TUSENBACH: *(Not listening.)* I have this passion, this thirst for life, for struggle, for work, and this feeling flows deep in my soul with my love for you, Irina, and because you are so beautiful, why then all of life is beautiful, too! Tell me what you're thinking.

IRINA: You say that life is beautiful. Yes, perhaps it is, but what if only seems to be! For us, for we three sisters, life has not been beautiful, life has choked us, like weeds…I'm weeping. I mustn't weep…*(Hastily wipes away the tears, smiles.)* Work, we must work. That is why we're so sad, why we look upon life with such sorrow, because we are strangers to work. We are born of those who disdained work…

NATALYA IVANOVNA enters; she is wearing a pink dress with a green belt.

NATASHA: Oh, no, they've already sat down to lunch…I'm late…*(Glances fleetingly in the mirror, touches up her hair.)* My hair doesn't look too bad, does it? (Sees IRINA.) Dearest Irina Sergeevna, congratulations! *(Gives her a big, prolonged kiss.)* You have so many guests, I'm ashamed, really I am…Hello, Baron!

OLGA: *(Entering the drawing room.)* And here's Natalya Ivanovna. Hello, my dear!

They kiss.

NATASHA: Congratulations. Look how much company you have, I'm terribly embarrassed…

OLGA: Never mind, really, it's only family and friends. *(In a low voice, slightly horrified.)* You're wearing a green belt! Darling, it just won't do!

NATASHA: Really, why not? Is it bad luck?

OLGA: No, it's just that it doesn't go with the dress…I mean, it looks rather unusual…

NATASHA: *(In a tearful voice.)* It does? But it's not really green, is it, I thought it was…sort of…neutral. *(Follows OLGA into the hall.)*

In the hall, everyone is seated for the luncheon; not a soul is left in the drawing room.

KULYGIN: I wish you a fine fiancé, Irina. It's time you got married.

CHEBUTYKIN: Natalya Ivanovna, I wish you a little fiancé, too.

KULYGIN: Natalya Ivanovna already has a little fiancé.

MASHA: *(Taps her fork against a plate.)* I'll have a glass of that wine, too! Ah, what the hell, life is sweet!

KULYGIN: A C-minus for conduct.

VERSHININ: This fruit liqueur is delicious! What is it made of?

SOLYONY: Cockroaches.

IRINA: *(In a tearful voice.)* Ugh! That's disgusting!

OLGA: And for supper, we're having roast turkey and apple tart. Thank God, I'm home all day long, all evening, too…Ladies and gentlemen, you're all invited to come again this evening!

VERSHININ: Allow me to come again, too!

IRINA: With pleasure.

NATASHA: Everyone's welcome here.

CHEBUTYKIN: *(Singing.)* "We're put on earth for love and love alone…" *(Laughs.)*

ANDREY: *(Angrily.)* Stop it, everyone! Haven't you had enough!

FEDOTIK and RODE enter with a large basket of flowers.

FEDOTIK: Look, they're already having lunch.

RODE: *(In a loud voice, with a slightly guttural accent.)* Lunch? Yes, they're already having lunch…

FEDOTIK: Wait! Hold for just a moment! *(Takes a photograph.)* One! Hold again for just a bit more…*(Takes another photograph.)* Two! There, all set!

They take the basket and goes into the hall, amidst a clamor of greetings.

RODE: *(In a loud voice.)* Congratulations, I wish you everything, everything!

The weather is superb today, simply magnificent. All morning long I was out walking with the students. I teach gymnastics at the high school...

FEDOTIK: It's all right, Irina Sergeevna, you can move now! *(Takes a photograph.)* You look charming today. *(Takes a top out of his pocket.)* Oh, by the way, look, here is a top...It makes an amazing sound...

IRINA: How lovely!

MASHA: "In a cove by the sea, a green oak stands,
    A golden chain wound round...
    A golden chain wound round..."
(Tearfully.) Why, oh why do I keep saying this? It's been haunting me since this morning...

KULYGIN: There are thirteen at the table!

RODE: *(In a loud voice.)* Ladies and gentlemen, surely, you're not superstitious?

Laughter.

KULYGIN: If there are thirteen at the table, that means someone's in love. Don't tell me it's you, Ivan Romanich, God forbid...

Laughter.

CHEBUTYKIN: Who me, I'm just an old so-and-so, although why Natalya Ivanovna is blushing, really, I simply can't understand it...

Huge laughter: NATALYA IVANOVNA rushes out of the hall into the drawing room; ANDREY follows after.

ANDREY: There, there, don't pay attention to them! Wait...stop, I beg of you...

NATASHA: I'm so ashamed...I don't know what's wrong, they're making so much fun of me. And I know it was disgraceful to jump up from the table, but I simply couldn't bear it...I couldn't...*(Covers her face with her hands.)*

ANDREY: My darling, I beg of you, I beseech you, don't get so upset. I assure you, they were only joking, it was all in fun. My darling, my dearest, they're all such good, kind-hearted people, they love us both very much. Come over here by the window, they can't see us here...*(Looks around.)*

NATASHA: I'm not used to social occasions!...

ANDREY: Oh, youth, sweet, sublime youth! My darling, my dearest, don't get so upset!...Believe me, believe me...I feel so wonderful, my heart is full of love, I'm in ecstasy…. No, no, they can't see us! They can't! Why, why did I fall in love with you, when did I fall in love with you — oh, I don't understand it at all. My darling, my dearest, my angel, be my wife! I love you, love you…as I've never ever loved before…

They kiss.

Two officers enter and, seeing the couple kissing, pause in astonishment.

CURTAIN

ACT TWO

The same setting as in Act I. It is eight o'clock in the evening. Offstage, on the street, the faint sound of an accordion is heard. It is dark. Enter NATALYA IVANOVNA in a dressing gown, carrying a candle; she walks about the room, stopping by the door which leads to ANDREY's room.

NATASHA: Andryusha, what are you doing in there? Are you reading? Never mind, I was only wondering...*(She continues along, opens another door, looks within, shuts it.)* There aren't any lights on, are there?...

ANDREY: *(Enters with a book in his hand.)* What is it, Natasha?

NATASHA: I'm making sure there aren't any lights on...It's carnival time, the servants aren't themselves, you have to keep an eye out, just in case...Last night I was walking through the dining room at midnight, and I found a candle burning. I haven't been able to find out who lit it...not yet. *(Puts the candle down.)* What time is it?

ANDREY: *(Glancing at his watch.)* A quarter past eight.

NATASHA: And Olga and Irina still aren't here. They haven't returned yet. They're still toiling away, poor things. Olga's at a faculty meeting, Irina's at the telegraph office...*(Sighs.)* Only this morning I said to your sister: "Take care of yourself, Irina, dear," I said. And she just doesn't listen. A quarter past eight, did you say? I'm afraid our little Bobik isn't feeling well. Why is he so cold? Yesterday, he had a fever, and today he's cold all over...I'm so worried!

ANDREY: It's nothing, Natasha. He's a healthy little boy.

NATASHA: Still, it would be better to put him on a diet. I'm worried. And tonight at ten o'clock, they tell me, the mummers are supposed to come, it would be better if they didn't, Andryusha.

ANDREY: Well, I don't know, really. They've already been invited.

NATASHA: This morning, that darling little boy woke up and he looked at me, and do you know what he did? — he smiled, he recognized me. "Bobik," I said, "good morning! Good morning, darling!" And he laughed. Children understand, they truly understand. Anyway, as I was saying. Andryusha, the mummers aren't to come.

ANDREY: *(Tentatively.)* But really, isn't that up to my sisters? They run the household.

NATASHA: And so they do. I'll just have to tell them, then. They're very understanding...*(She continues walking.)* I've ordered some yoghurt for supper. The doctor says you should eat only yoghurt, or else you'll never lose weight. *(Stops.)* Bobik is cold. You know, I'm afraid the room he has is simply too cold for him. He'll have to be moved to another room, at least until the weather gets warmer. Now Irina's room, for example, is ideal for a baby; it's dry, and it gets sunlight all day long. She must be told she'll just have to move in with Olga for the time being...And anyway, what difference does it make, she's not home all day long, she only sleeps here.

Pause.

Andryusha, sweet, why are you so quiet?

ANDREY: What, oh, I was just thinking...No, nothing, really, what is there to say?

NATASHA: Right...What else did I want to tell you...Oh yes, Ferapont has just come from the district council office, he's asking for you.

ANDREY: *(Yawning.)* Tell him to come in.

NATASHA exits; ANDREY, leaning over the candle she has forgotten, reads a book. Enter FERAPONT; he is wearing a shabby, threadbare coat, his collar is turned up, and his ears are covered.

Hello, old fellow. What's up?

FERAPONT: The chairman has sent over a book and some papers. Here they are...*(Gives him the book and a parcel.)*

ANDREY: Thank you. Very good. Why didn't you come earlier? It's past eight, already.

FERAPONT: How's that?

ANDREY: *(Louder.)* I said, you've come so late, it's already past eight o'clock.

FERAPONT: Well, that's just it. I did come over, while it was still light out, but they wouldn't let me in. The master's busy, they said. Well, all right. If he's busy, he's busy, I'm in no hurry to go anywhere. *(Thinking that ANDREY has asked him about something.)* How's that?

ANDREY: Nothing. *(Leafs through the book.)* Tomorrow is Friday, there won't be a meeting, but I'll go in anyway...I like to keep busy. It's boring at home...

Pause.

Isn't it strange, old fellow, how life tricks you, how life deceives you! Today, out of sheer boredom, I picked up this book — my old university lectures, and I saw how ludicrous it all was…My God, I am the secretary of the district council, the very council chaired by Protopopov, I am the secretary, and the most I can ever hope for is to become a *member* of the district council! I, a member of the local district council, I who dream every night of becoming a professor at Moscow University, a celebrated scholar, admired throughout all of Russia!

FERAPONT: I can't say, sir…I'm a bit hard of hearing…

ANDREY: If indeed you could hear what I've been saying, then perhaps I wouldn't be talking to you. I've got to talk to somebody, my wife doesn't understand me, I'm afraid of my own sisters, somehow, afraid they'll laugh at me, make a fool of me…I don't drink, I don't like taverns, but right now, what I wouldn't give to be sitting in a restaurant in Moscow — Testov's, say, or the Bolshoy Moskovsky, my dear fellow.

FERAPONT: The other day, at the district council office, one of the builders was saying how, in Moscow, there were these merchants sitting in a restaurant, eating blinis, and there was one merchant who ate forty blinis, and apparently he died. Forty, or perhaps it was fifty. I don't remember.

ANDREY: In Moscow, you sit in an enormous restaurant, you don't know anyone, and no one knows you, and yet all the while you never feel like a stranger. And here, you know everyone and everyone knows you, and somehow you're a stranger, a stranger…A stranger and alone.

FERAPONT: How's that?

Pause.

And that same builder was saying — well, maybe he was lying, — that apparently, they're stretching a rope across the whole of Moscow.

ANDREY: Whatever for?

FERAPONT: Can't say for sure. That's what the builder said.

ANDREY: Nonsense. *(Reads his book.)* Have you ever been to Moscow?

FERAPONT: *(After a pause.)* Can't say that I have. It wasn't God's will.

Pause.

Am I to go now?

ANDREY: Yes, go. Be well.

FERAPONT exits.

Be well. *(Reads.)* And tomorrow morning you'll come, and you'll pick up these papers…So, go then…

Pause.

He's gone.

A bell rings.

Yes, papers, papers…*(Stretches, and slowly exits into his room.)*

Offstage, a nurse is heard singing a lullaby to a child. Enter MASHA and VERSHININ. While they are talking, a maid lights the lamp and the candles.

MASHA: I don't know.

Pause.

Really, I don't know. Of course, it all depends on what you're used to. After father died, for example, it took us forever to get used to the fact that there weren't so many military orderlies around any more. But apart from that, I think it's fair to say, it may not be so in other places, but in our town, the most decent, the most honorable, the most cultivated people are the military.

VERSHININ: I'm thirsty. I wouldn't mind some tea.

MASHA: *(Glances at the clock.)* They'll bring it in, soon. They married me off when I was eighteen, and, oh, was I terrified of my husband then, well, after all, he was a teacher, and I'd only just finished school myself. He seemed so terribly learned, so brilliant, so important. Not any more, I'm sorry to say.

VERSHININ: Yes…I see.

MASHA: But, it's not my husband I'm talking about, I've gotten used to him. It's just that among the civilian population in general there are so many rude, ill-bred, uneducated people. Rudeness offends me, it upsets me, I suffer when I see people who lack sensitivity, gentility, refinement. And when I'm in the company of the other faculty, my husband's colleagues, oh, how I suffer…

VERSHININ: Yes, indeed…But, it seems to me, it makes no difference whatsoever whether they're civilian or whether they're military, they're all dull, at least they are in this town. No difference at all! If you listen to a member of the local intelligentsia, civilian or military, why, he's bored to tears, he's fed up with his wife, he's fed up with his house, he's fed up with his estate, he's fed up with his horses…A Russian prides himself on nobility of mind, loftiness of thought, he seeks the higher ground, so then tell me, why in real life does he sink so low? Why?

MASHA: Why?

VERSHININ: Why is he fed up with his children, why is he fed up with his wife? And why are his wife and children fed up with him?

MASHA: You're in a funny mood tonight.

VERSHININ: Perhaps. I haven't had any dinner yet, I've had nothing to eat since this morning. My daughter's ill, and when my little girls aren't well, I'm tormented by anxiety, tortured by my conscience, by the fact that they have such a mother! Oh, if only you could have seen her today! What a wretched creature she is! We started quarreling at seven this morning, and at nine I walked out and slammed the door.

Pause.

I never talk about this, isn't it strange, not to anyone but you, you alone. *(Kisses her hand.)* Don't be angry with me. Without you, I have no one, no one…

Pause.

MASHA: What a strange noise there is, coming from the stove…Shortly before Father died, there was a moaning in the chimney. It sounded just like that.

VERSHININ: Are you superstitious?

MASHA: Yes.

VERSHININ: Strange. *(Kisses her hand.)* What a dazzling, ravishing woman you are. Dazzling, ravishing! It's dark in here, but I can see your eyes shining.

MASHA: *(Sits in another chair.)* It's lighter over here.

VERSHININ: I love you, I love you, I love you…. I love your eyes, your every movement, you come to me in my dreams…A dazzling, ravishing woman!

MASHA: *(Laughs softly.)* You speak to me like that, and I can't help laughing, even though it petrifies me. Don't say it again, I beg of you…*(In a lower voice.)* Oh, go ahead, say it anyway, I don't care…*(Covers her face with her hands.)* I don't care. They're coming, talk about something else…

Enter IRINA and TUSENBACH through the hall.

TUSENBACH: I have a triple-hyphenated family name...And it goes like this: Baron Tusenbach-Krone-Altschauer, but I'm Russian through and through, pure orthodox, just like you. All right, so I've got a little German left in me, but really, only a little — stubbornness and perseverance, that's all, and I get on your nerves, I know I do. I accompany you home every evening.

IRINA: I'm so tired!

TUSENBACH: And every day, I shall come to the telegraph office and accompany you home for the next ten – twenty years to come, until you banish me from your sight...*(Seeing MASHA and VERSHININ, cheerfully.)* Oh, it's you! Hello!

IRINA: I'm home, home at last. *(To MASHA.)* A woman just came in, she wanted to send a telegraph to her brother in Saratov, to tell him her son had died today, and she just couldn't remember his address. So she sent it without an address, simply marked: 'Saratov.' She was weeping. And I was rude to her, for no reason at all. "I have no time for this," I said to her. It was all so horridly stupid. Are the mummers coming here tonight?

MASHA: Yes.

IRINA: *(Sits in an armchair.)* Rest, I need rest. I'm so tired.

TUSENBACH: *(With a smile.)* When you come home from work, you look so young, so forlorn...

Pause.

IRINA: I'm so tired. No, I don't like the telegraph office, I don't like it at all.

MASHA: You look thinner...*(She whistles.)* And younger, your face looks like a little boy's...

TUSENBACH: It's just the coiffure.

IRINA: I must find a new position, this one is not for me. Everything I longed for, everything I dreamed of, and it's nowhere to be found, not there, at least. Work without poetry, without meaning...

A knock on the floor.

It's the doctor knocking. *(To TUSENBACH.)* Be a dear, and answer, would you . . I don't have the strength...I'm so tired....

TUSENBACH knocks on the floor in response.

And now he'll come up. Something must be done about this. Yesterday, the doctor was at the club with our Andrey, and they lost, again. They say Andrey lost two hundred rubles.

MASHA: *(Indifferently.)* But what can we do about it, really!

IRINA: Two weeks ago he lost, in December he lost. Well, the sooner he loses everything, I suppose, the sooner we can leave this town. Dear Lord God, I dream of Moscow every night, every night, I think I'm going mad. *(Laughs.)* We're moving there in June, and till June we still have…February, March, April, May…a half a year, almost!

MASHA: Only Natasha mustn't find out that Andrey's lost.

IRINA: What would she care!

Enter CHEBUTYKIN, having just woken up from his afternoon nap — he enters the hall, combing his beard, then he sits at the table and takes a newspaper from his pocket.

MASHA: Here he comes…Has he paid his rent yet?

IRINA: *(Laughs.)* No. Not in eight months, not even a kopek. It seems he's forgotten.

MASHA: *(Laughs.)* Look how he sits there on his throne!

They all laugh; a pause.

IRINA: Why are you so quiet, Aleksandr Ignatich?

VERSHININ: I don't know. I'd love some tea. "My kingdom for a cup of tea!" I haven't had a thing to eat all day…

CHEBUTYKIN: Irina Sergeevna!

IRINA: What do you want?

CHEBUTYKIN: Come here, please. "Venez ici."

IRINA goes to him and sits at the table.

I can't live without you.

IRINA lays out the cards for a game of solitaire.

VERSHININ: Well, what do you say? If they're not serving tea, then, at least, let's philosophize.

TUSENBACH: Yes, let's. What about?

VERSHININ: What about? Let us dream…of what life will be like for those who come after us, say, in two hundred – three hundred years.

TUSENBACH: What about it? Those who live after us, they'll fly around in hot air balloons, the style of their clothing will change, perhaps they'll even discover a sixth sense and develop it, but life will remain just as it is, difficult, full of joys and mysteries. And even after a thousand years, people will sigh and say: "Ach, life is hard!" — just as they do today, even then they will fear death and will not want to die.

VERSHININ: *(After a moment's thought.)* How can you say that? It seems to me that everything on earth must change, little by little, indeed, it is changing even now, right before our very eyes. After two hundred – three hundred years, after a thousand years, even, — it's not the length of time that matters — a new life will finally dawn, a life of happiness. And we shall not take part in that life, of course, but we are living for it now, we are working for it, yes, even suffering for it, we are creating it — and this, and this alone, is our reason for being, indeed, this is our happiness.

MASHA laughs softly.

TUSENBACH: What is it?

MASHA: I don't know. I'm been laughing like this since this morning.

VERSHININ: I finished school where you did, though I didn't attend the academy; I read a lot, but I don't choose my books well, perhaps I'm still not reading what I should, and yet, the longer I live, the more I long to know. My hair is growing gray, I'm an old man, almost, and yet how little I know, ah, how very little I know! But, all the while, it seems to me, the most important truth in life, now *that* I know, I know *that* all too well. Oh, how I want to prove to you that there will be no happiness for us, not now, not ever…We can only work and work, and happiness — that is for our children to come.

Pause.

No, not for me, but for my children's children.

FEDOTIK and RODE appear in the hall; they sit and sing softly, playing the guitar.

TUSENBACH: According to you, we mustn't even dream of happiness! But what if I'm happy!

VERSHININ: You're not.

TUSENBACH: *(Throwing up his hands and laughing.)* Obviously, we don't understand one another. So, tell me, how can I convince you?

MASHA laughs softly.

(Holds up a finger.) Go ahead, laugh! *(To VERSHININ.)* Not after two hundred, not after three hundred, not even after a million years, will life be any different than it has been; it will never change, it will forever stay the same, following its own fixed laws, which are no concern of yours, or, which, in any case, you'll never discover. Migratory birds, cranes, for example, they fly and they fly, and whatever thoughts may wander through their heads, great or small, still they keep on flying, not knowing where to or what for. On and on they fly, and whatever philosophers appear among them, let them philosophize to their hearts' content, so long as they keep flying…

MASHA: And the meaning of all this is…?

TUSENBACH: Meaning?…Look, it's snowing outside. What is the meaning of that?

Pause.

MASHA: I think man must have faith, or he must seek faith, or else his life is empty, empty…To live and not know why the cranes fly, why children are born, why there are stars in the sky…Either we know why we live, or else it's all nonsense, it's pointless…

Pause.

VERSHININ: Such a pity, isn't it, that our youth has gone…

MASHA: "How depressing it is to live in this world, ladies and gentlemen!" That's from Gogol.

TUSENBACH: "How hard it is to argue with you, ladies and gentlemen!" That's from me…I give up…

CHEBUTYKIN: *(Reading the newspaper.)* Balzac was married in Berdichev.

IRINA hums softly.

I shall make a note of it, right here in this little book. *(Makes a note.)* Balzac was married in Berdichev. *(Reads the newspaper.)*

IRINA: *(Playing a game of solitaire, deep in thought.)* Balzac was married in Berdichev.

TUSENBACH: The die is cast. Did you know, Maria Sergeevna, I'm resigning from the military.

MASHA: I heard. And what good will that do? I don't like civilians.

TUSENBACH: It doesn't matter...*(Stands.)* Anyway, I'm not handsome enough to be a soldier. No, really, it doesn't matter at all...I shall work. I shall work so that, even if only for one day in my life, I might come home in the evening, collapse on my bed, and fall fast asleep with exhaustion. *(Goes into the hall.)* Workers sleep soundly, you know!

FEDOTIK: *(To IRINA.)* Look what I just bought you at Pyzhikov's in Moskovskaya Street — a set of pretty colored pencils. And this sweet little pen knife...

IRINA: You treat me like a child, but really, I'm all grown up now...*(Takes the pencils and knife, delighted.)* How charming!

FEDOTIK: And I bought myself a penknife, too...here, look...there's one, two, three blades, this one's for picking your ears, this one's a pair of scissors, this one's for cleaning your nails...

RODE: *(In a loud voice.)* Doctor, how old are you?

CHEBUTYKIN: Me? Thirty-two.

Laughter.

FEDOTIK: Let me show you another card game...*(Lays out the cards.)*

The samovar is brought in. ANFISA tends to it; a few moments later, NATASHA enters and also busies herself at the table; SOLYONY enters, greets everyone, and sits at the table.

VERSHININ: Listen to the wind!

MASHA: Yes. I'm sick of winter. I've already forgotten what summer is like.

IRINA: It's in the cards, I see it. We're going to Moscow.

FEDOTIK: No, it's not in the cards. Look, an eight on the two of spades. *(Laughs.)* That means you're not going to Moscow.

CHEBUTYKIN: *(Reads the newspaper.)* Tsitsikar. There's a smallpox epidemic there.

ANFISA: *(Approaching MASHA.)* Masha, dearie, have some tea. *(To VERSHININ.)* Please, your honor…forgive me, dearie, I've forgotten your name…

MASHA: Bring it here, nanny. I'm not coming over there.

IRINA: Nanny!

ANFISA: Co—ming!

NATASHA: *(To SOLONY.)* Little babies understand perfectly, you know. "Hello, Bobik," I said to him, "Hello, darling!" He gave me such a special look. Now I know what you're thinking: "That's his mother talking," but no, no, I assure you! This is an extraordinary child.

SOLONY: If that child were mine, I'd fry him up in a frying pan and eat him. *(Takes his glass into the drawing room and sits in a corner.)*

NATASHA: *(Covers her face with her hands.)* You crude, vulgar man!

MASHA: Happy is he, who knows not whether it is summer or winter. And, if I were in Moscow, I wouldn't care one bit about the weather…

VERSHININ: The other day, I was reading the diary of a French minister, written while he was in prison. It was the minister who was convicted for his part in the Panama affair. With what rapture, what ecstasy, he writes of the birds he sees through the bars of his prison window, birds he'd never noticed before when he was in the ministry. Now that he's released from prison, of course, he no longer notices the birds, just as he never had before. So, too, shall you never notice Moscow, after you're living there. Happiness is not ours to have, not now, not ever, we can only long for it.

TUSENBACH: *(Takes the box from the table.)* Where's the candy?

IRINA: Solyony ate it all up.

TUSENBACH: All of it?

ANFISA: *(Serving tea.)* A letter has come for you, dearie.

VERSHININ: For me? *(Takes the letter.)* From my daughter. *(Reads it.)* Yes, of course…Forgive me, Maria Sergeevna, I'll go quietly. There'll be no tea for me. *(Stands, upset.)* It's the same old story…

MASHA: What's happened? Can't you tell me?

VERSHININ: *(Quietly.)* My wife's tried to poison herself again. I must go. Don't worry, I'll slip away unnoticed. How terribly unpleasant it all is. *(Kisses MASHA's hand.)* My darling, my adorable, wonderful woman…I'll go out this way, quietly:…*(Exits.)*

ANFISA: Where's he going? And I've just poured the tea…How do you like him!

MASHA: *(Losing her temper.)* Leave me alone! Will you stop bothering me, you get on my nerves…*(Takes her cup to the table.)* I'm sick to death of you, old woman!

ANFISA: But how have I offended you? Darling!

ANDREY's voice: "Anfisa!"

(Mocking.) "Anfisa." There he sits...(Exits.)

MASHA:(At the table in the hall, angrily.) Move over! (Messes up the cards.) You've got cards all over the place! Go on, drink your tea!

IRINA: Mashka, you're in a bad mood.

MASHA: Right, I'm in a bad mood, so don't talk to me. Don't touch me.

CHEBUTYKIN: (Laughing.) Don't touch her, don't touch...

MASHA: Sixty years old, and you're just like a little boy, God only knows what comes out of your mouth.

NATASHA: (Sighs.) Darling Masha, why use such language in polite conversation? With those lovely looks, and I mean this sincerely, you'd be simply charming in proper society, if it weren't for all those little expressions of yours. "Je vous prie pardonnez moi, Marie, mais vous avez des manières un peu grossières."

TUSENBACH: (Stifling a laugh.) Please pass...the...There's some cognac over there, I think...

NATASHA: "Il paraît, que mon Bobik déjà ne dort pas," he's awake. He hasn't been feeling well today. I'm going to him, excuse me...(Exits.)

IRINA: And where did Aleksandr Ignatich go?

MASHA: Home. His wife again, something out of the ordinary.

TUSENBACH: (Goes over to SOLYONY, holding a decanter of cognac in his hand.) You're always sitting off alone — and no one knows what you're brooding about. Come, peace. Let's drink a glass of cognac.

They drink.

And I shall probably have to play the piano all night long, play all kinds of nonsense. Whatever!

SOLYONY: Peace? Why make peace? I have nothing against you.

TUSENBACH: You always make me feel as if there's something between us. Face it, you're a strange man.

SOLYONY: (Reciting.) "I'm strange, who isn't strange!" "Be not wrathful, Aleko!"...

TUSENBACH: Aleko...you mean from Pushkin?...what's Aleko got to do with this?

Pause.

SOLYONY: When I'm alone with someone, I'm fine, I'm just like anyone else, but when I'm out in public, I get depressed, I'm ill at ease…I say all kinds of foolish things. But I'm far more honorable and noble than so many others…And I can prove it.

TUSENBACH: I get angry with you, you're constantly teasing me in public, but for some reason, I feel sorry for you, really, I do. Whatever, come what may, tonight, I'm going to get drunk. Come on, drink up!

SOLYONY: Drink up.

They drink.

I've never had anything against you, Baron, really. But I have the soul of Lermontov. *(Softly.)* I even look a little like Lermontov…so they say…*(Takes a flask of scent from his pocket and sprinkles it on his hands.)*

TUSENBACH: I'm tendering my resignation. Basta! For five years, I've mulled it over, and now, finally, I've decided. I'm going to work.

SOLYONY: *(Reciting.)* "Be not wrathful, Aleko"…"Forsake thy dreams, forsake them…"

While they are speaking, ANDREY enters quietly with a book and sits by the candlelight.

TUSENBACH: I shall work…

CHEBUTYKIN: *(Entering the drawing room with IRINA.)* It was an authentic Caucasian feast: onion soup, and then for the meat dish, chekhartma.

SOLYONY: Cheremsha is not a meat dish, not at all, it's made from a plant similar to our onion.

CHEBUTYKIN: No no, my angel. Chekhartma is not onion, it's roast mutton.

SOLYONY: And I'm telling you that cheremsha is onion.

CHEBUTYKIN: And I'm telling you that chekartma is mutton.

SOLYONY: And I'm telling you that cheremsha is onion.

CHEBUTYKIN: Why should I waste my time arguing with you? You've never been in the Caucasus, and you've never eaten chekhartma.

SOLYONY: I've never eaten it, because I can't stand it. It has a god-awful smell, like garlic.

ANDREY: *(Imploring.)* Enough, gentlemen! I beg of you!

TUSENBACH: When are the mummers coming?

IRINA: They promised to come about nine; that means they'll be here any minute now.

TUSENBACH: *(Embraces ANDREY, singing.)* "Ah you, porch, my porch, my porch, so new…"

ANDREY: *(Dancing and singing.)* "Of maple wood, I sing to you…"

CHEBUTYKIN: *(Dancing.)* "All latticed…"

Laughter.

TUSENBACH: *(Kisses ANDREY.)* What the hell, let's drink, Andryusha, let's drink to our friendship. And I'll go with you to Moscow, Andryusha, to the university.

SOLYONY: Which one? There are two universities in Moscow.

ANDREY: There is one university in Moscow.

SOLYONY: And I'm telling you there are two.

ANDREY: Why not three. The more the merrier.

SOLYONY: There are two universities in Moscow.

Murmuring and hushing sounds.

There are two universities in Moscow: the old one and the new one. And if you choose not to listen to me, if my words offend you, why then I shall not speak. I might even remove myself to another room…*(Exits through one of the doors.)*

TUSENBACH: Bravo, bravo! *(Laughs.)* Ladies and gentlemen, come, I shall play for you! Funny fellow, that Solyony…*(Sits at the piano, plays a waltz.)*

MASHA: *(Waltzes alone.)* The baron is drunk, the baron is drunk, the baron is drunk!

Enter NATASHA.

NATASHA: *(To CHEBUTYKIN.)* Ivan Romanich! *(Says something to CHEBUTYKIN, then exits quietly.)*

CHEBUTYKIN touches TUSENBACH on the shoulder and whispers something to him.

IRINA: What is it?

CHEBUTYKIN: Time for us to go. Be well.

TUSENBACH: Good night. Time to go.

IRINA: But, may I ask…what about the mummers?…

ANDREY: *(Disconcerted.)* There aren't going to be any mummers. You see, my darling, Natasha says that Bobik's not feeling that well, and so…What I mean is, I don't know, really, it doesn't matter to me…

IRINA: *(Shrugs her shoulders.)* Bobik's not feeling well!

MASHA: Look what we have come to! We're being thrown out, and so it seems, we must depart. *(To IRINA.)* It's not Bobik who is sick, it's her…Here! *(Taps her finger against her forehead.)* The little bourgeois!

ANDREY exits into his room stage right; CHEBUTYKIN follows him; farewells are said in the hall.

FEDOTIK: What a shame! I was counting on spending the evening here, but if the baby's ill, well, then, of course…I'll bring him a little toy tomorrow…

RODE: *(In a loud voice.)* I purposely took a nap today after lunch, I expected to be up dancing all night. And it's only nine o'clock.

MASHA: Let's go out on the street and talk there. We'll decide what to do next.

Voices are heard: "Good-bye! Be well!" TUSENBACH's merry laughter can be heard. They all exit. ANFISA and the maid clear away the table and extinguish the lights. A nurse's voice can be heard, singing to a child. Enter ANDREY, wearing a coat and hat, and CHEBUTYKIN, quietly.

CHEBUTYKIN: I never managed to get married, somehow, life flashed by, like lightning…oh, yes, and also because I was madly in love with your mother, who happened to have been married at the time…

ANDREY: Don't bother getting married; don't…it's depressing.

CHEBUTYKIN: Easy for you to say, but what about the loneliness. Philosophize all you want, but loneliness is a terrible thing, my boy…Although the truth of it is, of course, it doesn't matter, not in the slightest!

ANDREY: Hurry up.

CHEBUTYKIN: Why hurry? We've got all the time in the world.

ANDREY: I'm afraid my wife will stop me.

CHEBUTYKIN: Ah!

ANDREY: Tonight I won't play, I'll only sit and watch. I don't feel very well…What do you do, Ivan Romanich, for shortness of breath?

CHEBUTYKIN: You're asking me! I don't remember, my boy. Really, I don't know.

ANDREY: Let's go out through the kitchen.

A bell rings, once, then again; voices, laughter. They exit.

IRINA: *(Enters.)* Who's there?
ANFISA: *(In a whisper.)* Mummers!

A bell rings.

IRINA: Tell them no one's home, nanny. Ask them to forgive us, please.

*ANFISA exits. IRINA wanders about the room, deep in thought; she is upset.
Enter SOLYONY.*

SOLYONY: *(Perplexed.)* No one's here…Where is everyone?
IRINA: They've all gone home.
SOLYONY: That's strange. Are you alone?
IRINA: Alone.

Pause.

Good night.

SOLYONY: I behaved inappropriately just now, I was tactless, I lost control.
But you're so unlike the others, you're noble and pure, you see the truth in
everything…You and you alone can understand me. I love you, profound-
ly, passionately, I love you without limit…
IRINA: Good night! Go away.
SOLYONY: I can't bear to live without you. *(Follows after her.)* O my bliss! *(In
tears.)* O ecstasy! Those lovely, luminous eyes, glorious eyes, no other
woman on earth has eyes like yours…
IRINA: *(Coldly.)* Stop it, Vasily Vasilyich!
SOLYONY: For the very first time I speak to you of love, and I'm not on this earth,
I'm on some other planet! *(Rubs his forehead.)* Ah well, what does it matter.
Love cannot be coerced, of course…But, I shall have no rivals…None…I
swear to you by all that's holy, I shall murder any rival…O angel!

NATASHA crosses with a candle.

NATASHA: *(Looks in one door, then another, and passes by the door to her hus-
band's room.)* Andrey's in there. Let him read. Excuse me, Vasily Vasilyich,
I didn't know you were here, I'm not dressed for visitors…
SOLYONY: What do I care! Good night! *(Exits.)*
NATASHA: And you're so tired, my poor darling girl! *(Kisses IRINA.)* You
should have been in bed ages ago.

IRINA: Is Bobik sleeping?

NATASHA: Yes. But not soundly. By the way, dear, I wanted to tell you something, and either you were always out or else I just didn't have the time... Bobik's room, the one he's in now, the nursery, well, you know, really, it feels so cold and damp in there. Now your room would be ideal for a baby. Be a dear, would you, and move into Olya's room for a little while!

IRINA: *(Not comprehending.)* Where?

A troika is approaching the house; the little bells are heard ringing.

NATASHA: You and Olya can share a room, just for the time being, and Bobik can have your room. He is such a sweetie, today I said to him: "Bobik! You're mine! Mine!" And he looked up at me with those precious little eyes of his.

A bell rings.

That must be Olga. How late she is!

A MAID approaches NATASHA and whispers something in her ear.

Protopopov? What a funny man. Protopopov's here, he's invited me to go for a ride with him in his troika. *(Laughs.)* Men are so strange...

A bell rings.

Someone's here. Well, maybe just a short ride, a quarter of an hour or so, that's all. *(To the MAID.)* Go on, tell him, hurry.

A bell rings.

There's the bell...that must be Olga...*(Exits.)*

The MAID runs out; IRINA sits, deep in thought; enter KULYGIN, OLGA, then VERSHININ.

KULYGIN: Well, that's a fine how-do-you-do. They told us there was going to be a party here tonight.

VERSHININ: That's strange, I just left here, not even half an hour ago, and they were expecting the mummers...

IRINA: They're all gone.

KULYGIN: Masha, too? Where did she go? And why is Protopopov waiting outside in his troika? Whom is he waiting for?

IRINA: Stop asking questions…I'm tired.

KULYGIN: My, aren't we sensitive…

OLGA: The meeting just ended. I'm exhausted. Our headmistress is ill, so now I've had to take her place. My head, my head aches, it aches so…*(Sits.)* Yesterday, Andrey lost two hundred rubles at cards…The whole town is talking about it…

KULYGIN: Yes, I'm tired out from that meeting, too. *(Sits.)*

VERSHININ: My wife decided to frighten me just now, she almost poisoned herself. But, everything is under control, and I'm glad, now I can rest…So, are we to go, then? Well, allow me to wish you all a very good night. Fyodor Ilyich, let's go somewhere. I can't stay at home, I just can't…Come!

KULYGIN: I'm tired. I'm not going anywhere. *(Stands.)* So tired. Has my wife gone home?

IRINA: She must have.

KULYGIN: *(Kisses IRINA's hand.)* Farewell. Tomorrow and the day after tomorrow, I shall rest all day. Good night! *(Exiting.)* I'm dying for a cup of tea. I was counting on spending the evening in pleasant company, and now — "o fallacem hominum spem!" The accusative case with the exclamatory…

VERSHININ: Well then, I'll go out alone. *(Exits with KULYGIN, whistling.)*

OLGA: My head, my head aches so Andrey lost…the whole town's talking…I'm going to bed. *(Exiting.)* Tomorrow, I'm free…Oh, dear God, how blissful! Tomorrow I'm free, the day after tomorrow I'm free…My head, my head aches so…*(Exits.)*

IRINA: *(Alone.)* They're all gone. No one's left.

An accordion plays on the street, a nanny sings a lullaby.

NATASHA: *(Crosses the room wearing a furcoat and cap; a MAID follows behind.)* I'll be home in half an hour. Just a short ride, that's all. *(Exits.)*

IRINA: *(Left standing alone, with longing.)* To Moscow! To Moscow! To Moscow!

CURTAIN

OLGA and IRINA's room. To the left and right are beds, blocked off by screens.
It is after two in the morning. Offstage, an alarm is sounding for a fire, which
has broken out a while ago. Evidently, no one in the household has gone to bed
yet. MASHA is lying on the sofa, dressed, as always, in black. Enter OLGA and
ANFISA.

ANFISA: They're sitting downstairs right now, underneath the staircase…I said
to them: "Please, come upstairs," I said, "You can't stay there like that,"—
but they kept on crying. "Papa," they said, "we don't know where Papa is.
God forbid, he's burned to death," they said. Imagine that! And others are
outside, too, with no clothes on.

OLGA: *(Takes dresses from the wardrobe.)* Here, take this grey one…And this
one…and this blouse, too…And take this skirt, nanny…What is going on
here, dear God! Kirsanovsky Lane burned to the ground, apparently…
Take this…Take this…*(Tosses the dresses into her hands.)* The Vershinin's,
poor things, they're frightened to death. Their house nearly burned down,
too. They can spend the night here…we can't let them go home…And
everything at poor Fedotik's is gone, there's nothing left, nothing…

ANFISA: Better call Ferapont, Olyushka, I can't carry all this myself…

OLGA: *(Rings.)* No one's answering…*(At the door.)* Whoever is out there, come in!

Through the open door, a window is visible, red from the fire's glow; the fire
brigade is heard going past the house.

What a nightmare! I'm so sick of it!

Enter FERAPONT.

Here, take this downstairs…The Kolotilin girls are waiting underneath the
staircase…give them this. And this too…

FERAPONT: Yes, mistress. In the year 1812, Moscow burned to the ground,
too. Good God almighty! Were those Frenchmen surprised!

OLGA: Go on, hurry.

FERAPONT: Yes, mistress. *(Exits.)*

OLGA: Nanny, darling, give it all away. We don't need any of it, give it all away,
nanny…I'm so exhausted, I can hardly stand on my feet…We can't let the

Vershinins go home…Let the little girls sleep in the drawing room, and put Aleksandr Ignatyevich downstairs with the baron…Fedotik can stay with the baron, too, or else let him sleep here in the hall…The doctor's drunk, horribly drunk, tonight of all nights, no one can stay with him. And let Vershinin's wife sleep in the drawing room, too.

ANFISA: *(Exhausted.)* Olyushka, darling, don't throw me out! Don't throw me out!

OLGA: You're talking nonsense, nanny. No one's going to throw you out.

ANFISA: *(Lays her head on OLGA's breast.)* My treasure, my own, I've toiled, I've slaved…And now that I've grown weak, everyone will say: Get rid of her! And where am I to go? Where? I'm eighty years old. Eighty-one…

OLGA: Sit, nanny…Poor thing, you're tired…*(Sits her down.)* Rest, my dearest. How pale you are!

Enter NATASHA.

NATASHA: They say we should form a committee as soon as possible, to aid those who've lost their homes in the fire. Well, why not? It's a fine idea. It's always the duty of the rich to help the poor. Bobik and little Sophie are fast asleep, they're sleeping as if nothing in the world has happened. There are people all over the place, everywhere you go, the house is full of them. And there's influenza going around town, I'm afraid the children might catch it.

OLGA: *(Not listening to her.)* You can't see the fire from this room, it's peaceful here…

NATASHA: Yes…I must look frightful. *(Before the mirror.)* They say I've put on weight…but it just isn't true! Not in the slightest! And Masha's fast asleep, she's tired out, poor thing…*(To ANFISA, furiously.)* Don't you dare sit in my presence! Get up! Go on, get out of here!

ANFISA exits; pause.

Why you keep that old woman here, I just don't understand!

OLGA: *(Stunned.)* Forgive me, I, too, don't understand…

NATASHA: She has no place here. She's a peasant, she should be living in the country…You've spoiled her! I like order in my household! There's no place for useless people here. *(Strokes her cheek.)* Poor thing, you're tired. Our headmistress is tired! And when my little Sophie grows up and enters high school, I shall be afraid of you.

OLGA: I'll never be headmistress.

NATASHA: Oh yes, you will, they'll choose you, Olyechka. It's already been decided.

OLGA: Then I shall decline. I can't...I haven't the strength...*(Drinks water.)* You were so rude to nanny just now...Forgive me, I'm simply can't bear it...it makes me feel faint...

NATASHA: *(Agitated.)* Forgive me, Olya, please, forgive me...I didn't mean to upset you.

MASHA gets up, takes her pillow and leaves, angrily.

OLGA: Please, try to understand, dear...perhaps we were brought up in a peculiar way, but I just can't bear it. That kind of behavior depresses me, it makes me feel ill...I simply lose heart!

NATASHA: Forgive me, forgive me...*(Kisses her.)*

OLGA: The slightest rudeness of any sort, even a single unkind word, upsets me...

NATASHA: I talk too much sometimes, it's true, but don't you agree, my dear, she should be living in the country.

OLGA: She's been with us for thirty years.

NATASHA: But, really, she can't work any more! Either I don't understand you, or else you just don't want to understand me! She's not capable of work, she only sleeps or sits around.

OLGA: Then let her sit.

NATASHA: *(Astonished.)* What do you mean, let her sit? She's a servant, isn't she? *(In tears.)* I don't understand you, Olya. I have a nanny, I have a wet nurse, we have a maid, we have a cook...what do we need this old woman for? Tell me, what?

Offstage, an alarm bell sounds.

OLGA: I've aged ten years tonight.

NATASHA: We need to settle this matter once and for all, Olya. You're at school, I'm at home, you have your teaching, I run the household. And if I say something regarding the servants, I know what I'm talking about; I-know-what-I'm-talking-about...And see to it that that old thief is out of here by tomorrow, that old hag...*(stamps her foot)* that witch!...Don't you dare provoke me! Don't you dare! *(Composes herself.)* Really, if you don't move downstairs, we'll be quarreling like this forever. It's terrible.

Enter KULYGIN.

KULYGIN: Where's Masha? It's time we were going home. They say the fire's subsiding. *(Stretches.)* Only one quarter burned down, but there was so much wind at first, it seemed the whole town was in flames. *(Sits.)* I'm all worn out. Olyechka, my darling…I often think: if it weren't for Masha, I'd have married you, Olyechka. You're so good…I'm exhausted. *(He listens for something.)*

OLGA: What is it?

KULYGIN: Tonight of all nights, the doctor's been drinking, he's terribly drunk. Tonight of all nights! *(Stands up.)* Wait, I think he's coming…Do you hear him? Yes, here he comes…*(Laughs.)* He's something, isn't he!…I'll go hide…*(Goes to the wardrobe and stands in the corner.)* What a devil!

OLGA: For two years he's been sober, and now all of a sudden he goes and gets drunk tonight…*(Goes upstage with NATASHA.)*

Enter CHEBUTYKIN; he walks steadily around the room as if he were sober, stops, looks, then crosses to the washstand and starts to wash his hands.

CHEBUTYKIN: *(Sullenly.)* To hell with them…with all of them…They think I'm a doctor, that I can cure all kinds of illnesses, and what do I know? absolutely nothing, I've forgotten everything I ever knew, I remember nothing, absolutely nothing.

Exit OLGA and NATASHA, unnoticed.

To hell with them. Last Wednesday I took care of a woman in Zasyp — she died, and it was my fault, that she died. Yes…I might have known something twenty-five years ago, but now, I remember nothing. Nothing. Perhaps I'm not even human, I only seem to have arms, and legs, and a head; perhaps I don't even exist at all, I only seem to walk, and eat, and sleep. *(Weeps.)* Oh, if only I didn't exist at all! *(Stops weeping, sullenly.)* Who the hell knows…The other day at the club, they were talking, about Shakespeare, about Voltaire…I've never read them, never read any of them, but I seemed to have read them, I gave the impression that I had. And there were others there like me, too. The vulgarity! The vileness of it all! And that woman I murdered on Wednesday, I thought of her…I thought of everything, and such an ugly, nasty, foul feeling of loathesomeness descended upon my soul…so I started to drink…

Enter IRINA, VERSHININ, and TUSENBACH; TUSENBACH is in new, stylish civilian attire.

IRINA: Let's sit here. No one else can come in.

VERSHININ: If it weren't for the soldiers, the whole town would have burned to the ground. Brave men! *(Rubs his hands together with pleasure.)* Fine fellows! Ah, what brave, brave men!

KULYGIN: *(Crossing to him.)* What time is it, gentlemen?

TUSENBACH: After three, already. It's growing light out.

IRINA: Everyone's sitting in the hall, no one's leaving. And that Solyony of yours is there...*(To CHEBUTYKIN.)* You ought to go to bed, doctor.

CHEBUTYKIN: Don't mind me, mam'selle...Thank you very much...*(Combs his beard.)*

KULYGIN: *(Laughs.)* You're soused, Ivan Romanich! *(Claps him on the shoulder.)* Well done, well done! "In vino veritas," as the ancients say.

TUSENBACH: They're asking me to arrange a recital on behalf of those who have lost their homes in the fire.

IRINA: But who will play...

TUSENBACH: I'll arrange it, if you like. Now Maria Sergeevna, in my opinion, plays piano marvelously.

KULYGIN: Yes, doesn't she, marvelously!

IRINA: She's already forgotten how. She hasn't played in three years...or four, even.

TUSENBACH: No one in this entire town knows a thing about classical music, not a soul, but I do, I know music, and I assure you, on my word of honor, that Maria Sergeevna plays magnificently, why, she's almost a virtuoso.

KULYGIN: Right you are, baron. I adore her, my Masha. She is superb.

TUSENBACH: To be able to play so brilliantly, knowing all the while that no one appreciates you, no one!

KULYGIN: *(Sighs.)* Yes...But would it be proper for her to take part in a concert?

Pause.

Really, ladies and gentlemen, I know nothing about such matters. That is, I mean, it might be quite appropriate. Now it must be said that our headmaster is a fine individual, yes, in fact, a very fine, very intelligent individual, but, you know, he has these views...Now, of course, this is none of his business, but nevertheless, if you like, I might have a word with him on the subject.

CHEBUTYKIN *takes a porcelain clock in his hands and examines it.*

VERSHININ: I'm all sooty from the fire, I must look like nothing on earth.

Pause.

Yesterday, I heard a rumor that they want to move our brigade, somewhere far away from here. Some say to Poland, others say to Eastern Siberia.

TUSENBACH: I heard that, too. Well, the town will be completely deserted, then.

IRINA: And we'll go away!

CHEBUTYKIN: *(Drops the clock, which breaks into pieces.)* Smashed to smithereens!

Pause; everyone is chagrined and disconcerted.

KULYGIN: *(Picking up the pieces.)* To break such a valuable thing — ach, Ivan Romanich, Ivan Romanich! Zero minus for conduct!

IRINA: That clock belonged to Mama.

CHEBUTYKIN: Perhaps it was Mama's, perhaps it wasn't Mama's. Perhaps I didn't break it, it only seems I did. Perhaps it only seems we exist, whereas in reality, we don't. I know nothing, no one knows anything. *(At the door.)* What are you looking at me for? Natasha's having an affair with Protopopov, and you don't see it…You sit here and you see nothing, and meanwhile, Natasha's having an affair with Protopopov… *(Sings.)* "Won't you please take this sweet fig…" *(Exits.)*

VERSHININ: Yes… *(Laughs.)* How strange it all is, really!

Pause.

When the fire broke out, I rushed home as fast as I could; and as I approached, I saw our house standing there, safe and unharmed, out of danger, but there were my two little girls in the doorway, clad only in their underclothes, with no mother in sight, while all around them people were rushing, dogs and horses were running, and there on my little girls' faces was an indescribable look, a look of horror, of terror, entreaty; how my heart sank, when I saw those sweet faces. Dear God, I thought, what have these little girls yet to endure in the course of a long, long lifetime! I gathered them into my arms, I ran, and yet all I could think of was what they have yet to endure on this earth!

An alarm bell; pause.

I arrived here, and their mother was waiting, with cries and reproaches.

Enter MASHA with a pillow; she sits on the couch.

And while my little girls were standing in that doorway, clad only in their underclothes, streets crimson from the flames, terrifying noises all around, I thought, that this is how it must have been so many years ago, when suddenly an enemy invaded, pillaged, plundered, burned…Yet, meanwhile, in truth, what a difference there is between what came before us and what is today! And still more time will pass, some two – three hundred years or so, again they will look back upon us with terror and disdain, again our present lives will seem so dreadful and so difficult, so painful and so strange. Oh, what a life there is to come, yes, surely, what a life! *(Laughs.)* Forgive me, I'm philosophizing again. Allow me to continue, ladies and gentlemen. I so desperately want to philosophize, it's just the mood I'm in.

Pause.

Everyone's asleep. As I was saying: What a life there is to come! You can only imagine it…Today, there are only three like you in this town, but in the coming generations there will be more, and more and more, and there will come a time when everything will change according to your way, and they will live as you have lived, and then, as you grow older, others will be born, whose lives are better than yours…*(Laughs.)* I'm in such a rare mood tonight. I want to live dangerously…*(Sings.)* "Young or old do love obey,/ Held within her gentle sway…" *(Laughs.)*

MASHA: Tram-tam-tam…
VERSHININ: Tam-tam…
MASHA: Tra-ra-ra?
VERSHININ: Tra-ta-ta. *(Laughs.)*

Enter FEDOTIK.

FEDOTIK: *(Dances.)* Burned, all burned! To the ground!

Laughter.

IRINA: What's so funny? Everything?

FEDOTIK: *(Laughs.)* To the ground! Everything I own, there's nothing left. My guitar burned, all my photographs burned, all my letters…And I so wanted to give you this lovely little notebook, and that burned too.

Enter SOLYONY.

IRINA: No, please, go away, Vasily Vasilyich. You may not come in here.

SOLYONY: Why is it that the baron may, while I may not?

VERSHININ: In fact, we all should be going. How is the fire?

SOLYONY: Subsiding, so they say. No, really, it's positively strange, why is it that the baron may, while I may not? *(Takes out a flask of scent and sprinkles himself.)*

VERSHININ: Tram-tam-tam?

MASHA: Tram-tam.

VERSHININ: *(Laughs, to SOLYONY.)* Come, let's go into the hall.

SOLYONY: Very well, sir, and we shall make a note of this.

"I'll answer you, although I fear
It might disturb the geese, my dear."

(Looks at TUSENBACH.) Tsip, tsip, tsip…*(Exits with VERSHININ and FEDOTIK.)*

IRINA: That Solyony has filled the room with smoke…*(Perplexed.)* The baron's asleep! Baron! Baron!

TUSENBACH: *(Awake.)* I'm so tired, really…The brick factory No, I'm not delirious, not at all, soon I shall be going to the brick factory, I shall work…It's all settled. *(To IRINA, tenderly.)* You're so pale, so beautiful, so enchanting…Your paleness illuminates the darkness, like light…You're sad, you're not content with life…Oh come away with me, we'll work together…

MASHA: Nikolai Lvovich, go away.

TUSENBACH: *(Laughing.)* You're here, too? I didn't see you. *(Kisses IRINA's hand.)* Farewell, I'm leaving…I see you now, and I remember how once, so long ago, on your nameday, you were radiant and gay, you spoke of the joys of work…What a vision of a happy life arose before me then! Where is it? *(Kisses her hand.)* You have tears in your eyes. Go to sleep, it's already light out…morning has come…If only you'd let me dedicate my life to you!

MASHA: Nikolai Lvovich, go away! Really, now…

TUSENBACH: I'm leaving…*(Exits.)*

MASHA: *(Lying down.)* Are you asleep, Fyodor?

KULYGIN: What?

MASHA: You ought to go home.

KULYGIN: My darling Masha, my precious Masha…

IRINA: She's exhausted. Let her rest, Fedya.

KULYGIN: I'm going, right away…My wife, she's so lovable, so adorable…I love you, my only one…

MASHA: "Amo, amas, amat, amamus, amatis, amant."

KULYGIN: *(Laughs.)* No, really, she's wonderful. I've been married to you for seven years, and yet it seems we were married only yesterday. Word of honor. No, really, you're a wonderful woman. I'm content, I'm content, I'm content!

MASHA: I'm miserable, miserable, miserable… *(Sits up and speaks.)* And I can't get it out of my head…It's simply disgraceful. It's like a nail boring into my brain, I can't keep silent. I'm talking about Andrey…He's mortgaged this house to the bank, and his wife has appropriated all the money, but this house doesn't belong to him alone, it belongs to all four of us! Surely, he must know that, if he were in the least bit honorable, that is.

KULYGIN: Must you, Masha? What's the point? Andryusha owes money to everyone, God bless him.

MASHA: Whatever, it's disgraceful. *(Lies down.)*

KULYGIN: We're not poor, you and I. I work, I go to the high school, I give lessons…I'm an honest man. A simple man…"Omnia mea mecum porto," as they say.

MASHA: I don't need anything, it's just that I can't bear the injustice, it enrages me.

Pause.

Go home, Fyodor!

KULYGIN: *(Kisses her.)* You're tired, rest for half an hour, I'll sit up and wait for you. Sleep… *(Exiting.)* I'm content, I'm content, I'm content. *(Exits.)*

IRINA: No, really, how our Andrey's aged, how he's weakened, how he's wasted away, living with that woman. Once, he was going to become a professor, and now, only yesterday, he's boasting that he's finally been appointed to the local district council. Andrey, a member of the local district council, whose chairman is Protopopov…The whole town is talking about him, laughing at him, and he alone doesn't know it and doesn't see it…Look, how everyone runs to the fire, and he sits in his room, oblivious to it all. Playing his violin. *(Upset.)* Oh, how awful it is, how awful, how awful! *(Weeps.)* I can't bear it any longer, I can't!…I can't, I can't!…

Enter OLGA, she tidies the area near her table.

(Sobs loudly.) Throw me out, throw me out, I can't bear it any longer!...

OLGA: *(Frightened.)* What is it, what is it? Darling!

IRINA: *(Sobbing.)* Where? Where has it all gone to? Where? Oh my God, my God! I've forgotten everything, everything...It's all muddled up in my head...I can't remember the word in Italian for 'window,' or 'ceiling'...I've forgotten everything. Every day I keep forgetting, and life is passing by us, never to return, never, we'll never go to Moscow...I see it now, we'll never go, ever...

OLGA: Darling, darling...

IRINA: *(Containing herself.)* Oh, how unhappy I am...I can't work, I can't bear to work. It's enough, enough! I worked in the telegraph office, now I work for the town council and I hate, no, I despise everything they give me to do...I'm almost twenty-four years old, I've been working forever, and my brain has shrivelled up, I've grown old, and thin, and ugly, and nothing, nothing gives me any satisfaction whatsoever, and meanwhile time passes by, and it's almost as if we're disappearing, fading away from all hope of a truly beautiful life, fading further and further away into some kind of abyss. I despair, and why I'm alive, why I haven't killed myself by now, I don't understand.

OLGA: Don't cry, my child, don't cry...I suffer so.

IRINA: I won't cry, I won't...Enough...There, you see, I'm not crying any more. Enough...Enough!

OLGA: Darling, I'm speaking to you as a sister, as a friend, if you want my advice, marry the baron!

IRINA weeps softly.

You respect him, you do, you admire him...He's not handsome, it's true, but he's so decent, so pure...We don't marry for love, really we don't, we marry for duty. That's what I think, at least, and I'd marry without love, I would. Whoever proposed to me, it wouldn't matter, I'd marry him, as long as he were decent. I'd even marry an old man...

IRINA: I've waited forever, to move to Moscow, to meet my own true love, I've dreamed of him, loved him...But it's all turned out to be such nonsense, such nonsense...

OLGA: *(Embraces her sister.)* My darling, my beautiful sister, I understand everything; when Baron Nikolai Lvovich left the military service and came to visit in civilian clothes, he looked so homely, I burst into tears..."Why are you crying?" he asked. How could I tell him! But if it's God's will that you marry him, then that would make me happy. That, you see, is different, altogether different.

NATASHA crosses silently from the door stage right to the door stage left, carrying a candle.

MASHA: *(Sits.)* She walks around here as if she started the fire herself.
OLGA: Masha, you're silly. You're the silliest one in the family. Forgive me, please…

Pause.

MASHA: I have something to confess, darling sisters, My soul is in anguish. I shall confess it to you and you alone, and never again to anyone, anywhere…And I shall tell it to you now. *(Softly.)* It is my secret, but you should know everything…I cannot keep silent…

Pause.

I love, I love…I love this man…You've only just seen him. There, now you know. I love Vershinin…
OLGA: *(Goes behind her screen partition.)* Stop it. It doesn't matter, I'm not listening.
MASHA: What can I do! *(Holds her head in her hands.)* At first, I thought him strange, then I pitied him…then I fell in love with him…I fell in love with his voice, his words, his misfortunes, his two little girls…
OLGA: *(From behind the screen.)* It doesn't matter, I'm not listening. Whatever foolish things you're saying, it doesn't matter, I'm not listening.
MASHA: You're the foolish one, Olya. I love him — that, you see, is my fate. That is my lot in life, you see…And he loves me…It's all so awful. Isn't it? Isn't it terrible? *(Takes IRINA by the hand, draws her close.)* Oh my darling…Somehow we shall live through life, whatever it has in store for us…You know, when you're reading some novel or other, and everything seems so predictable, so obvious, and then you fall in love yourself, then, only then do you see, that no one knows anything, and each of us must find her own way…My darlings, my sisters…There, I've confessed to you, and now I shall be silent…Like Gogol's madman…silence…silence…
Enter ANDREY, followed by FERAPONT.

ANDREY: *(Angrily.)* What do you want? I don't understand.

FERAPONT: *(At the door, impatiently.)* But, Andrey Sergeevich, I've already told you ten times.

ANDREY: First of all, it's not Andrey Sergeevich, it's "Your honor."

FERAPONT: It's about the firemen, your honor, they're asking permission to pass through the garden to get to the river. Otherwise they'll have to go all the way 'round the house, 'round and 'round. And that, well, that's a big problem.

ANDREY: All right. Tell them it's all right.

FERAPONT exits.

I'm sick of all this. Where's Olga?

OLGA appears from behind the screen.

I've come to ask you for the key to the wardrobe, I've lost mine. You've got a little key, haven't you?

OLGA gives him the key, silently. IRINA goes behind her screen partition. Pause.

What an enormous fire! It's dying down, now. That Ferapont, damn it, he gets on my nerves, and then I say the stupidest things to him..."Your honor"...

Pause.

Why are you so quiet, Olya?

Pause.

It's time to stop all this foolishness and resentment, there's no reason for it. You're here, Masha, Irina's here, so, well, good — let's have it all out, once and for all. What do you have against me? What?

OLGA: Stop it, Andryusha. We'll talk it over tomorrow. *(Upset.)* What a cruel night!

ANDREY: *(Very flustered.)* Don't get upset. I'm completely calm and collected, and I'm asking you: What do you have against me? Tell me the truth.

VERSHININ's voice: "Tram-tam-tam!"

MASHA: *(Stands, loudly.)* Tra-ta-ta! *(To OLGA.)* Good-bye, Olya, God bless you. *(She goes behind the curtain, kisses IRINA.)* Sleep well...Good-bye, Andrey. Go, they're all worn out...we'll talk it over tomorrow...*(Exits.)*

OLGA: Really, Andryusha, let's leave it till tomorrow...*(Goes behind her screen partition.)* It's time for sleep.

ANDREY: Just let me say it, then I'll go. All right...First of all, you have something against Natasha, my wife, this I have known from the day of my wedding. Natasha is a fine, decent person, honest, and honorable — that is my opinion. She is my wife, I love and respect her, do you understand, I respect her, and I demand that others respect her as well. I repeat, she is an honest, honorable person, and your disapproval, forgive me, is simply an indulgence.

Pause.

Second, you're angry with me, apparently, that I'm not a professor, that I didn't become a scientist. But I serve the district, I am a member of the local district council, that is my service, and I consider it to be as sacred and as noble as the service to science. I am a member of the local district council, and proud of it, if you really want to know...

Pause.

Third...I still have more to say...I have mortgaged the house, without asking your permission...I am guilty of this, yes, and I ask your forgiveness. My debts drove me to it...Thirty-five thousand...I no longer play cards, that I gave up a long time ago, but the main thing, and may I say this in my own defense, is that you girls, you all receive a pension, whereas I've had no...income myself, so to speak...

Pause.

KULYGIN: *(In the doorway.)* Masha's not here? *(Anxiously.)* Where is she, then? That's strange...*(Exits.)*

ANDREY: They aren't listening. Natasha is a outstanding person, a person of the highest integrity. *(He roams about the stage in silence, then stops.)* When I married her, I thought we'd be happy...so very happy...But my God... *(Weeps.)* My dearest sisters, my darling sisters, don't believe me, don't believe me...*(Exits.)*

KULYGIN: *(In the doorway, anxiously.)* Where's Masha? Masha's not here? That's surprising. *(Exits.)*

The alarm bell sounds, the stage is empty.

IRINA: *(From behind the screen.)* Olya! Who is knocking on the floor?

OLGA: It's the doctor, Ivan Romanich. He's drunk.

IRINA: What a bewildering night!

Pause.

Olya! *(Peers out from behind the screen.)* Did you hear? They're taking the brigade from us, they're moving it somewhere far far away.

OLGA: It's only a rumor.

IRINA: And then we shall be left alone...Olya!

OLGA: What?

IRINA: Dearest, darling, I respect the baron, I admire him, I do, he's a fine person, I'll marry him, I'll agree to it, only then let us go to Moscow! I beg of you, let us go! There is no place else on earth for us but Moscow! Let's go, Olya! Let's go!

CURTAIN

ACT FOUR

The old garden beside the Prozorov house. A long avenue lined with fir trees, at the end of which is a view of the river. On the other side of the river is a forest. To the right is the terrace of the house; there, on a table, are bottles and glasses; evidently, champagne has just been served. It is noon. From time to time, passersby cross through the garden from the road to the river; a group of five soldiers hurries by. CHEBUTYKIN sits in a comfortable chair in the garden, waiting to be summoned; he is calm, a mood which stays with him during the entire act; he wears a military cap and holds a walking stick. Standing on the terrace are IRINA, TUSENBACH, and KULYGIN, now clean-shaven and wearing a medal around his neck. They are saying good-bye to FEDOTIK and RODE, who are coming down the steps; both officers are in marching uniform.

TUSENBACH: *(Kisses FEDOTIK.)* You're a good man, we've been great friends. *(Kisses RODE.)* Once again…Farewell, my dear fellow!

IRINA: Till we meet again!

FEDOTIK: No, no, it's good-bye, we shall never see each other again!

KULYGIN: Who knows! *(Wipes his eyes, smiling.)* Look, I'm starting to cry.

IRINA: We'll meet again, some day.

FEDOTIK: What, in ten – fifteen years? We'll scarcely even recognize each other, we'll hardly give each other the time of day…*(Takes a photograph.)* Hold it…One last time.

RODE: *(Embraces TUSENBACH.)* We'll never see each other again…*(Kisses IRINA's hand.)* Thank you for everything, everything!

FEDOTIK: *(Annoyed.)* Hold still!

TUSENBACH: Please God, we'll meet again. Write to us. Without fail, write.

RODE: *(Glances around the garden.)* Good-bye, trees! *(Calls.)* Hup-hup!

Pause.

Good-bye, echo!

KULYGIN: Who knows, maybe you'll get married in Poland…Your Polish wife will hug you and squeeze you and call you: "Kokhane!" *(Laughs.)*

FEDOTIK: *(Glancing at his watch.)* We've less than an hour left. Solyony's the only one from our battery traveling on the barge, the rest of us are going with the artillery unit. Today, three divisions are going, tomorrow three more will go — and soon peace and tranquility will descend upon the town.

TUSENBACH: And deadly boredom.

RODE: Where's Maria Sergeevna?

KULYGIN: Masha's in the garden.

FEDOTIK: We'll say good-bye to her.

RODE: Farewell, we must go, or else I'll start to weep...*(Quickly embraces TUSENBACH and KULYGIN, kisses IRINA's hand.)* How wonderful it was, to have lived here for a while...

FEDOTIK: *(To KULYGIN.)* Take this as a souvenir...a notebook with a little pencil...We'll go this way to the river...

As they walk off, both turn and look back.

RODE: *(Calls out.)* Hup-hup!

KULYGIN: *(Calls out.)* Good-bye!

Upstage, FEDOTIK and RODE meet MASHA and say good-bye; she exits with them.

IRINA: They're gone...*(Sits on the lowest step of the terrace.)*

CHEBUTYKIN: They forgot to say good-bye to me.

IRINA: And what about you?

CHEBUTYKIN: Well, yes, I forgot, too. Never mind, I'll see them again, all too soon, I'm going away tomorrow. Yes...Only one more day left. And in a year, they'll give me my retirement, and I'll come right back here again, to live out the rest of my earthly days near you...Only one more year till I get my pension...*(Puts a newspaper into his pocket, takes out another.)* I'll come home to you, and I'll mend my ways...I'll become meek and mild, and what else...well-behaved...

IRINA: Yes, you must change your ways, dear. You must, somehow.

CHEBUTYKIN: Yes. I feel it, too. *(Sings softly.)* "Ta-ra-ra...boom- de-ay...Ta-ra-ra boom-de-ay..."

KULYGIN: You're incorrigible, Ivan Romanich! Incorrigible.

CHEBUTYKIN: Yes, and why don't I come to you for instruction. That would straighten me out.

IRINA: Fyodor has shaved off his moustache. I can't bear to look at him!

KULYGIN: Why not?

CHEBUTYKIN: I could tell you what you look like, but I won't.

KULYGIN: Oh come, now! It's quite proper, this 'modus vivendi.' Our headmaster shaved off his moustache, and so did I, as soon as I got promoted,

I shaved mine right off. No one really likes it this way, but I don't care. I'm content. With or without a moustache, either way, I'm content. *(Sits.)*

Deep in the garden, ANDREY wheels a sleeping baby in a carriage.

IRINA: Ivan Romanich, my own dear Ivan Romanich, I'm so terribly anxious. You were down on the boulevard yesterday, tell me, what happened?

CHEBUTYKIN: What happened? Nothing happened. It's all nonsense. *(Reads the newspaper.)* It doesn't matter!

KULYGIN: They say that, apparently, Solyony and the baron met on the boulevard yesterday near the theatre…

TUSENBACH: Stop it! I mean, really…*(Waves his hand and exits into the house.)*

KULYGIN: Near the theatre…Solyony started to provoke the baron, and he just couldn't stand it any more, so he insulted him…

CHEBUTYKIN: What do I know. It's all nonsense.

KULYGIN: Once, in one of the seminaries, a teacher wrote the word 'nonsense' on an essay, and the student thought it said 'non sequitur' — he thought the teacher had written it in Latin…*(Laughs.)* Absolutely hilarious. They say that apparently Solyony is in love with Irina and has developed a hatred for the baron…Well, that's understandable. Irina is a very fine girl. She's even a little like Masha, you know…intense. Only you have a somewhat more gentle nature, Irina. On the other hand, Masha is very very good-natured, too, I mean, really. I adore her, my Masha.

Deep in the garden, offstage, cries of: "A-oo! Hup-hup!"

IRINA: *(Shudders.)* Everything frightens me today, somehow.

Pause.

All my things are packed and ready, I'm sending them off after dinner. Tomorrow, the baron and I shall be married, tomorrow, we're going away to the brick factory, and the day after tomorrow, I shall already be in school…our new life will have begun. God will help me, somehow! When I took the teachers' examination, I wept with joy, I felt blessed…

Pause.

The carriage is coming soon for our things…

KULYGIN: That's all very well, only why get so serious about everything? Ideas are ideas, they shouldn't be taken so seriously. Never mind, I wish you everything, from the bottom of my heart.

CHEBUTYKIN: *(Tenderly.)* My precious, my treasure…my jewel…You're going away, far away, and we shall never catch up with you. And I shall be left behind, a decrepit bird who's grown too old to fly. Fly, my lovely, fly with God's blessing!

Pause.

You've shaved off that moustache in vain, Fyodor Ilyich.

KULYGIN: That'll do! *(Sighs.)* The troops are leaving today, and everything will be as it was before. Whatever they may say, Masha is a fine, honorable woman, I love her very much, I have been blessed, fate has been very kind to me…People have different fates…There's a fellow here named Kozyrev, he works in the local tax bureau. He was a classmate of mine, they failed him in the fifth year because he couldn't understand the rules of 'ut consecutivum.' And now he lives in terrible poverty, he's ill, and whenever I meet him, I say to him: "Hello, 'ut consecutivum.'" "Yes," he says, "that's me, 'consecutivum,'" and then he coughs…I've been lucky all my life, I'm happy, I've even received a decoration, the order of St. Stanislav, second class, and now I myself teach others the laws of 'ut consecutivum.' Of course, I'm an intelligent man, more intelligent than most, but that's not what brings happiness…

In the house, someone is playing "The Maiden's Prayer" on the piano.

IRINA: And tomorrow evening I won't have to hear "The Maiden's Prayer" any more, I won't have to see Protopopov…

Pause.

Protopopov's sitting there in the drawing room; he came by again today…

KULYGIN: Our headmistress still hasn't arrived yet?

IRINA: No. They've sent for her. If only you knew, how hard it's been for me to live here alone, without Olya…She lives at the high school; she's headmistress now, she's busy all day long, and I'm lonely, I'm bored, I have nothing to do, I hate the room I live in…And so I've decided: If it is not meant for me to go to Moscow, so be it. It's fate, you see. There's nothing you can do about it…It's all God's will, and that's the truth. Nikolai Lvovich has proposed to me…And so? I thought about it, and I made up my mind. He's a good man, really, it's remarkable, how good he is…And suddenly it was as if my soul grew wings and took flight…I felt joyous, and free, I wanted to work and work, all over again…Only, yesterday something happened, it's a secret, and a cloud is hanging over me…

CHEBUTYKIN: Non sequitur. Nonsense.

NATASHA: *(At the window.)* The headmistress!

KULYGIN: The headmistress has arrived. Let's go.

He exits into the house with IRINA.

CHEBUTYKIN: *(Reads the newspaper, sings softly.)* "Ta-ra-ra…boom de-ay…Ta-ra-ra boom de-ay…"

MASHA approaches; upstage, ANDREY pushes the baby carriage.

MASHA: There he sits, he sits and sits…

CHEBUTYKIN: What's your problem?

MASHA: *(Sits.)* Nothing…

Pause.

Did you love my mother?

CHEBUTYKIN: Very much.

MASHA: Did she love you?

CHEBUTYKIN: *(After a pause.)* Now *that* I don't remember.

MASHA: Is 'my man' here? Once upon a time, we had a cook named Marfa, and that's what she called her policeman: 'my man.' Is 'my man' here?

CHEBUTYKIN: Not yet.

MASHA: When you snatch at happiness in bits and pieces, and then you lose it, as I have, then little by little you grow coarse, and bitter…*(Points to her breast.)* Deep inside me, a rage is burning…*(Looks at her brother ANDREY who is passing by, wheeling the carriage.)* There's Andrey, our little brother… All hopes lost. Once, thousands of people lifted a great bell, with much toil and travail, a fortune spent to raise it, and then all of a sudden, it fell and shattered. Without warning, without cause. So, too, with Andrey...

ANDREY: When shall we ever have peace and quiet in this house? There's such a din.

CHEBUTYKIN: Soon. *(Looks at his watch.)* I have an old watch...it strikes...*(He winds up the watch; it strikes.)* The first, second, and fifth divisions leave exactly at one...

Pause.

And I go tomorrow.

ANDREY: Forever?

CHEBUTYKIN: Don't know. Perhaps I'll return in a year. Although, who the hell knows...it doesn't matter...

Somewhere far away, a harp and violin are playing.

ANDREY: The town will be deserted. It's as if they're covering it over with a shade.

Pause.

Something happened yesterday near the theatre; everyone's talking, and I don't know a thing about it.

CHEBUTYKIN: Nothing. Foolishness. Solyony was teasing the baron, the baron lost his temper and insulted him, and the upshot of it is that Solyony felt obliged to challenge the baron to a duel. *(Looks at his watch.)* It's almost time...At half past twelve, at a designated grove of trees, you can see it from here across the river...Bang-bang. *(Laughs.)* Solyony thinks he's Lermontov, he even writes poetry. I mean, it's all very well and good to joke about it, but it's already his third duel.

MASHA: Whose?

CHEBUTYKIN: Solyony's.

MASHA: And what about the baron?

CHEBUTYKIN: What about the baron?

Pause.

MASHA: My head is spinning…I'm telling you, they mustn't be allowed to go through with this. He might wound the baron, or even kill him.

CHEBUTYKIN: The baron's a good man, but one baron more, one baron less — what difference does it make? Let it be! It doesn't matter!

Beyond the garden, there are cries of: "A-oo! Hup-hup!"

Wait. That's Skvortsov calling, he's the second. He's sitting in the boat.

Pause.

ANDREY: In my opinion, to participate in a duel, or to be present at one, even in the capacity of a physician, is simply immoral.

CHEBUTYKIN: It only seems to be…We're not really here, there's nothing left on earth, we don't exist, it only seems that we exist…And anyway, what does it matter!

MASHA: All day long they talk, they talk and they talk…*(Walks.)* You live in a climate, where it might snow at any moment, and what do you do? Talk… *(Stops.)* I'm not going into that house, I can't set foot in there…When Vershinin comes, tell me…*(Walks along the avenue of trees.)* Already the birds are flying south…*(Looks up.)* Swans, or perhaps they're geese…My lovely ones, my lucky ones…*(Exits.)*

ANDREY: Our house will be deserted. The officers are going away, you're going away, my sister's getting married, and I'll be left alone in the house.

CHEBUTYKIN: What about your wife?

Enter FERAPONT with the papers.

ANDREY: A wife is a wife. She's honest, virtuous, yes, good-hearted, too, but with it all there is something about her that reduces her to a petty, blind, treacherous little beast. Whatever, she's not really human. I speak to you as a friend, the only person to whom I can bare my soul. I love Natasha, I do, but sometimes she seems to me so astonishingly vulgar, and then I'm lost, I can't understand why it is that I love her so, or, at least, loved her, once…

CHEBUTYKIN: *(Stands.)* My friend, I'm going away tomorrow, perhaps we'll never see each other again, so let me give you some parting advice. Listen — put on your hat, pick up your stick, and start walking…walk on and on and on, never look back. And the farther you go, the better.

SOLYONY crosses upstage with two officers; spotting CHEBUTYKIN, he turns to him; the officers continue on.

SOLYONY: Doctor, it's time! It's half past twelve, already. *(Greets ANDREY.)*
CHEBUTYKIN: Right away. I'm tired of all of you. *(To ANDREY.)* If someone asks for me, Andryusha, say I'll be right back…*(Sighs.)* Oh-ho-ho!
SOLYONY: "He scarce had time to cry 'beware,'
              When he was taken by the bear."
      (Walking with him.) What are you groaning about, old man?
CHEBUTYKIN: Please!
SOLYONY: How are you feeling now?
CHEBUTYKIN: *(Angrily.)* "Like butter from a cow."
SOLYONY: The old man's upset for no reason. I'll restrain myself, I'll only wing him, like a woodcock. *(Takes out the scent and sprinkles some on his hands.)* I've used up a whole flask today, and still they smell. They smell like a corpse.

Pause.

Yes, sir…And do you remember the verse?
      "He sought the ocean's mighty roll,
      To calm the storm within his soul."

CHEBUTYKIN: Yes.
      "He scarce had time to cry 'beware,'
      When he was taken by the bear."
      (Exits with SOLYONY.)

There are cries of: "Hup-hup! A-oo." Enter FERAPONT.

FERAPONT: Papers to be signed…
ANDREY: *(Agitated.)* Leave me alone! Leave me alone! I beg of you! *(Exits with the baby carriage.)*
FERAPONT: What are papers for, if not for signing. *(Exits upstage.)*

Enter IRINA and TUSENBACH in a straw hat; KULYGIN crosses the stage, calling: "A-oo, Masha, a-oo!"

TUSENBACH: There goes the only man in town, it seems, who is glad that the soldiers are leaving.

IRINA: That's understandable.

Pause.

Our town will be deserted now.

TUSENBACH: *(Looking at his watch.)* Darling, I'll be right back.

IRINA: Where are you going?

TUSENBACH: I have to go into town…to see some friends off.

IRINA: That's not the truth…Nikolai, why are you so distracted today?

Pause.

What happened yesterday near the theatre?

TUSENBACH: *(With an impatient gesture.)* I'll return in an hour, and we shall be together again. *(Kisses her hand.)* My beloved…*(Looks into her eyes.)* I have loved you for five years, and still, I can't believe it, and here you are before me, more beautiful than ever. What marvelous, exquisite hair! What eyes! Tomorrow, I'm taking you away, we shall work, we'll grow rich, all my dreams will come true. You will be happy. There's only one thing, and one thing, only: You don't love me!

IRINA: It's not within my power. I shall be your wife, I'll be faithful and obedient, but I don't love you, what can I do! *(Weeps.)* I've never been in love, never, not once in my life. Oh, how I have dreamed of love, I've dreamed of it for so long, day and night, but my heart is like a priceless piano, locked up tight, and the key is lost forever.

Pause.

You look so perturbed.

TUSENBACH: I didn't sleep all night long. There is nothing so terrible in my life, nothing that frightens me more than that lost key, it torments my soul, it robs me of my sleep…Say something.

Pause.

Say something…

IRINA: What? What can I say? What?

TUSENBACH: Anything.

IRINA: Enough! Enough!

Pause.

TUSENBACH: Isn't it ridiculous, sometimes, how silly little things suddenly take on a greater significance in life, for no reason at all. Before, you laugh them off, you think them nonsensical, and yet there they are again, and you feel that you haven't the power to stop them. Oh, let's not talk about it! I'm feeling joyful. It's as if, for the very first time in my life, I'm seeing these trees, firs, maples, birches, and they're all looking back at me curiously, waiting. How beautiful these trees are, indeed, how beautiful all of life must be around them.

Cries of: "A-oo! Hup-hup!"

I must go, it's time...That tree, there, you see, it has withered, and yet still it sways alongside the others in the wind. So, too, it seems, if I should die, I'll still take part in life in one way or another. Farewell, my darling...*(Kisses her hands.)* The papers you gave me, they're on the desk under the calendar.

IRINA: I'm going with you.

TUSENBACH: *(Anxiously.)* No, no! *(He starts off quickly, then stops at the avenue of trees.)* Irina!

IRINA: What?

TUSENBACH: *(Not knowing what to say.)* I haven't had my coffee yet today. Tell them to make some for me...*(Exits quickly.)*

IRINA stands, deep in thought, then goes upstage and sits in a swing. Enter ANDREY with the baby carriage; FERAPONT appears.

FERAPONT: Andrey Sergeich, these papers, they aren't mine, they're official ones. I didn't dream them up myself.

ANDREY: Oh where is it, my past, where has it gone, when I was young, and bright, and gay, when I dreamed elegant dreams, thought enlightened thoughts, when my present and my future shone with hope? How is it that we, who have hardly begun to live, have already become dull, grey, boring, lazy, indifferent, useless, miserable...Our town has existed for two hundred years, it has one hundred thousand inhabitants, and yet there isn't a single person here who doesn't resemble all the rest, not one visionary, past or present, not one scholar, not one artist, not one single person in the least bit illustrious, who might arouse envy or a passionate desire to emulate…No, here they only eat, drink, sleep, and then die…and others are born who also eat, drink, sleep, and so as not to be numbed with boredom, enliven their lives with vicious gossip, vodka, card-playing, malicious fraud and intrigue, and wives deceive their husbands, while husbands deceive themselves, pretending they see nothing, hear nothing, and meanwhile their children are overcome by vulgar influences, God's flame in them is extinguished, and they become these pitiful, wretched corpses which you can't tell apart, one from the other, like their fathers and mothers before them…*(To FERAPONT, angrily.)* What do you want?

FERAPONT: How's that? Papers to be signed.

ANDREY: I'm sick of you.

FERAPONT: *(Gives him the papers.)* Just now, the porter from the revenue office was saying…well, yes, he was saying how apparently, this winter, there were two hundred degrees of frost in St. Petersburg.

ANDREY: The present is loathesome, and yet, when I think of the future, how glorious! Everything will be so easy, so light, so free; in the distance the dawn will break, and I see freedom ahead, for me, for my children, I see freedom from idleness, from kvass, from roast goose and cabbage, from naps after dinner, from vile slothfulness…

FERAPONT: Two thousand people froze to death, apparently. People were terrified, he said. Petersburg, or perhaps it was Moscow — I don't remember.

ANDREY: *(Overcome with emotion.)* My darling sisters, my wonderful sisters! *(In tears.)* Masha, my sister…

NATASHA: *(At the window.)* Who's talking so loud out there? Is that you, Andryusha? You'll wake little Sophie. "Il ne faut pas faire du bruit, la Sophie est dormée dejà. Vous êtes un ours." *(Loses her temper.)* If you want to talk, then give the baby carriage to someone else. Ferapont, take that baby carriage away from the master!

FERAPONT: Yes, mistress. *(Takes the carriage.)*

ANDREY: *(Disconcerted.)* I'm talking quietly.

NATASHA: *(From behind the window, affectionately, to her little boy.)* Bobik! Bad Bobik! Naughty, naughty Bobik!

ANDREY: *(Glancing at the papers.)* All right, I'll look them over, and, where necessary, I'll sign them, and then you can take them back to the council office…*(Exits into the house, reading the papers; FERAPONT pushes the carriage through the garden.)*

NATASHA: *(From behind the window.)* Bobik, what do you call your Mama? Darling, darling! And who is this? This is Aunty Olya, say: "Hello, Olya!"

Enter two vagabond musicians, a man and a girl, playing the violin and harp; VERSHININ, OLGA, and ANFISA come out of the house; they listen to the music for a moment, in silence; IRINA approaches.

OLGA: Our garden is like a thoroughfare, everyone passes through it. Nanny, give the musicians something!…
ANFISA: *(Gives the musicians money.)* Our thanks, God bless.

The musicians bow and exit.

The people are bitter. You don't play like that on a full stomach. *(To IRINA.)* Hello, Arisha! *(Kisses her.)* Hee-hee, my little one, what a life I'm living! What a life! A flat at the high school, my treasure, together with Olyushka, all paid for by the state — God is taking care of me in my old age. Never, ever in my life, have I lived like this, old sinner that I am…A big flat, I have a whole room and a little bed of my very own. All paid for by the state. I go to sleep at night and — o lord, mother of God, there's no happier soul on earth!
VERSHININ: *(Looking at his watch.)* We're leaving now, Olga Sergeevna. It's time.

Pause.

I wish you everything, everything…Where's Maria Sergeevna?
IRINA: She's somewhere in the garden…I'll go look for her.
VERSHININ: Be well. I must go, quickly.
ANFISA: I'll go look for her, too. *(Calls out.)* Mashenka, a-oo! *(Exits with IRINA upstage into the garden.)* A-oo, a-oo!
VERSHININ: Everything must come to an end. And so we shall part. *(Looks at his watch.)* The town gave us a farewell luncheon, we drank champagne, the mayor made a speech; I ate, I listened, but my heart was here, with you… *(Glances around the garden.)* I feel at home here.
OLGA: Shall we ever see each other again?
VERSHININ: Probably not.

Pause.

My wife and my little girls will stay on for another two months; please, if something should happen, if they need anything…

OLGA: Yes, yes, of course. Don't worry.

Pause.

Tomorrow, there won't be one soldier left in the entire town, it will all become a memory, and of course, for us, a new life will begin…

Pause.

Nothing turned out the way we had hoped. I didn't want to be head-mistress, and yet, I became one. And so, Moscow is not meant to be…

VERSHININ: Well…I thank you for everything…Forgive me if it all wasn't as it should have been…I talked a lot, I know — and for that, forgive me, please, remember me kindly.

OLGA: *(Wipes her eyes.)* Masha still hasn't come…

VERSHININ: What else can I say for a farewell? What shall we philosophize about?…*(Laughs.)* Life is hard. For many of us, life is lonely and hopeless, and yet, we know, that all the while, slowly but surely, it grows clearer and brighter, and the time will not be distant when we shall live in radiance and light. *(Looks at his watch.)* It's time, yes, it's time! Once, mankind was submerged in war, his entire existence caught up in campaigns, invasions, conquests, but now all that has died away, leaving in its aftermath a great, enormous emptiness, which has not yet been filled; man desperately searches for something to fill it, and of course he shall find it, he shall. Ah, if only but soon!

Pause.

If only, for example, to industry we might add learning, and to learning, industry. *(Looks at his watch.)* However, I must go…

OLGA: Here she comes.

Enter MASHA.

VERSHININ: I've come to say farewell.

OLGA stands to the side, so as not to interfere with their farewell.

MASHA: *(Looking into his eyes.)* Farewell…

A prolonged kiss.

OLGA: There, there…

MASHA sobs violently.

VERSHININ: Write to me…Don't forget! let me go…it's time…Olga Sergeevna, take her, I must go…It's time…I'm already late…*(Moved, he kisses OLGA's hands, then embraces MASHA once again and hurries out.)*
OLGA: There, there, Masha! Stop, darling.

Enter KULYGIN.

KULYGIN: *(Embarrassed.)* Never mind, let her cry, let her cry…My sweetest Masha, my dearest Masha…You're my wife, and I am happy, come what may…I'll never complain, I'll never reproach you, ever, not once…As Olya is my witness…We'll start our life all over again, just as it was before, and I won't say a word, I won't even hint at it…
MASHA: *(Restraining her sobs.)*
    "In a cove by the sea a green oak stands,
    A golden chain wound round…
    A golden chain wound round…"
    …I'm going out of my mind…
    "In a cove by the sea…a green oak…"
OLGA: Gently, Masha…Gently…Give her some water.
MASHA: I'm not crying any more.
KULYGIN: She's not crying any more . . She's so good…

A lonely gunshot is heard in the distance.

MASHA:"In a cove by the sea a green oak stands,
    A golden chain wound round…
    A green cat…A green oak…"
…I'm raving…*(Drinks some water.)* My life is a failure…what do I need, any more…There, I've calmed down…It doesn't matter…What does "in a cove by the sea" mean? Why does this phrase keep sticking in my head? I'm all mixed up.

Enter IRINA.

OLGA: Gently, Masha. There, there's a good girl. Let's go inside.

MASHA:*(Angrily.)* I'm not going in there. *(Sobs, then suddenly stops.)* I'll never set foot in that house again, I'm not going in…

IRINA: Let's sit here together, quietly. Tomorrow, I'm going away…

Pause.

KULYGIN: Yesterday in the third-year class, I took this from one of the little boys, this moustache and beard…*(Puts on the moustache and beard.)* I look like a German teacher…*(Laughs.)* Don't I? Funny fellows, those boys.

MASHA: Actually, you do look like a German teacher.

OLGA: *(Laughing.)* Yes.

MASHA weeps.

IRINA: There, there, Masha!

KULYGIN: I do, I really do…

Enter NATASHA.

NATASHA: *(Addresses a MAID.)* What? Leave little Sophie with Protopopov, Mikhail Ivanich, and let Andrey Sergeich take Bobik for a walk in the carriage. Children are such a nuisance…*(To IRINA.)* Irina, you're going away tomorrow — what a shame. Stay for just one week more. *(Sees KULYGIN, shrieks; he laughs and removes the moustache and beard.)* What are you doing? You frightened me! *(To IRINA.)* I've gotten used to having you around, do you think saying good-bye will be easy for me? I'm moving Andrey and his violin into your room, — let him saw away in there all he wants! — and we're putting little Sophie into Andrey's room. What an absolutely heavenly child she is! What a little sweetheart! Today she looked up at me with those darling eyes of hers and said — "Mama"!

KULYGIN: A remarkable child, it's true.

NATASHA: That means tomorrow I shall be all alone here. *(Sighs.)* First of all, I'm ordering them to cut down that row of fir trees, and then that maple over there…It's so unattractive in the evening…*(To IRINA.)* Darling, that belt doesn't suit you at all…It's in such bad taste…You do need something a bit brighter. And then I'm ordering them to plant little flowers everywhere, lovely little flowers to perfume the air...*(Severely.)* Why is there a fork lying here on the bench? *(Crossing into the house, to a MAID.)* Why is there a fork lying here on the bench, I ask you? *(Shrieks.)* Be quiet!

KULYGIN: What a temper!

Offstage, the band plays a march; everyone listens.

OLGA: They're leaving.

Enter CHEBUTYKIN.

MASHA: Our men are leaving. Well, what of it...May they travel safely! *(To her husband.)* We must go home...Where are my hat and cape?

KULYGIN: I brought them into the house...I'll go get them, right away. *(Exits into the house.)*

OLGA: Yes, now we can all go home. It's time.

CHEBUTYKIN: Olga Sergeevna!

OLGA: What?

Pause.

What?

CHEBUTYKIN: Nothing...I don't know how to tell you...*(Whispers in her ear.)*

OLGA: *(Horrified.)* It can't be!

CHEBUTYKIN: Yes...That's the story...I'm so tired, I'm exhausted, I don't want to say any more...*(Annoyed.)* Anyway, it doesn't matter!

MASHA: What's happened?

OLGA: *(Embraces IRINA.)* What a terrible day this is...I don't know how to tell you, my darling...

IRINA: What? Tell me quickly: what? For the love of God! *(Weeps.)*

CHEBUTYKIN: The baron has just been killed in a duel...

IRINA: *(Weeps softly.)* I knew it, I knew it...

CHEBUTYKIN: *(Sits on a bench upstage.)* I'm so tired...*(Takes a newspaper out of his pocket.)* Let them weep...*(Sings softly.)* "Ta-ra-ra boom-de-ay...Ta-ra-ra boom-de-ay..." What does it matter!

The three sisters stand, nestled against one another.

MASHA: Oh, how the music plays! They're leaving us, one of them has gone away forever, forever, and we are left alone, to begin our lives anew. We must live…We must live…

IRINA: *(Lays her head on OLGA's breast.)* The time will come, when we shall know what all of this is for, all this suffering, there will be no more mysteries, and till then we must live…we must work, only work! Tomorrow I shall go away alone, I shall teach in a school, I shall dedicate my life to those who need it. It's autumn now, soon winter will come, the snow will fall, and I shall work, I shall work…

OLGA: *(Embraces both sisters.)* The music plays so joyfully, so freely, we want to live! Oh, my God! Time will pass, and we shall disappear forever, they will forget us, forget our faces, our voices, how many of us there were, but all our suffering will turn to joy for those who follow after, and peace and happiness will descend on earth, and they will bless us and remember us with kindness, those of us who live today. Oh darling sisters, our life is not yet over. We shall live! The music plays with ecstasy, with rapture, and so it seems that time will pass and in a little while, we shall know why we live, why we suffer…If only we knew, if only we knew!

The music plays more and more faintly; KULYGIN, cheerful, smiling, carries the hat and cape, ANDREY pushes the baby carriage with Bobik.

CHEBUTYKIN: *(Sings softly.)* "Ta-ra-ra boom-de-ay…Ta-ra-ra boom-de-ay…" *(Reads the newspaper.)* It doesn't matter! It doesn't matter!

OLGA: If only we knew, if only we knew!

CURTAIN

Premiere
January 31, 1901

THE CHERRY ORCHARD

A Comedy in Four Acts

The premiere of this new translation was produced by the Philadelphia Festival Theatre for New Plays, Annenberg Center, opening night, January 22, 1995. Scenic Designer: David P. Gordon; Lighting Designer, Jerold R. Forsyth; Costume Designer: Vickie Esposito; Sound Designer: Conny Lockwood; Properties Designer: David Cottrill; Musical Director: John S. Lionarons; Choreographer: Andrea Paskman; Casting: Hilary Missan, Jennifer Childs; Stage Manager: Susan Merrill; directed by Carol Rocamora.

CAST (in order of appearance)

Lopakhin, Yermolai Alekseevich . . . . , , , William Wise
Dunyasha . . . . Jilline Ringle
Anya . . . . Nicole Marcks
Ranevskaya, Lyubov Andreevna . . . . Marcia Mahon
Varya . . . . Susan Wilder
Gaev, Leonid Andreevich . . . . Doug Wing
Charlotta Ivanovna . . . . Ceal Phelan
Simeonov-Pishchik, Boris Borisovich . . . . Don Auspitz
Yasha . . . . Pearce Bunting
Firs . . . . Fred Shaffmaster
Trofimov, Pyotr Sergeevich . . . . Alessandro Nivola
Yepikhodov, Semyon Panteleevich . . . . Rick Stoppleworth
Passerby/Stationmaster . . . . Antony Giampetro
Post Office Clerk . . . . Adam Petrick
Musicians . . . . John S. Lionarons
Alex Siniavsky
Joe Spinelli

Cast of Characters

RANEVSKAYA, Lyubov Andreevna, a landowner

ANYA, her daughter, aged seventeen

VARYA, her adopted daughter, aged twenty-four

GAEV, Leonid Andreevich, Ranevskaya's brother

LOPAKHIN, Yermolai Alekseevich, a merchant

TROFIMOV, Pyotr Sergeevich, a student

SIMEONOV-PISHCHIK, Boris Borisovich, a landowner

CHARLOTTA IVANOVNA, a governess

YEPIKHODOV, Semyon Panteleevich, a clerk

DUNYASHA, a maid

FIRS, a servant, an old man of eighty-seven

YASHA, a young servant

A PASSERBY

A STATIONMASTER

A POST OFFICE CLERK

Guests, servants

The action takes place on the estate of LYUBOV ANDREEVNA RANEVSKAYA.

The Cherry Orchard

Act One

A room, which is still called the nursery. One of the doors leads to ANYA's room. It is dawn, just before sunrise. It is already May, the cherry trees are all in bloom, but outside it is still cold; there is an early morning frost in the orchard. The windows in the room are closed.

Enter DUNYASHA with a candle, and LOPAKHIN with a book in his hand.

LOPAKHIN: The train's arrived, thank God. What time is it?

DUNYASHA: Almost two. *(Puts out the candle.)* It's already getting light out.

LOPAKHIN: So how late is the train, then? A couple of hours, at least. *(Yawns and stretches.)* Well, I've made a fool of myself, then, haven't I! Hm? Came all the way out here, just to meet the train, and fell fast asleep…Sat here waiting and dozed right off. Annoying, isn't it…You should have woken me up

DUNYASHA: I thought you'd already gone. *(Listens.)* Listen, I think they're here.

LOPAKHIN: *(Listens.)* No…They've got to get their baggage first, you know, that sort of thing…

Pause.

Lyubov Andreevna, she's been living abroad for five years, I don't know, I can't even imagine what's become of her now…She's a fine person, you know…a warm, kind person. I remember, once, when I was a boy, oh, about fifteen years old, say, and my father — he had a shop here in the village then — my father, he hit me in the face with his fist, blood was pouring from my nose…We'd come out into the courtyard together, somehow, and he was drunk. And there was Lyubov Andreevna, I remember her so vividly, so young then, so graceful, so slender, she took me by the hand, brought me over to the washstand, right into this very room, into the nursery.

"Don't cry, little peasant," she said, "it will heal before your wedding day…"

Pause.

Little peasant…Yes, my father was a peasant, it's true enough, and here I am in a three-piece suit and fancy shoes. A silk purse from a sow's ear, or something like that, isn't that how the expression goes…Yes…The only difference is, now I'm rich, I've got a lot of money, but don't look too closely, once a peasant…*(Leafs through the book.)* Look at me, I read through this entire book and didn't understand a word of it. Read it and dozed right off.

Pause.

DUNYASHA: The dogs didn't sleep at all last night, they can sense their masters are coming home.

LOPAKHIN: What's wrong with you, Dunyasha…

DUNYASHA: My hands are trembling. I'm going to faint, I know I am.

LOPAKHIN: You're much too high-strung, Dunyasha. And look at you, all dressed up like a young lady, hair done up, too. You mustn't do that. Remember who you are.

Enter YEPIKHODOV with a bouquet; he is wearing a jacket and highly polished boots, which squeak loudly; upon entering, he drops the bouquet.

YEPIKHODOV: *(Picks up the bouquet.)* Look what the gardener sent. Put them on the dining room table. That's what he said. *(Gives the bouquet to DUNYASHA.)*

LOPAHKIN: And bring me some kvass, will you?

DUNYASHA: Yes, sir. *(Leaves.)*

YEPIKHODOV: We have an early morning frost, we have three degrees below zero, and we have the cherry blossoms all in bloom. I don't approve of our climate. *(Sighs.)* Really, I don't. Our climate doesn't work, it just doesn't work. It's not conducive. And would you like to hear more, Yermolai Alekseich, well, then you will, because the day before yesterday, I bought these boots, and, trust me, they squeak so much, that they are beyond hope. Now how can I oil them? Tell me? How?

LOPAKHIN: Enough. You're getting on my nerves.

YEPIKHODOV: Every day some new disaster befalls me. A new day, a new disaster. But do I grumble, do I complain, no, I don't, I accept it, look, I'm smiling, even.

DUNYASHA enters, gives LOPAKHIN some kvass.

I'm going now. *(Stumbles against a chair, which falls down.)* There…*(As if vindicated.)* You see? I mean, that's the situation, and excuse me for saying so…Remarkable, even…isn't it! *(Exits.)*

DUNYASHA: Yermolai Alekseich, I have something to tell you…Yepikhodov has proposed to me.

LOPAKHIN: Ah!

DUNYASHA: But I don't know, really…He's a nice enough fellow, you know, quiet and all, it's just that whenever he starts to talk, I can't understand a word he's saying. I mean, it all sounds so sweet and sincere, only it just doesn't make any sense. I like him, I mean, I think I like him. And he? He adores me. But he's such an unfortunate fellow, you know, really, every day it's something else. They even have a name for him, do you know what they call him: "Mister Disaster"…

LOPAKHIN: *(Listens.)* I think they're coming…

DUNYASHA: They're coming! What's happening to me…I'm freezing, look, I'm shivering all over.

LOPAKHIN: They're really coming! Let's go meet them. Will she recognize me? We haven't seen each other in five years.

DUNYASHA: *(Agitated.)* I'm going to faint, I know I am…Look, I'm fainting!

Two carriages are heard pulling up to the house. LOPAKHIN and DUN-YASHA exit quickly. The stage is empty. Then there is noise in the adjacent rooms. FIRS hurries across the stage to meet LYUBOV ANDREEVNA; he is leaning on a cane, and is dressed in old-fashioned livery and a high hat; he mutters something to himself, but it is impossible to make out a single word. The offstage noise crescendos. A voice calls out: "Let's go this way, through here…" Enter LYUBOV ANDREEVNA, ANYA, and CHARLOTTA IVANOVNA with a little dog on a leash; they are all dressed in traveling clothes. Enter VARYA, wearing a coat and a shawl, GAEV, SIMEONOV-PISHCHIK, LOPAKHIN, DUN-YASHA carrying a bundle and an umbrella, SERVANTS carrying luggage — they all come through the room.

ANYA: This way! Mama, do you remember what room this is?

LYUBOV ANDREEVNA: *(Ecstatic, in tears.)* The nursery!

VARYA: How cold it is, my hands are numb. *(To LYUBOV ANDREEVNA.)* Look, Mamochka, your rooms, violet and white, just as you left them.

LYUBOV ANDREEVNA: My nursery, my darling nursery, my beautiful room…I slept here, when I was a child… *(Weeps.)* And now, I'm a child again… *(Kisses her brother, VARYA, and her brother again.)* And Varya looks the same as ever, just like a little nun. And Dunyasha I recognize, of course… *(Kisses DUNYASHA.)*

GAEV: The train was two hours late. How do you like that? How's that for efficiency!

CHARLOTTA: *(To PISHCHIK.)* My dog eats walnuts, too.

PISHCHIK: *(Amazed.)* Imagine that!

They all exit, except for ANYA and DUNYASHA.

DUNYASHA: We've been waiting forever… *(Takes ANYA's coat and hat.)*

ANYA: I didn't sleep one moment the whole journey long, four whole nights…and now I'm absolutely frozen!

DUNYASHA: You left during Lent, we had snow then, and frost, and now! My darling! *(Bursts out laughing, kisses her.)* I've waited forever for you, my precious, my joy…And I've got something to tell you, I can't wait one minute longer ….

ANYA: *(Listlessly.)* Now what…

DUNYASHA: Yepikhodov, the clerk, proposed to me just after Easter.

ANYA: Not again… *(Adjusts her hair.)* I've lost all my hairpins… *(She is exhausted; she almost sways on her feet.)*

DUNYASHA: No, really, I don't know what to think any more. He adores me, God, how he adores me!

ANYA: *(Gazes at the door to her room, tenderly.)* My very own room, my windows, it's as if I never left. I'm home! And tomorrow I'll wake up, and I'll run out into the orchard…Oh, if only I could rest! I'm so exhausted — I didn't sleep one moment the whole way, I was so worried.

DUNYASHA: Pyotr Sergeich arrived the day before yesterday.

ANYA: *(Overjoyed.)* Petya!

DUNYASHA: He's out in the bathhouse, asleep, that's where he's staying. "I'm afraid of being in the way," he said. *(Glances at her pocket watch.)* We ought to wake him up, but Varvara Mikhailovna gave us strict orders not to. "Don't you dare wake him up," she said.

Enter VARYA, a bunch of keys hanging from her belt.

VARYA: Dunyasha, go, quickly, bring the coffee…Mamochka wants coffee.

DUNYASHA: Right away. *(Exits.)*

VARYA: So, thank God, you're here. You're home at last! *(Embracing her.)* My darling's home! My angel is home!

ANYA: I've been through so much.

VARYA: I can imagine.

ANYA: I left during Holy Week, it was so cold then, remember? And Charlotta Ivanovna talked the whole way, talked and played card tricks. How could you have stuck me with Charlotta!…

VARYA: You can't travel alone, darling. At seventeen!

ANYA: When we arrived in Paris, it was cold there, too, and snowing. My French is terrible. Mama lived on the fifth floor, and when I finally got there, the flat was filled with all sorts of French people, ladies, an old Catholic priest with a little book, and, oh, it was so uncomfortable there, so stuffy, the room was filled with smoke. And suddenly I felt sorry for Mama, so very sorry, I threw my arms around her neck, I held her so tight, I couldn't let go. And Mama kept clinging to me, and weeping…

VARYA: *(In tears.)* Enough, enough…

ANYA: She had already sold the dacha near Menton, she had nothing left, nothing at all. And neither did I, not a single kopek, we hardly had enough money to get home. And Mama just doesn't understand it, still! There we are, sitting in the station restaurant, and she orders the most expensive thing on the menu, she gives the waiter a ruble tip for tea. Charlotta, too. And Yasha orders a complete dinner, it's simply terrible. Yasha is Mama's butler, you know. We brought him with us…

VARYA: I'm seen him, the devil…

ANYA: So, tell me! Have we paid the interest yet?

VARYA: With what?

ANYA: Dear God, dear God…

VARYA: And in August, the estate will be sold…

ANYA: Dear God…

LOPAKHIN: *(Peeks through the door and makes a 'bleating' sound.)* Ba-a-a…*(Exits.)*

VARYA: *(In tears.)* I'd like to give him such a…*(Makes a threatening gesture with her fist.)*

ANYA: *(Embraces VARYA, softly.)* Varya, has he proposed yet? *(VARYA shakes her head "no.")* But he loves you, he does…Why don't you talk about it, what are you two waiting for?

VARYA: I know nothing will ever come of it, nothing. He's so busy, he has no time for me, really…he pays no attention to me at all. Well, God bless him, but it's too painful for me even to look at him…Everyone talks about our wedding, everyone congratulates us, but the fact is, there's absolutely nothing to it, it's all a dream… *(Changes tone.)* Your brooch looks just like a little bee.

ANYA: *(Sadly.)* Mama bought it. *(She goes to her room, speaking in a gay, child-like voice.)* And in Paris, I went up in a hot air balloon!

VARYA: My darling's home! My angel is home!

DUNYASHA has already returned with the coffee pot and prepares the coffee.

(Stands by the doorway.) All day long, darling, I go about my business, I run the household, I do my chores, but all the time I'm thinking, dreaming. If only we could marry you off to a rich man, then I'd find peace, I'd go to a cloister, and then on a pilgrimage to Kiev, to Moscow, and on and on, from one holy place to the next…on and on. A blessing!

ANYA: The birds are singing in the orchard. What time is it?

VARYA: After two, it must be…Time for you to sleep, darling. *(Goes into ANYA's room.)* Yes, a blessing!

YASHA enters with a rug, and a traveling bag.

YASHA: *(Crosses the stage, discreetly.)* May I?

DUNYASHA: I wouldn't have recognized you, Yasha. How you've changed, since you've been abroad.

YASHA: Hm…And who are you?

DUNYASHA: When you left, I was about 'so' high…*(Indicates.)* Dunyasha, Fyodor Kozoedov's daughter. Don't you remember!

YASHA: Hm…Ripe as a cucumber! *(Glances around, and then grabs her and embraces her; she screams and drops a saucer. YASHA exits quickly.)*

VARYA: *(In the doorway, displeased.)* What's going on here?

DUNYASHA: *(In tears.)* I broke a saucer…

VARYA: That means good luck.

ANYA: *(Coming out of her room.)* We'd better warn Mama: Petya's here…

VARYA: I gave strict orders not to wake him up.

ANYA: *(Deep in thought.)* Father died six years ago, and one month later my little brother Grisha drowned in the river, a lovely little seven-year-old boy. Mama couldn't endure it, she ran away, she ran away without once looking back…*(Shudders.)* How well I understand her, if only she knew!

Pause.

And Petya Trofimov was Grisha's tutor, he might remind her of it all…

Enter FIRS, in a jacket and white waistcoat.

FIRS: *(Goes to the coffee pot, anxiously.)* The mistress will take her coffee here…*(Puts on white gloves.)* Is the coffee ready? *(Sternly, to DUNYASHA.)* You! Where is the cream?

DUNYASHA: Oh, my God…*(Rushes out.)*

FIRS: *(Fusses with the coffee pot.)* Pathetic fool……*(Mutters to himself under his breath.)* They've just returned from Paris…Now in the old days, the master used to go to Paris, too…by horse and carriage…*(Bursts out laughing.)*

VARYA: What is it, Firs?

FIRS: Yes, and what may I do for you? *(Overjoyed.)* My mistress has come home! I've waited for so long! Now I can die…*(Weeps with joy.)*

Enter LYUBOV ANDREEVNA, GAEV, LOPAKHIN, and SIMEONOV-PISHCHIK; SIMEONOV-PISHCHIK wears a lightweight coat, fitted at the waist, and wide trousers. As he walks, GAEV gestures, as if he were playing a game of billiards.

LYUBOV ANDREEVNA: How does it go? Wait — don't tell me, let me think…"Yellow into the corner pocket! Double into the middle!"

GAEV: "Cut shot into the corner!" Once upon a time, sister dearest, we slept in this very room, you and I, and now I'm fifty-one years old, strange, isn't?…

LOPAKHIN: Yes, time flies.

GAEV: Beg pardon?

LOPAKHIN: As I was saying, time flies.

GAEV: It smells of patchouli in here.

ANYA: I'm going to bed. Good night, Mama. *(Kisses her mother.)*

LYUBOV ANDREEVNA: My beloved child. *(Kisses her hands.)* Are you glad you're home? I simply can't get hold of myself.

ANYA: Good night, Uncle.

GAEV: *(Kisses her face, hands.)* God bless you. You are the image of your mother! *(To his sister.)* Lyuba, you looked exactly like this at her age.

ANYA gives her hand to LOPAKHIN and PISHCHIK; she exits, and closes the door behind her.

LYUBOV ANDREEVNA: She's exhausted, really.

PISHCHIK: A tiring journey, no doubt.

VARYA: *(To LOPAKHIN and PISHCHIK.)* So, gentlemen? It's almost three o'clock in the morning, let's not overstay our welcome.

LYUBOV ANDREEVNA: *(Laughs.)* You're the same as ever, Varya. *(Draws her close and kisses her.)* First I'll have my coffee, then we'll all go, yes?

FIRS places a cushion under her feet.

Thank you, dearest. I've gotten so used to coffee. I drink it day and night. Thank you, my darling old man. *(Kisses FIRS.)*

VARYA: I'll go see if they've brought everything in…*(Exits.)*

LYUBOV ANDREEVNA: Am I really sitting here? *(Bursts out laughing.)* I feel like jumping up and down, and waving my arms in the air! *(Covers her face with her hands.)* No, really, I must be dreaming! God knows, I love my country, I love it passionately, I couldn't even see out of the train window, I wept the whole way. *(In tears.)* Never mind, we must have our coffee. Thank you, Firs, thank you, my darling old man. I'm so glad you're still alive.

FIRS: The day before yesterday.

GAEV: He's hard of hearing.

LOPAKHIN: I'd better be going; I leave for Kharkov at five this morning. What a nuisance! I only wanted to see you, that's all, to talk to you a little… You're as lovely as ever…

PISHCHIK: *(Sighs heavily.)* Even lovelier…All dressed up, Parisian style…I'm head-over-heels, as they say!

LOPAKHIN: People like Leonid Andreich here, they say all sorts of things about me, call me a boor, a kulak, but really, it doesn't matter, I couldn't care less. Let them say whatever they like. I only want you to believe in me, as you always did, to look at me with those beautiful, soulful eyes, as you used to, once. Merciful God! My father was a serf, he belonged to your grandfather and then to your father, but it was you, yes, you, who did so much for me once, so much, and I've forgotten everything now, I love you like my own flesh and blood…more, even, than my own flesh and blood.

LYUBOV ANDREEVNA: I can't sit still, I'm in such a state…*(Jumps up and walks around the room, agitated.)* I simply can't bear all this joy…Go ahead, laugh at me, I'm being foolish, I know it…My dear little bookcase…*(Kisses the bookcase.)* My own little table.

GAEV: Nanny died while you were gone.

LYUBOV ANDREEVNA: *(Sits and drinks coffee.)* Yes, God rest her soul. They wrote me.

GAEV: Anastasy died, too. And cross-eyed Petrushka — you remember him — he ran away, he lives in town now, at the district superintendent's. *(Takes a box of fruit drops out of his pocket, pops one into his mouth.)*

PISHCHIK: My daughter, Dashenka...she sends her regards...

LOPAKHIN: I'd like to tell you some good news, if I may, some cheerful news, all right? *(Looks at his watch.)* I've got to go, there's no time to talk...so, very briefly, then. As you already know, your cherry orchard is being sold to pay off the debts, the auction date has been set for the twenty-second of August, but don't you worry, my dear, you don't have to lose any sleep over this, rest assured, there is a way out...Here's my plan. Your attention, please! Your estate is located only thirteen miles from town, roughly, a railroad runs nearby, so if the cherry orchard and the land along the river are divided up into plots and then leased for summer homes, why then you'll receive at least 25,000 in yearly income.

GAEV: Forgive me, but what nonsense!

LYUBOV ANDREEVNA: I don't quite understand you, Yermolai Alekseich.

LOPAKHIN: You'll receive at least twenty-five rubles a year per three acre plot from the summer tenants, and if you advertise right away, I'll guarantee you, by autumn, there won't be a single plot left, they'll all be bought up. In a word, congratulations, you're saved. The site is marvelous, the river is deep. Only, of course, you'll have to clear it out, get rid of some things...for example, let us say, tear down all the old buildings, and this house, too, which isn't much good for anything any more, cut down the old cherry orchard...

LYUBOV ANDREEVNA: Cut it down? Forgive me, my darling, but you have no idea what you're talking about. If there is one thing in the entire province that's of interest, that's remarkable, even, why it's our own cherry orchard.

LOPAHKIN: The only thing remarkable about this orchard is that it's so big. There's a cherry crop once every two years, and yes, there are a lot of them, but what good are they, nobody buys them.

GAEV: There is a reference to this cherry orchard in the Encyclopaedia.

LOPAKHIN: *(Looks at his watch.)* Unless we come up with a plan, unless we reach a decision, then on the twenty-second of August the cherry orchard and the entire estate will be auctioned off. Make up your minds, will you, please! There is no other way, I swear to you. None. Absolutely none.

FIRS: Once upon a time, forty – fifty years ago, they used to dry the cherries, soak them, marinate them, preserve them, and often...

GAEV: Hush, Firs.

FIRS: And often, they would send cart loads of dried cherries to Moscow and

Kharkov. Brought in heaps of money! And those dried cherries, oh, how soft they were, soft, sweet, plump, juicy, fragrant…They knew the recipe in those days…

LYUBOV ANDREEVNA: Yes, where is that recipe now?

FIRS: Forgotten. No one remembers it any more.

PISHCHIK: *(To LYUBOV ANDREEVNA.)* Tell us! What is it like in Paris? Did you eat frogs' legs?

LYUBOV ANDREEVNA: I ate crocodile.

PISHCHIK: Imagine that…

LOPAKHIN: Up until now, we've only had landowners and peasants living in our countryside, but now, the summer people are starting to appear among us. All the towns, even the smallest ones, are surrounded by summer homes now. And, it's possible to predict that, in twenty years or so, the summer population will multiply beyond our wildest dreams. Now they're just sitting out on their balconies, drinking their tea, but just wait, soon it will come to pass, you'll see, they'll start cultivating their little plots of land, and your cherry orchard will bloom again with wealth, prosperity, happiness…

GAEV: *(Indignant.)* What nonsense!

Enter VARYA and YASHA.

VARYA: Two telegrams came for you, Mamochka. *(Takes keys and unlocks the antique bookcase; the keys make a clinking sound.)* Here they are.

LYUBOV ANDREEVNA: From Paris. *(Rips them up, without reading them.)* I'm through with Paris.

GAEV: And do you know, Lyuba, how old this bookcase is? Only one week ago, I pull out the bottom drawer, I look, and what do I see — a mark burned into it, a number. This bookcase was built exactly one hundred years ago. How do you like that? Eh? We may now celebrate the jubilee anniversary of this bookcase, ladies and gentlemen. Yes, it's an inanimate object, of course, but nevertheless, it is still a *book* case.

PISHCHIK: *(Amazed.)* One hundred years old. Imagine that!…

GAEV: Yes…a work of art…*(Touching the bookcase.)* O venerable bookcase! I salute thy existence. For over a century, thou hast sought the pure ideals of truth and justice; thy silent exhortation for fruitful labor has not yet faltered these one hundred years, inspiring courage and hope for the brightest future *(in tears)* in generation after generation of our kin, and fostering in us the noble ideals of charity and good.

Pause.

LOPAKHIN: Yes...

LYUBOV ANDREEVNA: You haven't changed a bit, Lyonya.

GAEV: *(A bit embarrassed.)* "Off the ball...right-hand corner! Cut shot into the middle."

LOPAKHIN: *(Glances at his watch.)* Time for me to go.

YASHA: *(Gives LYUBOV ANDREEVNA medicine.)* Perhaps you'll take your pills now...

PISHCHIK: Why bother taking medicine, lovely lady...doesn't do any harm, doesn't do any good either...Do let me have them...dearest lady. *(Takes the pills, pours them into the palm of his hand, blows on them, puts them in his mouth, and washes them down with kvass.)* There!

LYUBOV ANDREEVNA: *(Frightened.)* You've gone mad!

PISHCHIK: Took them all.

LOPAKHIN: There's an appetite.

Everyone laughs.

FIRS: When he was here during Holy Week, he ate half a bucket of cucumbers...*(Mutters to himself.)*

LYUBOV ANDREEVNA: What is he saying?

VARYA: He's been muttering like that for three years now. We're used to it.

YASHA: Old age.

Enter CHARLOTTA IVANOVNA wearing a white dress; she is very thin and tightly laced, with a lorgnette on her belt; she crosses the stage.

LOPAKHIN: Forgive me, Charlotta Ivanovna, I didn't have the chance to greet you. *(Goes to kiss her hand.)*

CHARLOTTA IVANOVNA: *(Takes her hand away.)* If I let you kiss my hand, next you'll want to kiss my elbow, then my shoulder...

LOPAKHIN: Not my lucky day.

Everyone laughs.

So, Charlotta Ivanovna, show us a trick!

LYUBOV ANDREEVNA: Yes, Charlotta, show us a trick!

CHARLOTTA: I don't want to. I wish to sleep. *(Exits.)*

LOPAKHIN: We'll see each other again in three weeks. *(Kisses LYUBOV*

ANDREEVNA's hand.) Farewell for now. Time to go. *(To GAEV.)* A very good-bye to you. *(Kisses PISHCHIK.)* And to you. *(Shakes hands with VARYA, then with FIRS and YASHA.)* I don't feel like going. *(To LYUBOV ANDREEVNA.)* If you make up your mind about the summer homes, if you decide to proceed, just let me know, I'll lend you 50,000. Think about it, seriously.

VARYA: *(Angrily.)* So go, then!

LOPAKHIN: I'm going, I'm going…. *(Exits.)*

GAEV: What a boor. Oh, wait, "pardon"…Our Varya's going to marry him. That's our Varya's fiancé.

VARYA: Don't talk so much, Uncle.

LYUBOV ANDREEVNA: Why not, Varya, I'd be so pleased. He's a good man.

PISHCHIK: And a most worthy man, as they say, truth be told…Now my Dashenka…she also says, that…well, she says a variety of things. *(Snores, then suddenly awakes with a start.)* Nevertheless, dearest lady, oblige me, would you, please…lend me two hundred and forty rubles…tomorrow I must pay off the interest on my mortgage.

VARYA: *(Startled.)* We have no money! None!

LYUBOV ANDREEVNA: As a matter of fact, I don't, I have nothing, really.

PISHCHIK: Some will turn up, you'll see! *(Bursts out laughing.)* I never lose hope. There, I say to myself, all is lost, all is ruined, and then suddenly, what do you know — they build a railroad right through my land, and…they pay me for it! So just wait and see, something will happen, if not today, then tomorrow. My Dashenka is going to win 200,000…she has a lottery ticket.

LYUBOV ANDREEVNA: The coffee's finished, now we can go to bed.

FIRS: *(Brushes GAEV's clothes, scolding him.)* And you've gone and put on the wrong trousers again. What I am going to do with you?

VARYA: *(Softly.)* Anya's sleeping. *(Quietly opens the window.)* The sun is up now, it isn't cold any more. Look, Mamochka: what glorious trees! My God, the air! And the starlings are singing!

GAEV: *(Opens another window.)* The orchard is all in white. You haven't forgotten, Lyuba, have you? Look — that long row of trees stretching on and on, like a silver cord, on and on, do you remember, how it gleams on moonlit nights? You haven't forgotten, have you?

LYUBOV ANDREEVNA: *(Looks out the window onto the orchard.)* O, my childhood, my innocence! Once I slept in this very nursery, I'd look out on the orchard, right from here, and happiness would awaken with me, every morning, every morning, and look, it's all the same, nothing has changed. *(Laughs with joy.)* White, all white! O, my orchard! After the dark, dreary autumn, the cold winter, you're young again, blooming with joy, the heavenly angels have not forsaken you...If only this terrible weight could be lifted from my soul, if only I could forget my past!

GAEV: Yes, and the orchard will be sold to pay off our debts, strange, isn't it...

LYUBOV ANDREEVNA: Look, there's my mother, walking through the orchard...all in white! *(Laughs with joy.)* There she is.

GAEV: Where?

VARYA: God bless you, Mamochka.

LYUBOV ANDREEVNA: There's no one there, I only dreamed it...Look, to the right, on the way to the summer-house, a white sapling, bowing low, I thought it was a woman...

TROFIMOV enters, wearing a shabby, threadbare student's uniform, and spectacles.

What an astonishing orchard! Masses of white blossoms, radiant blue sky...

TROFIMOV: Lyubov Andreevna!

She turns and looks at him.

I only came to pay my respects, I'll go, right away. *(Kisses her hand passionately.)* They told me I had to wait till morning, but I couldn't bear it any longer...

LYUBOV ANDREEVNA looks at him with bewilderment.

VARYA: *(In tears.)* It's Petya Trofimov...

TROFIMOV: Petya Trofimov, former tutor to your Grisha...Have I really changed that much?

LYUBOV ANDREEVNA embraces him and weeps softly.

GAEV: *(Embarrassed.)* Now, now, Lyuba.

VARYA: *(Weeps.)* You see, Petya, didn't I tell you to wait till tomorrow.

LYUBOV ANDREEVNA: My Grisha...my little boy...Grisha...son...

VARYA: But what can we do, Mamochka. It's God's will.

TROFIMOV: *(Gently, in tears.)* There, there...

LYUBOV ANDREEVNA: *(Weeps softly.)* My little boy...lost...drowned...Why? Why, my friend? *(Softer.)* Anya's sleeping, and here I am, raising my voice... carrying on...So, now, Petya, tell me! Why have you grown so ugly? And so old, too!

TROFIMOV: There was an old peasant woman on the train once, she called me "a shabby-looking gentleman."

LYUBOV ANDREEVNA: You were just a boy then, a sweet, young student, and now look at you, you're hair's gotten thin, you wear glasses…Don't tell me you're still a student? *(Goes to the door.)*

TROFIMOV: And I shall be an eternal student, so it seems.

LYUBOV ANDREEVNA: *(Kisses her brother, then VARYA.)* Better go to bed now…You've gotten old, too, Leonid.

PISHCHIK: *(Follows her.)* Yes, time for bed…Ach, this gout of mine…I'll stay the night with you…Lyubov Andreevna, lovely lady, tomorrow morning, if only you would…two hundred and forty rubles…

GAEV: He never gives up.

PISHCHIK: Two hundred and forty rubles…to pay the interest on the mortgage.

LYUBOV ANDREEVNA: But I don't have any money, really, my sweet, I don't.

PISHCHIK: I'll pay you back, charming lady…Such a small amount…

LYUBOV ANDREEVNA: Oh, all right, Leonid will give it to you…Give it to him, Leonid.

GAEV: I should give it to him? Don't hold your pockets open.

LYUBOV ANDREEVNA: Give it to him, what else can we do…He needs it…He'll pay it back.

Exeunt LYUBOV ANDREEVNA, TROFIMOV, PISHCHIK, and FIRS. GAEV, VARYA, and YASHA remain.

GAEV: My sister just can't seem to hold on to her money. *(To YASHA.)* Move away, good fellow, you smell like a chicken coop.

YASHA: *(With a grin.)* And you, Leonid Andreich, you haven't changed a bit.

GAEV: Beg pardon? *(To VARYA.)* What did he say?

VARYA: *(To YASHA.)* Your mother's come from the village to see you, she's been waiting since yesterday in the servants' quarters…

YASHA: Good for her!

VARYA: Shame on you!

YASHA: Who needs her? She could have waited till tomorrow to come. *(Exits.)*

VARYA: Mamochka's the same as she's always been, she hasn't changed at all. If she could, she'd give away everything.

GAEV: Yes…

Pause.

If there are many remedies offered for a disease, then that means the disease is incurable. Now, I've been thinking, wracking my brain, and I've got lots of remedies, oh yes, lots and lots of remedies, and you know what that means, don't you, in essence, that means I don't have any. Wouldn't it be nice, for example, if we received a large inheritance from somebody or other, wouldn't it be nice to marry our Anya off to a very rich fellow, wouldn't it be nice to go to Yaroslavl and try and get some money from our aunt, the countess. Our aunty's very very rich, you know.

VARYA: *(Weeps.)* If only God would help us.

GAEV: Stop weeping. The old lady's very rich, it's true, but the fact is, she doesn't like us. For one thing, my dear sister went off and married a lawyer, and not a gentleman...

ANYA appears in the doorway.

She didn't marry a gentleman, and you can't really say she's led a particularly conventional life. I mean, she's a good, kind person, a splendid person, and I love her very very much, of course, but, whatever the extenuating circumstances may have been, let's face it, she hasn't exactly been the model of virtue. Why, you can sense it in everything about her, her slightest gesture, her movements.

VARYA: *(In a whisper.)* Anya's standing in the doorway.

GAEV: Beg pardon?

Pause.

Amazing, there's something in my right eye...I can't see a thing. And on Thursday, when I was at the circuit court...

ANYA enters.

VARYA: Why aren't you in bed, Anya?

ANYA: I can't fall asleep. I just can't.

GAEV: My little one. *(Kisses ANYA's face, hands.)* My child...*(In tears.)* You're not my niece, you're my angel, you're everything to me. Believe me, believe me...

ANYA: I believe you, Uncle, I do. Everyone loves you, everyone reveres you...but, darling Uncle, you must try to be quiet, really, just be quiet. What were you saying just now about my Mama, about your own sister? Why would you say such a thing?

GAEV: Yes, yes...*(Covers his face with her hand.)* As a matter of fact, it's terrible! My God! My God, save me! And today, I made a speech before a bookcase...

how foolish of me! And it was only after I'd finished, that I realized how foolish it was.

VARYA: It's true, Uncle dear, you should try to be quiet. Just be very quiet, that's all.

ANYA: And if you're quiet, you'll feel much better, really.

GAEV: I'll be quiet. *(Kisses ANYA's and VARYA's hands.)* I'll be quiet. Just one small matter. On Thursday I was at the circuit court, and, well, some people got together and started talking, you know, about this, that, the other thing, and so on and so on, and one thing led to another, and so it seems that a loan might be arranged, to pay off the interest to the bank.

VARYA: God willing!

GAEV: And, on Tuesday, I'm going to have another little talk with them again. *(To VARYA.)* Stop weeping. *(To ANYA.)* Your mama will have a word with Lopakhin; he won't refuse her, of course…As for you, as soon as you've had your rest, off you'll go to Yaroslavl to see the countess, your great-aunt. So that way, we'll mount a three-pronged attack — and presto! it's in the bag. We'll pay off that interest, I'm sure of it…*(Pops a fruit drop into his mouth.)* On my honor, I swear to you, if you like, this estate will not be sold! *(Excited.)* I swear on my happiness! I give you my hand, call me a worthless good-for-nothing, a dishonorable fellow, if I allow it to go up for auction! I swear on my entire being!

ANYA: *(She regains her composure; she is happy.)* How good you are, Uncle, how wise! *(Embraces her uncle.)* Now I'm content! I'm content! I'm happy, now!

Enter FIRS.

FIRS: *(Reproachfully.)* Leonid Andreich, have you no fear of God in you? When are you going to bed?

GAEV: In a minute, in a minute. Go on, Firs. Yes, it's all right, I'm quite capable of undressing myself. So, children dear, night-night…Details tomorrow, but now, it's time for bed. *(Kisses ANYA and VARYA.)* I am a man of the eighties…These are not laudable times, but nevertheless, I can say that I've suffered greatly for my convictions in this life. It's not without reason that the peasants love me. One must give the peasant his due! Give him his due, for…

ANYA: You're off again, Uncle!

VARYA: Uncle, be quiet!

FIRS: *(Angrily.)* Leonid Andreich!

GAEV: I'm coming, I'm coming…And so, to bed. "Off two cushions into the middle. Pocket the white…clean shot." *(Exits, with FIRS shuffling behind him.)*

ANYA: Now, I'm content. I don't want to go to Yaroslavl, not really, I don't like my great-aunt that much, but, all the same, I'm content. Thanks to Uncle. *(Sits.)*

VARYA: We must get to bed. I know I'm going to…Oh, an awful thing happened here while you were gone. You remember the old servants' quarters, well, only the old ones live there now: you know, Yefimyushka, Polya, Yevstigney, oh, and don't forget Karp…Anyway, they started letting some homeless folks stay the night with them — I didn't say anything at first. But then, I hear, they're spreading this rumor, that I'd been giving orders to feed them nothing but dried peas. Because I was being stingy, you see…And all this coming from Yevstigney…So I say to myself, fine. If that's the way you want it, I say, just you wait and see. So I call for Yevstigney…*(Yawns.)* And he comes in. And I say to him, how dare you, Yevstigney…you're such a fool. *(Looks at ANYA.)* Anyechka!

Pause.

She's asleep! *(Takes ANYA by the arm.)* Come to bed…Come !…*(Leads her.)* My darling's sleeping! Come…

They go.

Far beyond the orchard, a shepherd plays on a pipe. TROFIMOV enters, crosses the stage, and, seeing VARYA and ANYA, stops.

VARYA: Shh…She's asleep…fast asleep…Come, my precious.
ANYA: *(Softly, half-asleep.)* I'm so tired…do you hear the bells…Dearest Uncle… Mama and Uncle…
VARYA: Come, my precious, come…*(Exits into ANYA's room.)*
TROFIMOV: *(Tenderly.)* My sunlight! My springtime!

CURTAIN

ACT TWO

A field. There is a small, dilapidated old chapel, long deserted, and beside it, a well, an old bench, and several large stones, once apparently gravestones. The road to GAEV's country estate is visible. To the side, towering poplar trees loom darkly, where the cherry orchard begins. In the distance, there is a row of tele-graph poles, and far beyond that, on the horizon, is the indistinct outline of a large town, visible only in very clear, fine weather. Soon, it will be sunset. CHARLOTTA, YASHA, and DUNYASHA sit on the bench; YEPIKHODOV stands nearby and plays the guitar; all are lost in thought. CHARLOTTA is wearing an old, peaked military cap; she removes the rifle from her shoulder and adjusts the buckle on the rifle sling.

CHARLOTTA: *(Deep in thought.)* I have no passport, no real one…no one ever told me how old I was, not really…but I always have this feeling that I'm still very young. When I was a little girl, Papa and Mama traveled in a circus, they were acrobats, good ones. And I performed the "salto-mortale," the dive of death, and all kinds of tricks. And when Papa and Mama died, a German lady took me in, she raised me, gave me lessons. "Gut." I grew up, I became a governess. But where I am from, and who I am — I don't know…Who were my parents, were they ever married…I don't know. *(Takes a cucumber out of her pocket and eats it.)* I don't know anything.

Pause.

So now I feel like talking, but to whom…I have no one to talk to.

YEPIKHODOV: *(Plays guitar and sings.)* "What care I for wordly woe, /What care I for friend and foe…" How pleasant it is to play upon the mandolin!

DUNYASHA: That's a guitar, not a mandolin. *(Looks in a little mirror and powders her nose.)*

YEPIKHODOV: For the man, who is mad with love, it's a mandolin.*(Sings.)* "If my true love were requited, /It would set my heart aglow…"

YASHA joins in, harmonizing.

CHARLOTTA: These people sing terribly…Phooey! Like jackals.

DUNYASHA: *(To YASHA.)* How blissful, to have been abroad.

YASHA: Well, of course. I'm not going to disagree with you on that one. *(Yawns, then lights a cigar.)*

232 • ANTON CHEKHOV

YEPIKHODOV: But we know that already. Everything abroad is very well organized, and has been so for a long long time.

YASHA: Right.

YEPIKHODOV: I am a man of the world. I am. I read many many remarkable books. But, speaking for myself, personally, I have no clue, no clue as to what direction I, personally, want my life to take, I mean: Do I want to live, or do I want to shoot myself, in the head…So just in case, I always carry a revolver around with me. Here it is…*(Shows them a revolver.)*

CHARLOTTA: I'm finished. And now, I'm leaving. *(Puts on the rifle.)* You, Yepikhodov, you are a very intelligent man and also a very dangerous one; women must be mad for you. Brrr! *(Starts to leave.)* These clever people, they're all such fools, no one for me to talk to…Alone, all alone, I have no one…and who I am, why I am on this earth, no one knows *(Exit, without hurrying.)*

YEPIKHODOV: Now. Speaking for myself, personally, again, putting all else aside, that is, if I may, when it comes to me, I mean, personally, again, I ask myself: Does fate care? No, fate doesn't care, very much as a terrible storm doesn't care about a tiny boat upon the sea. Now. Let us assume I am wrong in this regard, so then, tell me, would you, please, why is it that this morning, yes, this morning, I wake up, just to give you an example, I look up, and there, sitting right on my chest, is this huge and terrifying spider…About 'so' big. *(Indicates with both hands.)* And then, to give you yet another example, I go to pick up a glass of kvass, you know, to drink it, I look inside it, and what do I see? Possibly the most offensive species on the face of this earth — like a cockroach.

Pause.

Have you ever read Buckle?

Pause.

May I trouble you, Avdotya Fyodorovna, for a word or two.

DUNYASHA: Speak.

YEPIKHODOV: It would be far more desirable to speak to you in private…*(Sighs.)*

DUNYASHA: *(Embarrassed.)* Oh, all right…only first, bring me my cloak…I left it near the cupboard…it's a bit chilly out…

YEPIKHODOV: Of course…Right away…Of course. Now I know what to do with my revolver…*(Takes the guitar and exits, strumming.)*
YASHA: Mister Disaster! He's hopeless, just between you and me. *(Yawns.)*
DUNYASHA: God forbid he should shoot himself.

Pause.

I'm so nervous, I worry all the time. I was just a girl when they took me in, you know, I'm not used to the simple life any more, look at my hands, how lily-white they are, like a young lady's. Can't you see, I've become so delicate, so fragile, so…so sensitive, every little thing upsets me…It's just awful. And if you deceive me, Yasha, I just don't know what will happen to my nerves.
YASHA: *(Kisses her.)* My little cucumber! Of course, a girl should know how to behave, I can't stand a girl who doesn't know how to behave.
DUNYASHA: I've fallen madly in love with you, you are so refined, you can talk about anything.

Pause.

YASHA: *(Yawns.)* Right!…Now, in my opinion, if a girl falls in love, that means she's immoral.

Pause.

Nice, isn't it, to smoke a cigar in the fresh, open air…*(Listens.)* Someone's coming…It's the ladies and gentlemen…

DUNYASHA embraces him impetuously.

Go home, pretend you've gone for a swim in the river, take that path there, or else they'll run into you and think I arranged this little rendezvous. I can't have that.
DUNYASHA: *(Coughs quietly.)* I've got a headache from all this cigar smoke… *(Exits.)*

YASHA remains; he sits by the chapel. Enter LYUBOV ANDREEVNA, GAEV, and LOPAKHIN.

LOPAKHIN: You must decide, once and for all — time waits for no one. The question's quite simple, you know. Will you or won't you agree to lease your land for conversion into summer homes? Answer in one word: yes or no? One word, that's all!

LYUBOV ANDREEVNA: Who has been smoking those disgusting cigars here... *(Sits.)*

GAEV: Since they've built the railroad, it's all become so convenient. *(Sits down.)* We took a little ride into town, we had our lunch..."yellow into the middle pocket!" Now, if only I'd gone home first, and played one little game...

LYUBOV ANDREEVNA: You'll have plenty of time.

LOPAHKIN: One word, that's all! *(Entreating.)* Give me your answer!

GAEV: *(Yawns.)* Beg pardon?

LYUBOV ANDREEVNA: *(Looks in her purse.)* Yesterday I had so much money, and today I have hardly any at all. My poor, thrifty Varya feeds everyone milk soup, the old folks in the kitchen get nothing but dried peas to eat, and I manage to let money slip right through my fingers. *(Drops her purse, gold coins scatter.)* There, you see, now I've gone and spilled it... *(She is annoyed.)*

YASHA: I'll get them, allow me. *(Collects the coins.)*

LYUBOV ANDREEVNA: Please do, Yasha. And why on earth did I go out to lunch...That ridiculous restaurant of yours with the music, and the table-cloths that smell of soap...And why drink so much, Lyonya? Why eat so much? Why talk so much? Today in the restaurant you went on and on again, on and on...About the seventies, about the decadents. And to whom? Talking to the waiters about the decadents!

LOPAKHIN: Yes.

GAEV: *(Waves his hand.)* I'm incorrigible, it's obvious... *(Irritably, to YASHA.)* What is it with you, you're always disturbing my line of vision...

YASHA: *(Laughs.)* I can't hear the sound of your voice without laughing.

GAEV: *(To his sister.)* It's either him or me...

LYUBOV ANDREEVNA: Go away, Yasha, go on...

YASHA: *(Gives LYUBOV ANDREEVNA her purse.)* Right away. *(Barely contains his laughter.)* At once... *(Exits.)*

LOPAKHIN: Your estate is going to be bought by that millionaire, Deriganov. He's coming to the auction himself, they say, in person.

LYUBOV ANDREEVNA: And where did you hear that?

LOPAKHIN: They were talking about it in town.

GAEV: Our aunty from Yaroslavl promised to send us something, but when and how much she will send, who knows…

LOPAKHIN: How much is she sending? One hundred thousand? Two hundred thousand?

LYUBOV ANDREEVNA: Oh, well,…ten – fifteen thousand, at most, and that much we can be thankful for…

LOPAKHIN: Forgive me, but such frivolous people as you, my friends, such strange, impractical people, I have never before met in my entire life. I'm speaking to you in the Russian language, I'm telling you that your estate is about to be sold, and you simply don't understand.

LYUBOV ANDREEVNA: But what on earth are we to do? Tell us, what?

LOPAKHIN: Every day I've been telling you. Every day I've been repeating the same thing, over and over again. The cherry orchard and the land must be leased for summer homes, it must be done immediately, as soon as possible — the auction is imminent! Do you understand! As soon as you decide, once and for all, about the summer homes, you'll have as much money as you'll ever want, and then you will be saved.

LYUBOV ANDREEVNA: Summer homes, summer people — forgive me, please, it all sounds so vulgar.

GAEV: I agree with you, absolutely.

LOPAKHIN: Either I'm going to burst out sobbing, or screaming, or else I'm going to fall on the ground, right here in front of you. I can't stand it any more! You're driving me mad! *(To GAEV.)* And you, you act like an old woman!

GAEV: Beg pardon?

LOPAKHIN: An old woman! *(Wants to leave.)*

LYUBOV ANDREEVNA: *(Frightened.)* No, don't go, please, stay, dearest. I beg of you. Who knows, perhaps we'll think of something!

LOPAKHIN: What's there to think of!

LYUBOV ANDREEVNA: Don't go, I beg of you. It's so much more cheerful when you're here…

Pause.

I keep waiting for something to happen, as if the house were going to tumble down on top of us.

GAEV: *(Deep in thought.)* "Double into the corner pocket…Croisé into the middle…"

LYUBOV ANDREEVNA: How we have sinned…

LOPAKHIN: What are you talking about, what sins...

GAEV: *(Pops a fruit drop in his mouth.)* They say I've squandered a entire fortune on fruit drops...*(Laughs.)*

LYUBOV ANDREEVNA: O my sins, my sins...I've always thrown money around, uncontrollably, like a madwoman, and I married a man, who did nothing but keep us in debt. My husband died from too much champagne — he drank himself to death, — then, for my next misfortune, I fell in love with another man, I began living with him...and just at that time, there came my first great punishment, and what a blow it dealt me — right here in this river...my little boy drowned, and so I fled, abroad, I simply fled, never to return, never to see this river again...I closed my eyes and I ran, not knowing where I was going, what I was doing, and *he* following after...ruthlessly, relentlessly. I bought a dacha near Menton, *he* had fallen ill there, and for three years I knew no rest, neither day nor night; his illness exhausted me, wasted me, my soul withered away. And then last year, when the dacha was sold to pay off the debts, I fled again, to Paris, and there he robbed me, he left me for another woman, I tried to poison myself...How stupid, how shameful...And suddenly I felt drawn again to Russia, to my homeland, to my daughter...*(Wipes away her tears.)* Dear God, dear God, be merciful, forgive me my sins! Don't punish me any longer! *(Pulls a telegram from her pocket.)* Today, I received this from Paris...He begs my forgiveness, beseeches me to return...*(Rips up the telegram.)* There's music playing, somewhere. *(Listens.)*

GAEV: It's our celebrated Jewish orchestra. Don't you remember, four violins, flute, and contrabass.

LYUBOV ANDREEVNA: Does it still exist? We ought to invite them sometime, plan a little soirée.

LOPAKHIN: *(Listens.)* I don't hear anything. *(Hums softly.)*

"An enterprising man, the Prussian,
He'll make a Frenchman from a Russian!"

(Laughs.) What a play I saw at the theatre last night, it was very funny, really.

LYUBOV ANDREEVNA: There probably wasn't anything funny about it. Why go to the theatre to see a play! Better to see yourselves more often. How grey your lives are, how endlessly you talk.

LOPAKHIN: It's the truth. And the truth must be told, our lives are foolish...

Pause.

My papa was a peasant, an ignorant fool, he understood nothing, taught me nothing, he only beat me when he was drunk, and always with a stick. And the fact of the matter is, I'm the same kind of ignorant fool that he was. I never learned anything, I'm ashamed of my own handwriting, it's not even human, it's more like a hoof-mark than a signature.

LYUBOV ANDREEVNA: You ought to get married, my friend.

LOPAKHIN: Yes…It's the truth.

LYUBOV ANDREEVNA: Why not to our Varya? She's a good girl.

LOPAKHIN: Yes.

LYUBOV ANDREEVNA: She's of simple origin, she works all day long, but the important thing is, she loves you. And you've been fond of her for a long time now.

LOPAKHIN: Well…I have nothing against it…She's a good girl.

Pause.

GAEV: They've offered me a job at the bank. 6,000 a year…Have you heard?

LYUBOV ANDREEVNA: You, in a bank! Stay where you are…

FIRS enters; he is carrying a coat.

FIRS: *(To GAEV.)* Please, sir, better put this on…it's chilly out.

GAEV: *(Puts on the coat.)* You get on my nerves, old man.

FIRS: Now, there's no need for that…You went out this morning, without telling anyone. *(Looks him over.)*

LYUBOV ANDREEVNA: How old you've grown, Firs!

FIRS: Yes, what may I do for you?

LOPAKHIN: She said: How old you've grown!

FIRS: Well, I've lived a long time. They were marrying me off, and your papa wasn't even in this world yet…*(Laughs.)* Then, when the emancipation came, I was already head valet…I didn't want my freedom, so I stayed with my masters…

Pause.

I remember how glad everyone was, but what they were glad about, they didn't even know themselves.

LOPAKHIN: Ah yes, the good old days. At least there was flogging.

FIRS: *(Not hearing.)* I'll say. The servants belonged to the masters, the masters belonged to the servants, but now everything's all mixed up, you can't tell one from the other.

GAEV: Hush, Firs. Tomorrow I've got to go to town. They've promised to introduce me to some general, he might give us a loan on a promissory note.

LOPAKHIN: Nothing will come of it. And you won't pay off the interest, rest assured.

LYUBOV ANDREEVNA: He's delirious. There are no generals, they don't exist.

Enter TROFIMOV, ANYA, and VARYA.

GAEV: Ah, here they come.

ANYA: Here's Mama.

LYUBOV ANDREEVNA: *(Tenderly.)* Come, come...My darling children... *(Embraces ANYA and VARYA.)* If only you knew how much I love you both. Sit here, right next to me.

They all get settled.

LOPAKHIN: Our eternal student is always in the company of the young ladies.

TROFIMOV: Mind your own business.

LOPAKHIN: And when he's fifty, he'll still be a student.

TROFIMOV: Stop your foolish joking.

LOPAKHIN: You're such a peculiar fellow! Why are you so angry with me, anyway?

TROFIMOV: Because you won't stop bothering me.

LOPAKHIN: *(Laughs.)* Permit me to ask you, if I may, what do you think of me?

TROFIMOV: Here is what I think of you, Yermolai Alekseich: You are a rich man, soon you'll be a millionaire. So, in the general scheme of things, that is, according to the laws of nature, we need you, we need predatory beasts, who devour everything which stands in their path, so in that sense you are a necessary evil.

All laugh.

VARYA: Petya, you do better when you talk about astronomy.

LYUBOV ANDREEVNA: No, let's continue yesterday's conversation.

TROFIMOV: What about?

GAEV: About pride. Pride in man.

TROFIMOV: That. We talked about that forever, but we did not come to any conclusion. According to your way of thinking, there is something mystical about the proud man, an aura, almost. Perhaps you are correct in your beliefs, but if you analyze the issue clearly, without complicating things, then why does this pride even exist, what reason can there be for pride, if a man is not physically distinguished, if the vast majority of mankind is coarse, stupid, or profoundly miserable. There is no time for the admiration of self. There is only time for work.

GAEV: We're all going to die, anyway, so what difference does it make?

TROFIMOV: Who knows? And what does it really mean — to die? For all we know, man is endowed with a hundred sensibilities, and when he dies, only the five known to us perish along with him, while the other ninety-five remain alive.

LYUBOV ANDREEVNA: How intelligent you are, Petya!...

LOPAKHIN: *(Ironically.)* Yes, terribly!

TROFIMOV: Mankind marches onward, ever onward, strengthening his skills, his capacities. All that has up until now been beyond his reach may one day be attainable, only he must work, indeed, he must do everything in his power to help those who seek the truth. In Russia, however, very few people actually do work. The vast majority of the intelligentsia, as I know them, do nothing, pursue nothing, and, meanwhile, have no predisposition whatsoever to work, they're completely incapable of it. They call themselves 'the intelligentsia,' and yet they address their servants with disrespect, they treat the peasants as if they were animals, they're dismal students, they're poorly educated, they never read serious literature, they're absolutely idle, they don't do a thing except sit around talking about science and art, about which they know nothing at all. And they're all so grim looking, they have tense, taut faces, they only talk about 'important things,' they spend all their time philosophizing, and meanwhile, right before their very eyes, the workers live atrociously, eat abominably, sleep without bedding, thirty-forty to a room, together with bedbugs, stench, dankness, depravity...And so it seems that all this lofty talk is simply meant to conceal the truth from themselves and others. Show me, please, where are the day nurseries, about which they speak so much and so often, where are the public reading rooms? They only write about them in novels, they never become a reality, never. There is only filth, vulgarity, barbarism...I dread their serious countenances, their serious conversations, I despise them. Better to be silent!

LOPAKHIN: You know, I get up before five every morning, I work from dawn until night, I deal with money, constantly, mine and others, and yes, I see how people really are. You only have to try to get something done to realize how few honest, decent people there are in this world. Sometimes, when I can't fall asleep, I lie there thinking: "Dear Lord, you have given us the vast forests, the boundless plains, the endless horizons, and we who live here on this earth, we should be true giants…"

LYUBOV ANDREEVNA: What good are giants…They're very nice in fairy tales, you know, but in true life, they're terrifying.

YEPIKHODOV crosses upstage, playing the guitar.

(Pensively.) There goes Yepikhodov.

ANYA: *(Pensively.)* There goes Yepikhodov.
GAEV: The sun has set, ladies and gentlemen.
TROFIMOV: Yes.
GAEV: *(Softly, as if reciting.)* O nature, wondrous nature, you shine on, radiant and eternal, beauteous and indifferent, you whom we call mother, you embody birth and death, you create and you destroy, you…
VARYA: *(Imploring.)* Uncle, dear!
ANYA: Not again, Uncle!
TROFIMOV: You're better off "pocketing the yellow…"
GAEV: I'll be quiet, I'll be quiet.

All sit, deep in thought. Silence. Only FIRS's muttering can be heard. Suddenly from far, far away, a sound is heard, as if coming from the sky, the sound of a breaking string, dying away in the distance, a mournful sound.

LYUBOV ANDREEVNA: What was that?
LOPAKHIN: Don't know. Somewhere far away, deep in the mines, a bucket broke loose and fell…But somewhere very far away.
GAEV: Or a bird of some kind…a heron, perhaps.
TROFIMOV: Or an owl…
LYUBOV ANDREEVNA: *(Shudders.)* Disturbing, somehow.

Pause.

FIRS: Right before the time of trouble, it was the same thing: The owl screeched, and the samovar hissed, it never stopped.
GAEV: What time of trouble?
FIRS: Why, before the emancipation of the serfs.

Pause.

LYUBOV ANDREEVNA: Let's go, dear friends, shall we, it's getting dark. *(To ANYA.)* You've got tears in your eyes...What is it, my pet? *(Embraces her.)*

ANYA: I'm fine, Mama. It's nothing.

TROFIMOV: Someone's coming.

A PASSERBY appears in a shabby, white cap and a coat; he is slightly drunk.

PASSERBY: Permit me to inquire, may I pass through here to get to the train station?

GAEV: You may. Go down that road.

PASSERBY: I'm deeply grateful. *(Coughs.)* What superb weather we're having...*(Recites.)* "My brother, my suffering brother...Come down to the Volga, whose moan..." *(To VARYA.)* Mademoiselle, please, give a poor starving Russian thirty kopeks...

VARYA cries out in fear.

LOPAKHIN: *(Angrily.)* This has gone too far!

LYUBOV ANDREEVNA: *(Stunned.)* Here...take this...*(Searches in her purse.)* I have no silver...Never mind, here's a gold piece...

PASSERBY: I'm deeply grateful! *(Exits.)*

Laughter.

VARYA: *(Frightened.)* I'm leaving...I'm leaving...Oh, Mamochka, the servants at home have nothing to eat, and you gave him a gold piece.

LYUBOV ANDREEVNA: What are you going to do with me, I'm such a silly fool! I'll give you everything I have. Yermolai Alekseich, please, lend me some more money!...

LOPAKHIN: Yes, madam.

LYUBOV ANDREEVNA: Come, ladies and gentlemen, time to go. Oh, yes, Varya, we've just made a match for you. Congratulations.

VARYA: *(In tears.)* Mama, you musn't joke about that.

LOPAKHIN: "Oh-phel-i-a, get thee to a nunnery..."

GAEV: It's been so long since I've played a game of billiards, my hands are shaking.

LOPAKHIN: "Oh-phel-i-a, o nymph, remember me in thy prayers!"

LYUBOV ANDREEVNA: Come, ladies and gentlemen. It's almost suppertime.

VARYA: How he frightened me. My heart is pounding.

LOPAKHIN: May I remind you, ladies and gentlemen: On the twenty-second of August, the cherry orchard will be sold. Think about it! Think!...

They all leave, except TROFIMOV and ANYA.

ANYA: *(Laughing.)* The stranger frightened Varya off, thank goodness, now we're alone.

TROFIMOV: Varya's afraid we'll fall madly in love, she hasn't let us out of her sight for days. She's so narrow-minded, she can't understand we're above love. To overcome all obstacles, real and imagined, which stand in the path of freedom and happiness, — that is our quest in life. Onward! We set forth, undaunted, toward that star, burning bright in the distance! Onward! Don't fall behind, my friends!

ANYA: *(Clasps her hands.)* How beautifully you talk!

Pause.

It's glorious here today!

TROFIMOV: Yes, the weather is amazing.

ANYA: What have you done to me, Petya, why don't I love the cherry orchard, as I did, once? I loved it so tenderly, I couldn't imagine any other place on earth more lovely than our orchard.

TROFIMOV: All Russia is our orchard. The land is vast and beautiful, there are many marvelous places in it.

Pause.

Just think, Anya: Your grandfather, your great-grandfather, and his forefathers before him, all were serf-owners, they all owned living souls, so isn't it possible, then, that in every blossom, every leaf, every tree trunk in the orchard, a human soul now gazes down upon us, can't you hear their voices...To own human souls — can't you see how this has transformed each and every one of us, those who have lived before and those who live today, so that you, your mother, your uncle, all of you, are no longer aware that you are alive at the expense of others, at the expense of those whom you would not even permit beyond your front hall...We have fallen behind, by two hundred years or so, at least, we have nothing left, absolutely nothing, no clear understanding of the past, we only philosophize, complain about our boredom, or drink vodka. And it's all so clear, can't you see, that to begin a new life, to live in the present, we must first redeem our past, put an end to it, and redeem it we shall, but only with suffering, only with extraordinary, everlasting toil and suffering. You must understand this, Anya.

ANYA: The house, in which we live, is no longer our house, and I shall leave it, I give you my word.

TROFIMOV: If you have the key, throw it in the well and run, run far, far away. Be free, like the wind.

ANYA: *(Ecstatic.)* How wonderfully you say it!

TROFIMOV: Believe me, Anya, believe me! I'm not even thirty yet, I'm young, I'm still a student, and yet, I've endured so much! Come winter, I'm hungry, sick, anxiety-ridden, poverty-stricken, like a beggar, and wherever fate carries me, there I shall be! And yet, all the while, every waking moment, day and night, my soul is filled with an indescribable premonition, a vision. A vision of happiness, Anya, I can see it now...

ANYA: *(Pensively.)* The moon is rising.

YEPIKHODOV is heard playing the guitar, the same melancholy song as before. The moon is rising. Somewhere near the poplars, VARYA is looking for ANYA and calling: "Anya! Where are you?"

TROFIMOV: Yes, the moon is rising.

Pause.

Here comes happiness, here it comes, closer and closer, I can already hear its footsteps. And if we don't see it, if we don't recognize it, then what does it matter? Others will!

VARYA'S voice: "Anya! Where are you?"

Varya, again! *(Angrily.)* It's disgraceful!

ANYA: I know! Let's go down to the river. It's lovely there.

TROFIMOV: Let's go.

They go.

VARYA's voice: "Anya! Anya!"

CURTAIN

The drawing room, separated from the ballroom by an archway. A chandelier burns brightly. A Jewish orchestra, the same one referred to in Act II, is heard playing in the entrance hall. It is evening. In the ballroom, the crowd is dancing the 'grand-rond.' The voice of SIMEONOV-PISHCHIK is heard: "Promenade à une paire!" The couples dance through the drawing room, as follows: first PISHCHIK and CHARLOTTA IVANOVNA; then TROFIMOV and LYUBOV ANDREEVNA; then ANYA and the POST OFFICE CLERK; then VARYA and the STATIONMASTER, and so on. VARYA is weeping quietly and wipes away her tears as she dances. DUNYASHA is in the last couple. They dance around the drawing room. PISHCHIK calls out: "Grand-rond, balancez!" and "Les cavaliers à genoux et remerciez vos dames!"

FIRS, wearing a tailcoat, carries a tray with seltzer water. PISHCHIK and TROFIMOV enter the drawing room.

PISHCHIK: I have high blood pressure, I've had two strokes already, it's difficult for me to dance, but, you know what they say: "If you run in a pack, whether you bark or not, you'd better wag your tail." Never you mind, I'm as healthy as a horse. My dear departed father, joker that he was, God rest his soul, always used to say, on the subject of our ancestry, that the Simeonov-Pishchiks are descended from the same horse that Caligula appointed to the Senate…*(Sits.)* The only trouble is: We don't have any money! And you know what they say: "A hungry dog believes only in meat…" *(Snores and suddenly wakes up.)* And that's my problem…all I ever dream about is money…

TROFIMOV: As a matter of fact, you do bear some resemblance to a horse.

PISHCHIK: And why not…a horse is a good animal…you can get a very good price for a horse, you know…

In the next room, the sound of a billiard game is heard. VARYA appears in the archway to the hall.

TROFIMOV: *(Teasing.)* Madame Lopakhina! Madame Lopakhina!…

VARYA: *(Angrily.)* The shabby-looking gentleman!

TROFIMOV: Yes, I'm a shabby-looking gentleman, and proud of it!

VARYA: *(Bitterly.)* We've gone and hired the musicians, now how are we going to pay for them? *(Exits.)*

TROFIMOV: *(To PISHCHIK.)* Think about it: The energy you've wasted your whole life through in search of money to pay off the interest on your debts, if only you'd spent that energy elsewhere, then, no doubt, you could have changed the world.

PISHCHIK: Nietzsche...the philosopher...the supreme, the exalted...a man of the greatest genius, this man once said, in his own writings, that it's all right to forge banknotes.

TROFIMOV: Have you ever read Nietzsche?

PISHCHIK: Well...Dashenka told me that one. And anyway, given my situation, even if I could forge banknotes...Day after tomorrow, I owe a payment of three hundred and ten rubles...I've already scraped up one hundred and thirty so far...*(Searches in his pockets, anxiously.)* My money's gone! I've lost my money! *(In tears.)* Where is my money! *(Overjoyed.)* Here it is, in the lining...Look, I even broke into a sweat...

Enter LYUBOV ANDREEVNA and CHARLOTTA IVANOVNA.

LYUBOV ANDREEVNA: *(Humming the 'lezginka.')* Why has Leonid been gone so long? What is he doing in town? *(To DUNYASHA.)* Dunyasha, offer the musicians some tea...

TROFIMOV: The auction didn't take place, in all probability.

LYUBOV ANDREEVNA: And of all times to invite the musicians and give a ball...Oh well, never mind...*(Sits and hums softly.)*

CHARLOTTA: *(Gives PISHCHIK a deck of cards.)* Here is a deck of cards, think of a card, any card.

PISHCHIK: I've got one.

CHARLOTTA: Now shuffle the deck. Very good. Give it to me, oh my dear Mr. Pishchik. Eins, zwei, drei! Now go look, it's in your side pocket...

PISHCHIK: *(Takes a card from his side pocket.)* The eight of spades, you're absolutely right! *(Amazed.)* Imagine that!

CHARLOTTA: *(Holds out the deck of cards in her palm to TROFIMOV.)* Tell me, quickly, which card is the top card?

TROFIMOV: What? Oh, the queen of spades.

CHARLOTTA: Right! *(To PISHCHIK.)* So? Which card is the top card?

PISHCHIK: The ace of hearts.

CHARLOTTA: Right! *(Claps her hands, and the deck of cards disappears.)* My, what lovely weather we're having today!

A mysterious female voice answers her as if coming from underneath the floor: "Oh yes, the weather is splendid, dear lady."

You are the image of perfection...

Voice: "And you I like very much too, dear lady."

STATIONMASTER: *(Applauds.)* Madame Ventriloquist, bravo!

PISHCHIK: *(Amazed.)* Imagine that! Most enchanting Charlotta Ivanovna...I'm head-over-heels in love...

CHARLOTTA: In love? *(Shrugs her shoulders.)* How could you possibly be in love? "Guter Mensch, aber schlechter Musikant."

TROFIMOV: *(Claps PISHCHIK on the shoulder.)* Well done, old horse...

CHARLOTTA: Your attention please, for one more trick. *(Gets a lap robe from a chair.)* Here is a very lovely lap robe, I wish to sell it...*(Shakes it.)* Doesn't anyone wish to buy it?

PISHCHIK: *(Amazed.)* Imagine that!

CHARLOTTA: Eins, zwei, drei! *(Quickly lifts the lap robe.)*

ANYA appears behind the lap robe; she curtsies, runs to her mother, embraces her, and runs out into the ballroom, amidst general delight.

LYUBOV ANDREEVNA: *(Applauds.)* Bravo, bravo!...

CHARLOTTA: Once more! Eins, zwei, drei! *(Lifts the lap robe.)*

VARYA appears behind the lap robe; she bows.

PISHCHIK: *(Amazed.)* Imagine that!

CHARLOTTA: The end! *(Throws the lap robe over PISHCHIK, curtsies, and runs out into the ballroom.)*

PISHCHIK: *(Hurries after her.)* Sorceress...how did you do it? How? *(Exits.)*

LYUBOV ANDREEVNA: And Leonid is still not back. What can he be doing in town this long, I don't understand it! Surely everything is over by now, either the estate has been sold or else the auction never took place, one or the other, so why must we be kept in the dark forever!

VARYA: *(Attempting to console her.)* Uncle has bought it, I'm sure of it.

TROFIMOV: *(Sarcastically.)* Yes.

VARYA: Great-aunt sent him power of attorney to buy the estate in her name and transfer the mortgage to her. She did it for Anya. And Uncle will buy it, with God's help, I'm sure of it.

LYUBOV ANDREEVNA: Great-aunt in Yaroslavl sent 50,000 to buy the estate in her name because she doesn't trust us, — and that wasn't even enough to pay the interest. *(Covers her face with her hands.)* Today my destiny will be decided, my destiny...

TROFIMOV: *(Teasing VARYA.)* Madame Lopakhina!

VARYA: *(Angrily.)* The eternal student! Twice you've been expelled from the university.

LYUBOV ANDREEVNA: Why are you so angry, Varya? He's teasing you about Lopahkin, but what does it matter? If you want to — marry Lopakhin, he's a fine man, a fascinating man. And if you don't want to — don't; no one is forcing you to, darling...

VARYA: I take this matter very seriously, Mamochka, I must tell you. He is a good man, I like him, I do.

LYUBOV ANDREEVNA: Then marry him. What are you waiting for, I don't understand!

VARYA: But Mamochka, I can't propose to him myself. For two years now everyone's been talking to me about him, everyone, and either he says nothing, or else he jokes about it. I understand. He's busy getting rich, he's preoccupied with his affairs, he has no time for me. Oh, if only I had money, only a little, a hundred rubles even, I'd give up everything, I'd run away as far as I could. I'd enter a convent.

TROFIMOV: Blessings on you!

VARYA: *(To TROFIMOV.)* A student's supposed to be intelligent! *(Gently, in tears.)* How ugly you've grown, Petya, and how old, too! *(To LYUBOV ANDREEVNA, no longer crying.)* I simply can't live without work, Mamochka. I must be doing something, every minute.

Enter YASHA.

YASHA: *(Hardly able to contain his laughter.)* Yepikhodov has broken a billiard cue!...*(Exits.)*

VARYA: Why is Yepikhodov here? Who allowed him to play billiards? I don't understand these people...*(Exits.)*

LYUBOV ANDREEVNA: Don't tease her, Petya, can't you see how miserable she is.

TROFIMOV: She's overbearing, that's what she is...always poking her nose into other people's business. She hasn't given Anya and me a moment's peace all summer, she's afraid we might fall in love. What business is it of hers, anyway? And how could she even think that of me, I'm far beyond such vulgarity. We are above love!

LYUBOV ANDREEVNA: And I suppose that means I must be beneath love. *(Tremendously agitated.)* Why isn't Leonid back yet? I only want to know: Is the estate sold or isn't it? This terrible business has gone too far, I don't know what to think any more, I'm at my wits' end…I might scream any minute…I might do something foolish. Save me, Petya. Say something, anything…

TROFIMOV: Whether the estate is sold today or not — does it really matter? It's over, it's been so for a long time, there's no turning back again, that path is long overgrown. Face it, dear friend. You mustn't delude yourself any longer, for once in your life you must look the truth straight in the eye.

LYUBOV ANDREEVNA: What truth? Oh, yes, of course, you see what is true and what is not true, while I have lost my vision, I see nothing. You boldly solve all the problems of the world, don't you, but tell me, my darling, isn't that because you're still so young, because you haven't even suffered through one of life's problems yet, not even one? You boldly look to the future, but isn't that because you see nothing so terrible lying ahead, because life is still safely hidden from your young eyes? You have more courage, more character, more honesty than any of us, so then why not have compassion, find it, somewhere in a corner of your heart, have mercy on me. I was born here, my mother and father lived here, my grandfather, too, I love this house, I can't comprehend a life without the cherry orchard, and if it must be sold, then sell me with it…(*Embraces TROFIMOV, kisses him on the forehead.*) My son drowned here…(*Weeps.*) Have pity on me, my good, kind fellow.

TROFIMOV: You know I do, with all my heart.

LYUBOV ANDREEVNA: Yes, but there must be another way to say it, another way…(*Takes out a handkerchief, a telegram falls on the floor.*) My soul is so heavy today, you can't possibly imagine. There is such a din here, I'm trembling with each and every sound, trembling all over, but I can't be alone, the silence would be terrifying. Don't judge me, Petya…I love you, as if you were my own child. And I'd gladly let you marry Anya, I would, I swear to you, only first you must finish your education, darling, get your degree. You don't do a thing, you just let fate carry you from place to place, and that's such a strange way to live…Isn't it? Well? And you simply must do something about that beard, to make it grow, somehow…(*Bursts out laughing.*) How funny-looking you are!

TROFIMOV: (*Picks up the telegram.*) I don't wish to be handsome.

LYUBOV ANDREEVNA: It's a telegram from Paris. Every day I receive one. Yesterday, and today, too. That terrible man is ill again, he's in trouble again…He begs my forgiveness, he beseeches me to return to him, I really ought to be going to Paris, to be near him. You should see your face now, Petya, so severe, so judgmental, but, really, what am I to do, darling, tell me, what can I do, he's ill, he's alone, unhappy, and who will take care of him, who will keep him from harm, who will nurse him through his illness? Oh, why hide it, why keep silent, I love him, it's the truth. I love him, I love him…He is the stone around my neck, and I shall sink with him to the bottom, and how I love this stone, I can't live without it! *(Presses TROFIMOV's hand.)* Don't think ill of me, Petya, and don't speak, please, not a word…

TROFIMOV: *(In tears.)* Forgive me for saying it, but for God's sake: This man robbed you, he cleaned you out!

LYUBOV ANDREEVNA: No, no, no, you mustn't talk like that…*(Covers her ears.)*

TROFIMOV: He's an absolute scoundrel, and you're the only one who doesn't know it! A petty thief, a good-for-nothing…

LYUBOV ANDREEVNA: *(With controlled anger.)* And you're twenty-six or twenty-seven years old, and still a schoolboy!

TROFIMOV: So be it!

LYUBOV ANDREEVNA: You're supposed to be a man, at your age you're supposed to understand how lovers behave. Why don't you know this by now…why haven't you fallen in love yourself? *(Angrily.)* Yes, yes! You and all your talk about purity…why, you're nothing but a prude, that's what you are, an eccentric, a freak…

TROFIMOV: *(Horrified.)* What is she saying!

LYUBOV ANDREEVNA: "I am above love." You're not above love, no, as Firs says, you're pathetic! At your age, not to have a lover!…

TROFIMOV: *(Horrified.)* This is terrible! What is she saying?! *(Rushes out into the ballroom, holding his head.)* This is terrible…I can't bear it, I'm leaving…*(Exits, but returns again immediately.)* It's all over between us! *(Exits into the front hall.)*

LYUBOV ANDREEVNA: *(Calls after him.)* Petya, wait! Don't be silly, I was only joking! Petya!

In the front hall, someone is heard dashing down the stairs, and suddenly falling the rest of the way with a crash. ANYA and VARYA cry out, but then, almost immediately, laughter is heard.

What happened?

ANYA runs in.

ANYA: *(Laughing.)* Petya fell down the stairs! *(Runs out.)*

LYUBOV ANDREEVNA: What a peculiar fellow that Petya is…

The STATIONMASTER stands in the middle of the ballroom, and starts to recite a poem: 'The Fallen Woman' by Alexey Konstantinovich Tolstoy. Everyone stops to listen, but after a few lines, the strains of a waltz are heard coming from the front hall, and the recitation is interrupted. Everyone dances. TROFIMOV, ANYA, VARYA, and LYUBOV ANDREEVNA pass through from the entrance hall.

Petya…my pure Petya…I beg your forgiveness…Come, dance with me… *(Dances with him.)*

ANYA and VARYA dance together. FIRS enters, and places his cane near the side door. YASHA also enters, and watches the dancing.

YASHA: So, what's new, grandpa?

FIRS: I don't feel very well. In the old days, we used to have generals, barons, admirals dancing at our balls; nowadays we have to send for the postal clerk and the stationmaster, and even they come reluctantly. And I'm getting weaker, somehow. In the old days, when anyone of us fell ill, my old master — that would be their grandfather — he would treat us all with sealing wax. I've taken a dose of sealing wax every day for twenty years now, even more, who knows; perhaps that's why I'm still alive.

YASHA: You get on my nerves, grandpa. *(Yawns.)* Maybe it's time for you to kick the bucket.

FIRS: And you're a pathetic fool, that's what you are. *(Mumbles.)*

TROFIMOV and LYUBOV ANDREEVNA dance in the ballroom, and then in the drawing room.

LYUBOV ANDREEVNA: "Merci." Let me sit down…*(Sits.)* I'm exhausted.

Enter ANYA.

ANYA: *(Agitated.)* There's a man out in the kitchen, he was just saying that the cherry orchard was sold today.

LYUBOV ANDREEVNA: To whom?

ANYA: He didn't say. He left. *(Dances with TROFIMOV.)*

Both exit into the ballroom.

YASHA: Some old fellow jabbering, that's all. A stranger.

FIRS: And Leonid Andreich is still not here, he's still not back yet. All he has on is a lightweight overcoat, one for in-between seasons, he's bound to catch cold. Oh, these young people nowadays!

LYUBOV ANDREEVNA: I think I'm going to die. Go, Yasha, hurry, find out to whom it was sold.

YASHA: Oh, he left a long time ago, that old fellow. *(Laughs.)*

LYUBOV ANDREEVNA: *(Slightly annoyed.)* And what are you laughing about? What's so funny?

YASHA: That Yepikhodov, he's a clown. The man is pitiful. "Mister Disaster."

LYUBOV ANDREEVNA: Firs, if the estate is sold, where will you go?

FIRS: Wherever you tell me, that's where I'll go.

LYUBOV ANDREEVNA: Why do you look like that? Are you ill? You should be in bed, you know…

FIRS: Yes…*(With a grin.)* I'll go to bed, and who will serve, who will manage everything? Hm? One servant for the whole household.

YASHA: *(To LYUBOV ANDREEVNA.)* Lyubov Andreevna! One small request, allow me, please! If you go to Paris again, take me with you, I beg of you. I can't stay here any more, it's absolutely impossible. *(Looks around, in a low voice.)* What can I say, you see for yourself, this is an ignorant country, the people are immoral, and anyway, life here is boring, the food they give you in the kitchen is disgusting, and you have Firs wandering around everywhere, muttering all kinds of nonsense. Take me with you, I beg of you!

Enter PISHCHIK.

PISHCHIK: May I have the pleasure…a little waltz, most charming lady…

LYUBOV ANDREEVNA joins him.

But, don't forget, one hundred eighty rubles, enchanting lady…That, I'll take…*(They dance.)* One hundred and eighty sweet little rubles…

THEY cross into the ballroom.

YASHA: *(Sings softly.)* "O, do you know how my heart is yearning…"

In the ballroom, a figure in a grey top hat and checkered trousers waves her hands and jumps up and down; there are cries of: "Bravo, Charlotta Ivanovna!"

DUNYASHA: *(Stops to powder her face.)* The mistress told me to dance — too many gentlemen, too few ladies, — but now my head is spinning from too much waltzing, my heart is pounding, and, do you know what else, Firs Nikolaevich, the postmaster just told me something that took my breath away.

The music dies down.

FIRS: What did he say?

DUNYASHA: "You," he said, "are like a little flower."

YASHA: *(Yawns.)* What ignorance... *(Exits.)*

DUNYASHA: "A little flower"...I'm such a sensitive young woman, you know, I adore a few tender words.

FIRS: You'll get yourself into a lot of trouble.

Enter YEPIKHODOV.

YEPIKHODOV: Avdotya Fyodorovna, you keep avoiding me...what am I, some sort of insect? *(Sighs.)* Ach, life!

DUNYASHA: Yes, what may I do for you?

YEPIKHODOV: And no doubt, probably, you're right. Of course. *(Sighs.)* Who can blame you. And yet, look at it from my point, of view, I mean, if I may say so myself, and I shall, so excuse me, but you have reduced me to a complete state of mind. Now I know my destiny in life, every day some new disaster befalls me, and have I accepted this? — yes, I have, I look upon my fate with a smile. You have given me your word, and though...

DUNYASHA: Can we have our little talk later, please? Leave me alone now. I'm in a fantasy. *(Plays with her fan.)*

YEPIKHODOV: A new day, a new disaster, and excuse me, I just keep smiling, I even laugh, sometimes.

Enter VARYA from the ballroom.

VARYA: You still haven't left yet, Semyon? Who do you think you are, really. *(To DUNYASHA.)* Get out of here, Dunyasha. *(To YEPIKHODOV.)* First you play billiards and you break a cue, then you parade around the drawing room like a guest.

YEPIKHIDOV: You should not reprimand me. Excuse me.

VARYA: I'm not reprimanding you, I'm telling you. All you do is float from one place to the next, you don't do a blessed bit of work. Why we keep you as clerk, God only knows.

YEPIKHODOV: *(Offended.)* Whether I work, or float, or eat, or play billiards, for that matter, excuse me, but that's a subject of discussion only for our elders.

VARYA: How dare you speak to me like that! *(Enraged.)* How dare you? Do you mean to tell me I don't know what I'm doing? Get out of here! This minute!

YEPIKHODOV: *(Cowering.)* Excuse me, may I ask that you express yourself in a more delicate fashion?

VARYA: *(Besides herself.)* Get out, this minute! Out!

He goes to the door, she follows him.

"Mister Disaster!" Never set foot in here again, do you hear! I never want to lay eyes on you!

YEPIKHODOV has exited; from behind the door, his voice is heard: "I am going to file a complaint against you."

So, you're think you're coming back, eh? *(Grabs the cane, which Firs has left by the door.)* Come on…come on…come on, I'll show you…So, are you coming back? Are you? This is for you, then…*(Swings the cane.)*

Just at this moment LOPAKHIN enters.

LOPAKHIN: I humbly thank you.

VARYA: *(Angrily and sarcastically.)* Sorry!

LOPAKHIN: Please, it's nothing. I'm most grateful for the warm reception.

VARYA: Don't mention it. *(She turns to go, then looks around and asks, meekly.)* I didn't hurt you, did I?

LOPAKHIN: No, of course not, it's nothing. Just a bump, an enormous one, that's all.

Voices in the ballroom: "Lopakhin has returned! Yermolai Alekseich!"

PISHCHIK: Well, well, well, and speaking of the devil!…*(Kisses LOPAKHIN.)*

I smell a touch of brandy, my dear, good fellow, yes, I do! And we've been celebrating here, too!

Enter LYUBOV ANDREEVNA.

LYUBOV ANDREEVNA: Yermolai Alekseich, you're back. Why did it take you so long? Where is Leonid?

LOPAKHIN: Leonid Andreich returned with me, he's coming...

LYUBOV ANDREEVNA: *(Upset.)* So? Was there an auction? Tell me!

LOPAKHIN: *(Disconcerted, afraid to reveal his excitement.)* The auction was over at four o'clock...We missed the train, we had to wait till nine-thirty. *(Sighs heavily.)* Oh! My head is spinning...

Enter GAEV. In his right hand he carries some packages; he wipes away the tears with his left hand.

LYUBOV ANDREEVNA: Lyonya, what is it? Lyonya? *(Impatiently, in tears.)* Tell me, quickly, for God's sake...

GAEV: *(Doesn't answer her, simply waves his hands; weeping, to FIRS.)* Here, take it...anchovies, and some kerch herring...I haven't had a thing to eat all day...What I have lived through!

The door to the billiard room is open; the clicking of billiard balls is heard, and YASHA's voice: "Seven and eighteen!" GAEV's expression changes; he is no longer crying.

I'm terribly tired. Help me change my clothes, Firs.
(Exits through the ballroom to his room, FIRS follows behind.)

PISHCHIK: What happened at the auction? Tell us! Please!

LYUBOV ANDREEVNA: Is the cherry orchard sold?

LOPAKHIN: It is sold.

LYUBOV ANDREEVNA: Who bought it?

LOPAKHIN: I bought it.

Pause. LYUBOV ANDREEVNA is stunned; she might have fallen, were she not standing near an armchair and table. VARYA takes the keys off her belt, throws them on the floor in the middle of the drawing room, and exits.

I bought it! Wait, ladies and gentlemen, bear with me, please, my head is spinning, I can't speak...*(Laughs.)* We arrived at the auction, and Deriganov was already there. Leonid Andreich only had 15,000, so right away Deriganov bid 30,000 over and above the debt on the mortgage. I saw how it was going, so I decided to take him on, I bid forty. And he bid forty-five. Then I bid fifty-five. You see — he'd raise it by five, I'd raise it by ten...And then, it was all over. I bid ninety over and above the debt, and that was it, it went to me. And now, the cherry orchard is mine! Mine! *(Roars with laughter.)* My God, ladies and gentlemen, the cherry orchard is mine! Tell me that I'm drunk, that I'm out of my mind, that I've made it all up...*(Stamps his feet.)* Don't you laugh at me! If only my father and my grandfather could get up from their graves and witness all these events, how their Yermolai, their ignorant little Yermolai, the one who was beaten, the one who ran barefoot in the bitter winter, how this same little Yermolai bought the estate, the most beautiful estate in the world. I bought the estate, where my grandfather and my father were slaves, where they were forbidden to set foot in the kitchen. No, I'm dreaming, I'm hallucinating, it's only an illusion...a figment of the imagination, shrouded in a cloak of mystery...*(Picks up the keys, smiles tenderly.)* She threw down the keys, she's saying she's not the mistress of the house any more...*(Jingles the keys.)* Ah, well, what does it matter.

The orchestra can be heard tuning up.

Eh, musicians, play, I want to hear you play! Everyone, come and see, how Yermolai Lopakhin will take an axe out into the cherry orchard, and all the trees will come crashing to the ground! And we'll build summer homes, and our grandchildren and great grandchildren will see a new life...Let's have music, play!

The music plays. LYUBOV ANDREEVNA lowers herself into a chair and weeps bitterly.

(Reproachfully.) Why, why didn't you listen to me? My, poor, dear friend, you'll never get it back now, never. *(In tears.)* Oh, the sooner all this is behind us, the sooner we can change our chaotic lives, our absurd, unhappy lives.

PISHCHIK: *(Takes him by the hand, in a low voice.)* She is weeping. Come into the ballroom, let's leave her alone...Come...*(Takes him by the hand and leads him into the ballroom.)*

LOPAKHIN: What's going on here? Let there be music! Loud, the way I want it! Let everything be the way I want it! *(With irony.)* Here comes the new master, the owner of the cherry orchard! *(Accidentally shoves against a table, almost turning over a candelabra.)* I can pay for it all, for everything! *(Exits with PISHCHIK.)*

There is no one left in the ballroom or the drawing room, except LYUBOV ANDREEVNA, who is sitting, huddled over, weeping bitterly. The music plays softly. ANYA and TROFIMOV rush in. ANYA goes to her mother and kneels before her. TROFIMOV stays at the entrance to the ballroom.

ANYA: Mama!...Mama, are you crying? My dear, good, kind Mama, my beautiful Mama, I love you...I bless you. The cherry orchard is sold, it's gone, it's true, it's true, but don't cry, Mama, you still have your whole life before you to live, and your pure and beautiful soul...Come with me, come, my darling, away from here, come!...We'll plant a new orchard, more glorious than this one, you'll see, you'll understand, and joy, a deep, peaceful, gentle joy will settle into your soul, like the warm, evening sun, and you will smile, Mama! Come, darling! Come!...

CURTAIN

ACT FOUR

The same setting as Act I. There are no curtains on the windows, no pictures on the walls; only a few pieces of furniture remain, stacked in a corner, as if for sale. There is a feeling of emptiness. There are suitcases, travel bags, etc. piled high upstage by the door leading to the outside. The door to stage left is open, from which the voices of VARYA and ANYA can be heard. LOPAKHIN stands there, waiting. YASHA holds a tray of glasses, filled with champagne. In the entrance hall, YEPIKHODOV is packing a case. Offstage, voices are heard — the peasants have come to say good-bye. GAEV's voice is heard: "Thank you, my friends, I thank you."

YASHA: The peasants have come to say good-bye. Now here's my opinion on that subject, Yermolai Alekseich: The people are good, but what do *they* know.

The noise dies down. LYUBOV ANDREEVNA and GAEV enter through the entrance hall; she is no longer crying, but she is very pale: she is trembling, and it is difficult for her to speak.

GAEV: You gave them everything in your purse, Lyuba. No! You mustn't do that!
LYUBOV ANDREEVNA: I couldn't help it! I couldn't help it!

Both exit.

LOPAKHIN: *(At the door, following after them.)* Please, I humbly beg you! A farewell toast! I didn't think to bring any from town…and I could only find one bottle at the station. Please!

Pause.

So, my friends! You don't want any? *(Steps away from the door.)* If I'd known, I wouldn't have bought it. Never mind, I won't have any, either.

YASHA carefully places the tray on the table.

Drink up, Yasha, why don't you.
YASHA: To those who are leaving! And to those who are staying behind! *(Drinks.)* This isn't real champagne, that much I can tell you.

LOPAKHIN: Eight rubles a bottle.

Pause.

Wickedly cold in here, isn't it.

YASHA: They didn't stoke up the stoves today, what's the point, everybody's leaving. *(Laughs.)*

LOPAKHIN: What are you laughing about?

YASHA: I'm happy.

LOPAKHIN: It's October, but outside it's sunny and mild, like summertime. Good weather for construction. *(Looks at his watch, at the door.)* Ladies and gentlemen, bear in mind, only forty-six minutes left until the train departs! That means we have to leave for the station in twenty minutes. Hurry, everyone!

TROFIMOV enters from the outside, wearing a coat.

TROFIMOV: I think it's time to go now. They've already brought the horses around. Where are my galoshes, damn it! They've disappeared. *(At the door.)* Anya, my galoshes aren't here! I can't find them!

LOPAKHIN: And I've got to get to Kharkov. I'll go with you as far as the station. I'm going to spend the winter in Kharkov. Yes. Here I am, standing around, talking to you, I'm lost when I'm not working. I can't live without work, I don't know what to do with my hands; isn't it strange, look, they're hanging there, as if they belonged to someone else.

TROFIMOV: We'll be leaving momentarily, and you'll return to all your worthy enterprises.

LOPAKHIN: Have a glass with me.

TROFIMOV: I can't.

LOPAKHIN: So, it's off to Moscow, then?

TROFIMOV: Yes, that's right, I'll go with them into town, and tomorrow, it's off to Moscow.

LOPAKHIN: Yes...Well, the professors haven't started their lectures yet, no doubt they're all waiting for you!

TROFIMOV: That's none of your business.

LOPAKHIN: How many years is it, then, since you've been at the university?

TROFIMOV: Think up something new, why don't you? That's a stale and feeble joke, it's not funny any more. *(Searches for his galoshes.)* It's very likely we may never see each other again, you know, so allow me, please, to give you some parting advice: Don't wave your arms around so much! Try to get out the habit of waving your arms when you talk, if you can. All this planning of yours, you know, building summer houses, creating a new generation of independent landowners, and so on and so forth, — why, that's just another form of waving your arms…Oh, well, never mind, all things considered, I like you…I do. You have delicate, sensitive fingers, the fingers of an artist…you have a delicate, sensitive soul…

LOPAKHIN: *(Embraces him.)* Good-bye, my friend. Thanks for everything. Just in case, here, take some money for the journey.

TROFIMOV: Why should I? I don't need it.

LOPAKHIN: But you don't have any!

TROFIMOV: Yes, I do, thank you very much. I've just received some money for a translation. Here it is, right here, in my pocket. *(Anxiously.)* Now where are my galoshes!

VARYA: *(From the other room.)* Here, take the filthy things! *(Tosses a pair of rubber galoshes on the stage.)*

TROFIMOV: Why are you so angry, Varya? Hm…These are not my galoshes!

LOPAKHIN: This spring I planted almost 3,000 acres of poppies, and made a clean profit of 40,000. And when my poppies bloomed, now what a sight that was! So, here's what I'm saying, I've just made 40,000 rubles, and I'm offering you a loan because I can afford to. Why do you look down your nose at me? I'm a peasant…what do you expect?

TROFIMOV: Your father was a peasant, mine was a chemist, none of it means a thing.

LOPAKHIN takes out his wallet.

Stop that, stop…Even if you were to give me 200,000, I wouldn't take it. I am a free man. And everything that is so sacred and dear to all of you, rich and poor alike, hasn't the slightest significance to me, it's all dust, adrift in the wind. I can survive without you, I can even surpass you, I am proud and strong. Mankind is on a quest to seek the highest truth, the greatest happiness possible on this earth, and I am in the front ranks!

LOPAKHIN: And will you reach your destination?

TROFIMOV: Yes, I shall.

Pause.

I shall, or else I'll show others the way.

In the distance, the sound is heard of an axe falling on a tree.

LOPAKHIN: So, good-bye, my friend. Time to go. Here we are, looking down our noses at one another, and all the while, life goes on, in spite of any of us. When I work, for days on end, without any rest, that's when my thoughts come most clearly, that's when I know why I am on this earth, why I exist. And how many of us are there in Russia, my friend, who still don't know why they exist. Ah well, what does it matter, that's not the point, is it. They say that Leonid Andreich has taken a position at a bank, 6,000 a year…He won't be able to keep it, though, he's too lazy…

ANYA: *(At the door.)* Mama asks you not to cut down the orchard till after she's gone.

TROFIMOV: Isn't it possible to show some tact…*(Exits through the entrance hall.)*

LOPAKHIN: Yes, yes, right away…Really.

ANYA: Have they sent Firs to the hospital yet?

YASHA: I told them about it this morning. I'm sure they did.

ANYA: *(To YEPIKHODOV, who is walking through the hall.)* Semyon Panteleich, please, go find out, would you, if they've taken Firs to the hospital yet.

YASHA: *(Offended.)* I told Yegor this morning. Why ask the same question over and over!

YEPIKHODOV: The ancient Firs, in my final opinion, is beyond repair; he should return to his forefathers. And I can only envy him. *(Places the suitcase on a hat box, and crushes it.)* Oh, well, of course. I knew it. *(Exits.)*

YASHA: *(Mocking.)* "Mister Disaster"…

VARYA: *(From behind the door.)* Have they taken Firs to the hospital?

ANYA: Yes, they have.

VARYA: Why didn't they bring the letter to the doctor?

ANYA: We'll just have to send it along…*(Exits.)*

VARYA: *(From the adjacent room.)* Where's Yasha? Tell him his mother's here, she wants to say good-bye to him.

YASHA: *(Waves his hand.)* I'm losing my patience.

During this, DUNYASHA has been busying herself with the luggage; now that YASHA is alone, she goes up to him.

DUNYASHA: Just one last look, Yasha. You're leaving…you're abandoning me…*(Weeps and throws her arms around his neck.)*

YASHA: What's there to cry about? *(Drinks champagne.)* In six days, I'll be in

Paris again. Tomorrow we'll board an express train, and off we'll go, that's the last you'll ever see of us. I just can't believe it. "Vive la France!"...This place is not for me, I can't live here...and that's all there is to it. I've seen a lot of ignorance — and I've had enough. *(Drinks champagne.)* What's there to cry about? Behave yourself properly, then you won't cry so much.

DUNYASHA: *(Powders her face, looks at herself in the mirror.)* Send me a letter from Paris. You know how much I have loved you, Yasha, I have loved you very, very much! I'm a sensitive creature, Yasha!

YASHA: They're coming. *(Busies himself with the luggage, hums softly.)*

Enter LYUBOV ANDREEVNA, GAEV, ANYA, and CHARLOTTA IVANOVNA.

GAEV: We really ought to be going. There's hardly any time left. *(Looks at YASHA.)* Who smells of herring in here?

LYUBOV ANDREEVNA: In ten minutes time we'll be getting into the carriages...*(Glances around the room.)* Good-bye, beloved home, home of my forefathers. Winter will pass, spring will come, and you'll no longer be here, they will have destroyed you. How much these walls have seen! *(Kisses her daughter passionately.)* My treasure, you're radiant, your eyes are sparkling, like two diamonds. Are you happy? Very happy?

ANYA: Very! We're starting a new life, Mama!

GAEV: *(Cheerfully.)* Everything's turned out quite well, as a matter of fact, yes, indeed. Before the cherry orchard was sold, we were all upset, we suffered a great deal, but then, when everything was settled, once and for all, finally and irrevocably, we all calmed down, we were even glad...And now I'm a bank official, a financier..."yellow into the middle pocket," and you, Lyuba, for all that we've been through, you're looking better than ever, no doubt about it.

LYUBOV ANDREEVNA: Yes, I'm calmer, it's true.

She is given her hat and coat.

I can sleep better now. Take my things out, Yasha. It's time. *(To ANYA.)* My darling child, we shall see each other again, soon...I am going to Paris, I shall live there on the money your great-aunt from Yaroslavl sent to buy the estate — God bless great-aunt! — but that money won't last very long.

ANYA: You'll come home soon, Mama, soon...won't you? And I'll study, take my examinations, and then I'll work, I'll take care of you. And we'll read all sorts of marvelous books together, Mama…Won't we? *(Kisses her mother's hands.)* We'll read through the long autumn evenings, we'll read so many books, and a wonderful new world will open before us…*(Dreaming.)* Come home, Mama…

LYUBOV ANDREEVNA: I'll come, my jewel. *(Embraces her daughter.)*

Enter LOPAKHIN, and CHARLOTTA, who is softly humming a tune.

GAEV: Charlotta is happy: she's singing!

CHARLOTTA: *(Picks up a bundle, resembling an infant in swaddling clothes.)* "My sweet little baby, 'bye, 'bye…"

The child's cry: "Wa, wa!…" can be heard.

"Hushabye, baby, my sweet little boy."

The child's cry: "Wa!…wa!…"

Poor baby! I feel so sorry for you! *(Throws the bundle down.)* Now, please, find me another job. I can't go on like this.

LOPAKHIN: We shall, Charlotta Ivanovna, don't worry.

GAEV: We're all being cast out, Varya's going away…suddenly no one needs us any more.

CHARLOTTA: There's nowhere for me to live in town. I must go away… *(Hums.)* It doesn't matter…

Enter PISHCHIK.

LOPAKHIN: One of nature's wonders!…

PISHCHIK: *(Out of breath.)* Oy, let me catch my breath…I'm all worn out…Most honorable friends…Give me some water…

GAEV: Looking for money, by any chance? I remain your humble servant, but, forgive me, I really must avoid the temptation…*(Exits.)*

PISHCHIK: I haven't been here in such a long, long, time…loveliest lady…*(To LOPAKHIN.)* And you are here, too…so good to see you…a man of the highest intelligence…here, take it…it's yours…*(Gives LOPAKIN some money.)* Four hundred rubles…I still owe you eight hundred and forty…

LOPAKHIN: *(Shrugs his shoulders in amazement.)* I must be dreaming…Where on earth did you get this?

PISHCHIK: Wait…So hot…Most extraordinary circumstances. Some Englishmen came to visit my estate, and what do you know, they found white clay in the earth…whatever that is…*(To LYUBOV ANDREEVNA.)* And here's four hundred for you…elegant, exquisite lady…*(Gives her some money.)* The rest will come later. *(Drinks the water.)* Just now, a young man on the train was telling us about this great philosopher…how he's advising everyone to jump off the roof…"Jump!" — he says, and that will solve everything. *(Amazed.)* Imagine that! Water!…

LOPAKHIN: What Englishmen are you talking about?

PISHCHIK: I leased them a plot of the land with the white clay for twenty-four years…But now, forgive me, please, I've run out of time…a long ride ahead…I'm going to the Znoykovs…to the Kardamonovs…I owe everybody…*(Drinks.)* Good day to you all…I'll drop by again on Thursday…

LYUBOV ANDREEVNA: We're just moving into town now, and tomorrow I'm going abroad…

PISHCHIK: What? *(Anxiously.)* Why to town? What's this I see…furniture…suitcases…Well, never mind…*(In tears.)* Never mind…Very very smart people, these Englishmen…people of the highest intelligence…Never mind…I wish you happiness…God will watch over you…Never mind…Everything on this earth must come to an end…*(Kisses LYUBOV ANDREEVNA's hand.)* And when you hear the news that my own end has come, remember this good old horse, won't you, and say: "Once upon a time there lived an old so-and-so…Simeonov-Pishchik…God rest his soul"…Magnificent weather we're having…Yes…*(Exits in great confusion, and immediately returns and speaks from the doorway.)* Dashenka sends her regards! *(Exits.)*

LYUBOV ANDREEVNA: And now we can go. But I'm leaving with two worries. The first is Firs — he's ill. *(Looks at her watch.)* We still have five minutes…

ANYA: Mama, they've already sent Firs to the hospital. Yasha sent him this morning.

LYUBOV ANDREEVNA: My second sorrow is Varya. She's used to getting up early and working, and now, without work, she's like a fish out of water. She's grown thin and pale, she weeps all the time, poor thing…

Pause.

You know very well, Yermolai Alekseich, I have dreamed…that one day she would marry you, in fact, it was obvious to everyone that you would be married. *(She whispers to ANYA, who motions to CHARLOTTA, and both exit.)* She loves you, you seem to be fond of her, and I don't know why, I simply don't know why it is that you go out of your way to avoid one other. I don't understand it!

LOPAKHIN: I don't understand it myself, to tell the truth. It's all so strange, somehow…If there's still time, then I'm ready to do it now…Basta! Let's settle it once and for all; without you here, I don't think I could possibly propose to her.

LYUBOV ANDREEVNA: Excellent. It only takes a minute, you know. I'll call her in right away…

LOPAKHIN: Oh yes, and there's champagne, too. *(Looks at glasses.)* It's empty, someone drank it all up.

YASHA coughs.

Or, should I say, lapped it all up…

LYUBOV ANDREEVNA: *(Excited.)* Splendid. We're leaving…Yasha, "allez"! I'll call her…*(At the door.)* Varya, stop what you're doing, and come here. Come! *(Exits with YASHA.)*

LOPAKHIN: *(Looks at his watch.)* Yes…

Pause.

Muffled laughter and whispering is heard from behind the door: finally, VARYA enters.

VARYA: *(In a lengthy search for something.)* That's strange, I can't find it anywhere…

LOPAKHIN: What are you looking for?

VARYA: I put it away myself, I can't remember where.

Pause.

LOPAKHIN: So where will you go now, Varvara Mikhailovna?

VARYA: Me? To the Ragulins'…I've agreed to work for them…you know…as a housekeeper.

LOPAKHIN: Aren't they in Yashnevo? That's about forty-five miles from here.

Pause.

And so, life has come to an end in this house…

VARYA: *(Searching among the things.)* Where can it be…Perhaps I put it in the trunk…Yes, life has come to an end in this house…and will be no more…

LOPAKHIN: And I'm off to Kharkov now…on the same train. I've got a lot of business there. But I'm leaving Yepikhodov here to look after things…I've hired him, you know.

VARYA: Really!

LOPAKHIN: Last year at this time it was already snowing, if you remember, and now it's so sunny and calm. Only it's quite cold…Three degrees of frost, almost.

VARYA: I hadn't noticed.

Pause.

Anyway, our thermometer's broken…

Pause.

A voice is heard calling from outside: "Yermolai Alekseich!…"

LOPAKHIN: *(As if he'd long been waiting for this call.)* Coming! *(He hurries out.)*

VARYA sits on the floor, puts her head on a bundle of clothing, and sobs quietly. The door opens, and LYUBOV ANDREEVNA enters cautiously.

LYUBOV ANDREEVNA: So?

Pause.

We'd better go.

VARYA: *(No longer weeping, wipes her eyes.)* Yes, Mamochka, it's time. If I don't miss the train, I might even get to the Ragulins' today…

LYUBOV ANDREEVNA: *(At the door.)* Anya, put your coat on!

Enter ANYA, then GAEV, CHARLOTTA IVANOVNA. GAEV is wearing a warm coat with a hood. The SERVANTS and CARRIAGE DRIVERS assemble. YEPIKHODOV is busy with the luggage.

Now, we can be on our way.

ANYA: *(Overjoyed.)* We're on our way!

GAEV: My friends, my dear, kind friends! Upon leaving this house forever, how can I be silent, how can I refrain, upon this our departure, from expressing those feelings, which now fill my very being...

ANYA:*(Imploring.)* Uncle!

VARYA: Uncle, must you!

GAEV: *(Dejected.)* "Double the yellow into the middle..." I'll be quiet...

Enter TROFIMOV, then LOPAKHIN.

TROFIMOV; All right, ladies and gentlemen, time to depart!

LOPAKHIN: Yepikhodov, my coat!

LYUBOV ANDREEVNA: I want to sit for just one minute longer. I never really noticed before, what walls this house has, what ceilings, and now I look at them with such longing, with such tender love...

GAEV: I remember, when I was six, on Trinity Sunday, I sat at this window and watched my father walking to church...

LYUBOV ANDREEVNA: Have they taken everything out?

LOPAKHIN: I think so. *(To YEPIKHODOV, who is putting on his coat.)* Yepikhodov, see to it that everything's been taken care of.

YEPIKHODOV: *(Speaking in a hoarse voice.)* Don't you worry, Yermolai Alekseich.

LOPAKHIN: What's the matter with your voice?

YEPIKHODOV: I just drank some water, and I must have swallowed something.

YASHA: *(Contemptuously.)* What ignorance...

LYUBOV ANDREEVNA: We're leaving — and not a soul will be left here...

LOPAKHIN: Until springtime.

VARYA: *(Pulls an umbrella out of a bundle — it appears as if she were about to strike someone; Lopakhin pretends to be frightened.)* What's wrong with you?...I wouldn't think of it...

TROFIMOV: Ladies and gentlemen, please, let's get into the carriages now...It's time to go! The train will arrive any minute!

VARYA: Petya, here they are, your galoshes, beside the suitcase. *(In tears.)* Look how old and muddy they are...

TROFIMOV: *(Putting on the galoshes.)* We're off, ladies and gentlemen!

GAEV: *(Very confused, afraid of bursting into tears.)* Train...station..."Croisé into the middle pocket, Double the white into the corner..."

LYUBOV ANDREEVNA: We're off!

LOPAKHIN: Is everyone here? No one left behind? *(Locks the side door stage left.)* There are some things stored in here, better lock up. We're off!

ANYA: Good-bye, house! Good-bye, old life!

TROFIMOV: Hello, new life!…*(Exits with ANYA.)*

VARYA glances around the room and exits without hurrying. Exit YASHA, and CHARLOTTA, with the little dog,

LOPAKHIN: And so, until springtime. Come now, ladies and gentlemen, we'd better be going…Once more, a very good-bye!!…*(Exits.)*

LYUBOV ANDREEVNA and GAEV are left alone together. It is as if they have been waiting for this moment; they throw themselves into each others' arms and sob quietly, with restraint, fearing they might be heard.

GAEV: *(In despair.)* My sister, my sister…

LYUBOV ANDREEVNA: O my precious orchard, my sweet, lovely orchard!… My life, my youth, my happiness, farewell!…Farewell!…

ANYA's voice calls out, merrily: "Mama!…"
TROFIMOV's voice calls out, gaily, excitedly: "A-oo!…"

LYUBOV ANDREEVNA: For the last time, let me look at these walls, these windows…how my mother loved to walk about this room…

GAEV: My sister, my sister!…

ANYA's voice: "Mama!…"
TROFIMOV's voice: "A-oo…"

LYUBOV ANDREEVNA: We're off!…

They exit.

The stage is empty. There is the sound of all the doors being locked, and then of the carriages pulling away. It grows very still. Through the stillness comes the remote sound of the axe falling on a tree, a lonely, melancholy sound. Footsteps are heard. FIRS appears at the door, stage right. He is dressed, as always, in a jacket and a white waistcoat, with slippers on his feet. He is ill.

FIRS: *(Goes to the door, tries the handle.)* Locked. They've gone…*(Sits on the sofa.)* They've forgotten about me…Never mind…I'll sit here for a just a bit…And Leonid Andreich, most likely, didn't put his fur coat on, went off wearing his light one…*(Sighs, anxiously.)* Just slipped my notice…These young people nowadays! *(Mutters something incomprehensible.)* And life has passed by, somehow, as if I never lived it at all. *(Lies down.)* I'll lie down for just a bit…Don't have too much strength left, now, do you, no, not much, not much at all…You pathetic old fool, you!…*(Lies there, immobile.)*

A distant sound is heard, as if coming from the sky, the sound of a breaking string, dying away, a mournful sound. Silence falls, and all that is heard, far off in the orchard, is the sound of the axe falling on a tree.

CURTAIN

Premiere
January 17, 1904

THE FALLEN WOMAN

by

Alexey Konstantinovich Tolstoy

A wave of laughter fills the hall!
O strike the cymbals, sound the call!
Commence the celebration!
Through portals decked in majesty
Of brocade-braided tapestry
The crowd swells with elation!

Past corridors gold- and crystal-gleaming
The joyous multitude comes streaming,
Around the feasting table they throng.
And while the hall is burning bright,
The coachmen wait into the night,
Their passengers will revel long.

Inspired by inebriation,
Their voices raise in wild oration,
Of Pilate's tyranny, Roman rule…

…

(etc.)

*Note: The opening lines of this poem
are quoted on page 251
in the text of* The Cherry Orchard.

Chronology of the Plays

PLATONOV*	1880–81
ON THE HIGH ROAD	1885
ON THE HARMFUL EFFECTS OF TOBACCO	1886 *(revised 5 times through 1902)*
SWAN SONG	1887–88
IVANOV*	1887–89
THE BEAR	1888
THE PROPOSAL	1888
TATYANA REPINA	1889
THE TRAGEDIAN IN SPITE OF HIMSELF	1889
THE WEDDING	1889
THE WOOD DEMON*	1889
THE JUBILEE	1891
THE NIGHT BEFORE THE TRIAL	1890s *(unfinished)*
THE SEAGULL*	1896** *(completed 1895)*
UNCLE VANYA*	1899** *(completed 1896)*
THE THREE SISTERS*	1901** *(completed 1900)*
THE CHERRY ORCHARD*	1904** *(completed 1903)*

*indicates the full-length works
**dates of their Moscow or St. Petersburg
premiere performances

Biographical Chronology
Anton Chekhov

1860   January 17. Anton Pavlovich Chekhov, born in Taganrog, a town on the Azov Sea, son of a shopkeeper. (One of six children: Aleksandr, Nikolai, Anton, Masha, Ivan, Mikhail). Of peasant lineage: His grandfather was a serf in the Voronezh province.

1869   Enters grammar school, is required to work in his father's grocery store and to sing in the church choir along with his other siblings.

1876   Anton's father's bankruptcy forces the family to flee to Moscow; Anton is left behind to complete his education; supports himself by tutoring.

1877   Sends his first serious full-length play (a lost manuscript whose title is purported to have been *Bezotsovshchina [Fatherless]*) to his brother Aleksandr, along with several short comedic ones, which Aleksandr sends to journals for publication.

1879   Passes his exams, joins his family in Moscow, enrolls in the medical school at Moscow University; to support his family and his education, begins writing sketches for humorous publications.

1880   First story published in *Strekoza (The Dragon Fly)*, a humorous journal; from 1880–87, writes over 400 stories and sketches for numerous journals under a variety of 'noms de plume.'

1882   Begins to contribute stories regularly to the weekly *Osolki (Splinters)* for a five year period; its editor, Leykin, limits him to comedic sketches of less than 1000 words, signed primarily by Antosha Chekhonte; this becomes the main source of income for himself and his family.

1884   Receives medical degree; begins to practice medicine; experiences his first hemorrhage; *Tales of Melpomena,* a collection of humorous short stories, is published.

1885   Begins to contribute weekly to the Petersburg Gazette — no longer limiting him to strictly humorous pieces, and permitting him to write more lengthy stories; his collection *Motley Stories* is published.

1886   Invited to contribute to *Novoe Vremya (New Time)* by its prestigious publisher, Suvorin, enabling him to begin his more serious work and to publish under his true name with no space restrictions; experiences his second hemorrhage; continues writing dozens of short stories.

1887   Premiere of *Ivanov* at the Korsh Theatre, Moscow; *At Twilight,* a volume of short stories, is published by Suvorin, establishing him as a writer of increased stature.

1888   Awarded Pushkin Prize in Literature by the Imperial Academy of Sciences in St. Petersburg; premiere of *The Bear* and *Swan Song;* publication of a story, *The Steppe* in *The Northern Herald,* his first appearance in a so-called 'thick journal,' the serious monthlies of the Moscow literary establishment, further enhancing his stature as a writer; *Stories,* a volume of short stories, is published by Suvorin.

1889   Premiere of *The Proposal* and *The Tragedian in Spite of Himself;* premiere of *The Wood Demon* in Moscow, which closed after three performances to uniformly negative reviews; death of his brother, Nikolai, of consumption; writes stories. *A Dreary Story, The Bet.*

1890   Journeys across Siberia to the island of Sakhalin off the Pacific Coast of Siberia to study the penal colony; experiences symptons of cough, heart palpitations; writes stories: *The Horse-Thieves, Gusev.*

1891   Travels in Western Europe; writes story *The Duel,* beginning the period of the longer and more serious short stories.

1892   Journeys to Novgorod province to join the fight against famine; purchases his 'estate' in Melikhovo, fifty miles south of Moscow, and moves from Moscow with his family; appointed honorary medical superintendent of Serpukhov, his district, in the fight against cholera; his notes on the Sakhalin journey are published in *Russian Thought;* writes stories: *Ward No. 6, The Grasshopper, In Exile, Neighbors, The Wife.*

1893   Increased sympotons of his illness: cough, heart palpitations, indigestion, headaches; writes stories: *An Anonymous Story, The Two Volodyas*.

1894   His cough worsens; writes stories: *The Black Monk, The Student, The Teacher of Literature*.

1895   Completes *The Seagull;* first meeting with Tolstoy; writes stories: *The Murder, Ariadne, Anna on the Neck*.

1896   October 17: *The Seagull* premieres at the Aleksandrinsky Theatre in St. Petersburg; it is a critical failure; writes stories: *The House with a Mezzanine, My Life*.

1897   Continues his humanitarian work in the Serpukhov district (Melikhovo), building schools (at his own expense), census-taking; experiences a major hemorrhage; is formally diagnosed with consumption and advised by his doctors to move to the south; Stanislavsky and Nemirovich-Danchenko make plans for the founding of the Moscow Art Theatre; Chekhov spends winter in France; writes stories: *Peasants, The Schoolmistress*.

1898   Inaugural season of the Moscow Art Theatre; December 17: *The Seagull* is produced there with great success; performances of *Uncle Vanya* are well received in the provinces; Chekhov shows interest in the Dreyfus affair; Chekhov's father dies; owing to his declining health, Chekhov buys a plot of land in Yalta and builds a house; writes stories: *Man in a Case, Gooseberries, About Love*.

1899   Sells Melikhovo and moves to the Yalta with his mother and sister; sells all the rights for his works, past and future, to St. Petersburg publisher Marks; October 26: *Uncle Vanya* is produced at the Moscow Art Theatre; writes stories: *The Darling, The Lady with the Dog, On Official Duty*.

1900   Spring: the Moscow Art Theatre comes to Yalta to visit the ailing Chekhov, and performs *Uncle Vanya* for Chekhov, with Gorky, Bunin, Kuprin and Rachmaninov in attendance. Chekhov is elected member of the Academy of Sciences; writies stories: *In the Ravine, At Christmas-Time*.

1901 January 31: *The Three Sisters* premieres at the Moscow Art Theatre; May 25, Chekhov marries Olga Knipper.

1902 Resigns from the Academy of Sciences in protest against exclusion of Gorky; writes story: *The Bishop.*

1903 His health declines; elected president of the Society of Russian Literature; writes his last story: *The Bride.*

1904 January 17: Chekhov's forty-fourth birthday is honored at the premiere of *The Cherry Orchard,* his last play; April: leaves Russia for Germany with Olga Knipper, on doctors' advice; July 2: Chekhov dies at a spa at Badenweiler, Germany. Buried in the cemetery of the Novo-Devichy Monastery in Moscow.

Please note that the dates of his one-act and full-length plays are set forth in a separate chronology. I have included mention of a few of his almost 500 short stories in this chronology, to show that Chekhov wrote stories every year of his life from the age of seventeen. The names of individual stories don't begin in this outline until 1889, since before then, they were so numerous and were published in collections.

Glossary

This glossary contains a brief explanation of selected literary, musical, and cultural allusions in the four plays. Its purpose is to enhance the understanding of the texts and their practical usage.

The Seagull
ACT I

Nekrasov
> Nikolai Alekseevich (1821–78): a great Russian poet, and leader of the school of "civic" poetry (poetry of social and political consciousness).

Duse
> Eleonora Duse (1859–1924): internationally celebrated Italian actress whose popularity peaked in the 1890's.

La Dame aux Camélias
> popular nineteenth century play, premiering in 1852, by Alexandre Dumas-fils (1824–95); the play was the basis for Verdi's opera *La Traviata* (1853).

Maupassant
> Guy de Maupassant (1850–1893): prolific French short story writer and novelist, whose technique Chekhov admired.

Tolstoy
> Lev Nikolaevich (1828–1910): great and prolific writer (of novels, short stories, plays), and towering figure in Russian literature; author of *War and Peace* (1865–69), *Anna Karenina* (1873–76), *The Death of Ivan Ilyich* (1888), and the play, *The Power of Darkness* (1888). Visited Chekhov in Yalta in his declining years, where they became great friends.

Zola
> Emile Zola (1840–1902): famous French novelist, dramatist and critic. Chekhov admired the stand Zola took against the French government in the Dreyfus case (1898 — *J'accuse*).

"In France, two grenadiers…"
> the opening lines of *Die Grenadiere,* a poem by Heinrich Heine (1797–1856), set to music in a popular 'lied' by Schumann (1810–56).

"Don't say that our youth has been wasted…"
> a 'romance' (popular Russian love song of the day) of a poem by Nekrasov.

"Again before you I stand…"

>the opening line of the poem *Stansy (Stanzas)* (1841) by V. I. Krasov, set to music in a popular 'romance.'

Chadin

>Russian actor, presumed fictitious.

Rasplyuyev

>a character in the well-known contemporary Russian comedy, *Krechinsky's Wedding* (1855), by Sukhovo-Kobylin (1817–1903).

Sadovsky

>Prov Mikhailovich: a famous contemporary Russian comedic actor of the Maly Theatre in Moscow.

"De gustibus, aut bene, aut nihil"

>Here, Shamraev combines two Latin sayings: "de gustibus non est disputandum" ("there's no arguing about taste") and "de mortuis aut bene, aut nihil" ("about the dead, say something good or say nothing at all") — resulting in the creation of the following: "when speaking about taste, say something good or nothing at all."

"O Hamlet…"

>from Shakespeare's *Hamlet,* Act III, sc. 4; Chekhov knew *Hamlet* from Polevoy's translations into Russian (Chekhov did not read English).

"Decadent School"

>Writers of the Russian symbolist movement in the 1890s were referred to as 'decadents.' Influenced by the French symbolists and considered to be 'avant-garde,' their literature and poetry was characterized by obscure and exotic themes, musical verse, and rich poetic vocabulary. The movement's precursor was Solovyov; some famous Russian symbolist poets include Blok, Bely, and Bryusov.

Silva

>Russian opera singer, presumed fictitious.

"An angel of silence…"

>a Russian expression, when there is a lull in the conversation.

THE SEAGULL: ACT II

'Tell her, my flowers…"

>The beginning of Siebel's aria from Act III of *Faust* (1859), an opera by Gounod (1818–93).

"like that poor fellow in Gogol's story…"

The reference is to 'Poprishchin,' a character in Gogol's *Diary of a Madman* (1835), the story of a petty clerk who harbors delusions of grandeur and romance, and who is ultimately committed to an asylum. Nikolai Gogol (1809–52) is one of Russia's greatest authors — humorist, dramatist (*The Inspector General* [1836]), short story writer (*The Nose* [1835]), novelist (*Dead Souls* [1842]), "The Overcoat" [1842]).

Turgenev

Ivan Sergeevich (1818–83), great Russian short story writer (*Sportman's Sketches* [1852]), novelist (*Father's and Sons* [1862]), dramatist (*A Month in the Country* [1850]).

THE SEAGULL: ACT III

"If ever you have need of my life, then come and take it…"

This actually is a quote from one of Chekhov's own short stories, *The Neighbors* (1892). In her memoirs *Chekhov in My Life* (published posthumously), the short story writer Lydia Avilova (1864–1943), a protégée of Chekhov, writes of a love relationship she maintains she had with Chekhov over a ten year period (1889–99), during which she herself presented him with a locket with that inscription in 1895. She theorizes that this is the inspiration for Nina's gift in *The Seagull.*

Suzdaltsev

Russian actor, presumed fictitious.

Izmailov

Russian actor, presumed fictitious.

Slavyansky Bazaar

famous hotel/restaurant in Moscow. Stanislavsky and Nemirovich-Danchenko met there in 1897, and as a result of this legendary meeting, the Moscow Art Theatre was founded.

THE SEAGULL: ACT IV

"The moon floats through the night sky…"

a opening line of *The Tiger Cub,* a popular 'romance' by Shilovsky (1849–93).

state councillor

a high rank in the prerevolutionary Russian civil service.

Pushkin's *Rusalka*

Aleksandr Sergeevich Pushkin (1799–1837), Russia's greatest poet, author of *Boris Godunov* (1831, a play in blank verse); *Eugene Onegin* (1823–31, a novel in verse); *The Bronze Horseman* (1833). In his *Rusalka* (*The Mermaid,* 1830), an old miller goes mad after his only daughter drowns herself, and imagines that he's a raven.

'The Man in the Iron Mask'
> The reference is to a mysterious French prisoner of state during the reign of Louis XIV, who died in the Bastille in 1703; his identity is the subject of many European literary works.

"Lucky is he…"
> Nina's (approximate) reference is to a line from Turgenev's novel *Rudin* (1856).

Translator's note. There are two omissions of literary allusions in this translation: the first, in Act I, Treplev's reference to a play The Turbulence of Life, *an obscure play by Markevich (1822–84), which would not be familiar to non-Russian audiences; the second, in Act III, Sorin's reference to his "gudgeon-like existence," an allusion to* The Wise Gudgeon, *a satire-fable by Saltykov-Shchedrin [1826–89], which would have had special meaning to contemporary Russian audiences who knew the play.*

Uncle Vanya
ACT I

privy councillor
> a high rank in prerevolutionary Russian civil service.

"With strained mind…"
> lines from a satirical poem *Other People's Views* (1794) by Ivan Dmitriev (1760–1837) (poet, author of odes, elegies, verse tales), in which he satirizes the contemporary literary fashion of ode-writing.

Ostrovsky
> Aleksandr Nikolaevich (1823–1886), leading Russian dramatist of the second half of the nineteenth century. Known for his realistic prose plays of which he wrote over forty, the most well-known being *The Storm* (1859). Many of his plays were already incorporated into the repertoires of established Russian theatres when Chekhov came on the scene.

"quantum satis"
> "as much as is needed" (Latin).

"perpetuum mobile"
   "perpetual motion" (Latin).

UNCLE VANYA: ACT II

Batyushkov
   (1787–1855) a leading Russian romantic poet.
"Dance, my stove…"
   lines from a traditional Russian folk song.
'brüderschaft'
   the German word for 'brotherhood,' here denoting a custom wherein two
   people pledge friendship by drinking from the same glass and thereafter
   addressing each other as 'thou' instead of 'you.' (In Russian, as well as in
   German and French, there remains this pronominal distinction, as con-
   trasted to contemporary English).

UNCLE VANYA: ACT III

"the inspector general"
   Here, Serebryakov quotes the famous first line of Gogol's play of the same
   name (1836) (for Gogol, see glossary under *The Seagull,* Act II).
"manet omnes una nox"
   "one night awaits us all" (Latin).
Dostoevsky
   Fyodor Mikhailovich (1821–1881) great Russian novelist (*Crime and
   Punishment* [1866], *The Idiot* [1868–9], *The Brothers Karamazov*
   [1879–80])

UNCLE VANYA: ACT IV

Aivazovsky
   (1817–1900) A popular and prolific nineteenth century Russian painter,
   famous for his marine subjects (his paintings numbered almost 6,000).
"finita la commedia"
   "the comedy is over" (Italian); also, the famous lines at the end of Leoncavallo's
   opera *I Pagliacci* (1892).

The Three Sisters
ACT I

nameday
> the day of the saint after whom a person is named.

Dobrolyubov
> Aleksandr Mikhailovich (1836–1861), a leading radical Russian critic.

"In a cove by the sea…"
> the opening lines to *Ruslan and Lyudmila* (1820), a famous poetic fairy tale by the great poet Pushkin (1799–1837), familiar to most educated Russians.

silver samovar
> here, Chebutykin has made a 'faux pas,' in giving a gift appropriate for a married couple on a silver wedding anniversary.

"He scarce had time…"
> from the fable *The Peasant and the Workman* by Ivan Andreevich Krylov (1769–1844), the leading Russian writer of fables, of which he wrote several hundred.

district council
> a system of local government in prerevolutionary Russia.

Novo-Devichy
> the cemetery of the famous Novo-Devichy Monastery in Moscow; Chekhov was buried there in 1904, three years after the opening of *The Three Sisters*.

"We're put on earth…"
> an obscure French operetta known in Russian as *The Werewolf*.

"Feci quod…"
> "I did what I could, and let him who can do better, do so" (Latin).

"mens sana…"
> "a sound mind in a sound body" (Latin).

THE THREE SISTERS: ACT II

"carnival time"
> Shrovetide carnival, during the last week before Lent.

(holds up a finger)
> reference to a Russian proverbial saying, in effect, that it's enough to hold up a finger to make someone laugh.

"How depressing…"

Masha's paraphrase of the final line in Gogol's famous short story *How Ivan Ivanovich Quarrelled with Ivan Nikiforovich* (1835); Gogol (1809–1852), celebrated Russian writer (see glossary under *The Seagull,* Act II)

"Balzac…Berdichev"

Honoré de Balzac, French novelist (1799–1850). Berdichev: a town in the Ukraine.

Panama Affair

Baillot (1843–1908), a French Minister implicated in the Panama Canal scandal (1888), and imprisoned for five years; from his *Notes of a Prisoner.*

"je vous prie…"

"Forgive me, Marie, but your manners are a bit uncouth" (Natasha's French grammar is flawed).

"il parait…"

"It appears that my Bobik is not asleep" (again, Natasha's French grammar is flawed).

"I'm strange…"

Solyony quotes from *Wit Works Woe,* a popular Russian satire (1822–24), written by Aleksandr Sergeevich Griboedov (1795–1829), leading playwright of the early nineteenth century.

"Aleko"

a reference to Aleko, the violent and jealous hero of Pushkin's poem *The Gypsies* (1824), who kills his wife and her lover.

Lermontov (1814–1841)

Mikhail Yurevich, celebrated Russian romantic poet and prose writer. Famous works include *Masquerade* (1835–36) (prose drama), *The Demon* (1839) (long poem), *A Hero of Our Time* (1840) (novel), and many poems. Killed in a duel. Chekhov wrote to Tikhomirov (an actor in the cast of *The Three Sisters)* that "Solyony *thinks* he resembles Lermontov, but, of course, he doesn't…" (1/14/01).

"cheremsha"/"chekhartma"

both definitions by Chebutykin and Solyony are correct.

"Ah, you, porch …"

Russian folk song.

"O, fallacem…"

"O illusory human hope" (Latin).

THE THREE SISTERS: ACT III

1812
> reference to the great fire of Moscow during the French invasion and occupation under Napoleon.

"in vino veritas"
> "in wine, there is truth" (Latin).

"Won't you please take this sweet fig…"
> lines from a Russian operetta which was once performed at the Hermitage; Chekhov wrote (to Tikhomirov, 1/14/01) that he couldn't remember the name of the operetta.

"Young or old do love obey…"
> lines from Pushkin's *Eugene Onegin* (1823–31); in Act III of Tchaikovsky's opera of the same name (1879), these lines also began a famous aria sung by the character Gremin.

"I'll answer you…"
> a quote from Krylov's fable *The Geese*.

"Amo, amas…"
> "I love, you love" etc. (Latin declension).

"Omnia mea…"
> "All I have, I carry with me" (Latin).

"Gogol's madman"
> the character 'Poprishchin' in Gogol's *Diary of a Madman* (1835) (see glossary under *The Seagull*, Act I).

THE THREE SISTERS: ACT IV

"kohkane"
> "darling" (Polish).

"Ta-ra-ra boom-de-ay"
> the opening of a popular contemporary Russian song (the second line literally translates: "I'm sitting on a curbstone") (actually, this song is a version of a popular English music-hall song written in 1890).

"ut consecutivum"
> Latin law of syntax.

The Maiden's Prayer
> a popular piano piece by Polish composer Badarzevska-Baranowska (1838–1862).

"He sought…"
> the final lines of Lermontov's famous poem *The Sail* (1832).

"Il ne faut pas faire du bruit…"

"You mustn't make any noise, little Sophie is sleeping. You are a bear."
(Natasha's French grammar is still flawed).

The Cherry Orchard
ACT I

"it will heal before your wedding day"
>a Russian saying.

Holy Week
>the week before Easter.

"eternal student"
>revolutionary students were prevented from taking their exams because they had police records (due to their political activities).

"a man of the eighties"
>the connotation here is of a liberal idealist living in a reactionary time. The 1880s in Russia were considered to have been a reactionary period following the assassination of Czar Alexander II in 1881.

THE CHERRY ORCHARD: ACT II

'salto mortale'
>acrobatic term for somersault (Italian).

"What care I…"
>lyrics from a popular contemporary 'romance' of the period.

Buckle
>Henry Thomas Buckle (1821–1862), an English historian popular in Russia in the 1880s, author of *A History of English Civilization.*

"the seventies"
>the 1870s in Russia were considered to have been a period of liberal reform.

"the decadents"
>another name for "symbolists," a literary movement in the 1890s (see glossary under *The Seagull,* Act I).

"An enterprising man, the Prussian…"
>most probably, lyrics from a contemporary vaudeville of the period.

the emancipation of the serfs
>In 1861, 15 million serfs were freed in Russia.

"My brother, my suffering brother…"
>a misquote of a poem by the poet Semyon Yakovlevich Nadson (1862–1887), a well-known "civic" poet.

"Come down to the Volga, whose moan…"

a quote from the famous poem *Thoughts at the Portals* (1858) by the "civic" poet Nekrasov (1821–1878) (see glossary for *The Seagull,* Act I), who wrote of the Russian peasantry and their suffering. Here, the passerby combines lines of two famous contemporary poems into one fragmented recitation.

the sound of the breaking string

while fishing one summer on an estate in the Ukraine when he was young, Chekhov heard a strange, distant sound, which later was identified as that of a bucket falling down a mineshaft.

"Oh-phel-i-a, get thee to a nunnery"

"Oh-phel-i-a, o nymph, remember me in thy prayers"

in attempting to reproduce two quotes from *Hamlet,* Lopakhin mispronounces the name of Polonius's daughter and misquotes the second line (the correct quote from *Hamlet,* Act III, Sc. I, is: "Soft you now!/The fair Ophelia! Nymph, in thy orisons/Be all my sins remember'd").

THE CHERRY ORCHARD: ACT III

"Promenade à une pair"

"grand rond, balancez"

"les cavaliers à genoux et remerciez vos dames"

"promenade with your partner"

"take your positions for the 'grand rond'"

"gentlemen, kneel, and thank your ladies"

All of the above are French terms of instruction for popular social dances of the day.

"Güter mensch, aber schlecter musikant"

a German expression, literally: "a good man, but a bad musician," which Charlotta uses here in reference to Pishchik's romantic potential.

The Fallen Woman by Alexey Konstantinovich Tolstoy

(1817-75) — a long poem in six parts (written in 1857) about a courtesan who is converted to Christianity; not considered to be his best poem.

"O, do you know how my heart is yearning"

one of the most popular romances of the day, by Rzhevskaya.

THE CHERRY ORCHARD: ACT IV

Trinity Sunday

The Sunday after Whitsunday, observed as a feast in honor of the Trinity; the cherries are ripe on the trees at that time of year.

Pronunciation Guide

For the actor, the most significant aspect of the pronunciation of Russian names is the accentuation of the correct syllable, indicated below by an accent mark (′) after the syllable to be stressed. Once the actor masters this, the narrative will flow, and the names will provide the richness that resonates in the original Russian. Note that the Russian name and patronymic is used for formality in address. Occasionally, the patronymic is contracted in the dialogue (e. g. "Sergeevich" sometimes becomes "Sergeich"). In general, accented "a" is pronounced as in "father," accented "e" as in "yet"; accented "o" as in "for." Note: This guide is only approximate, since the pronunciation of some Russian vowels changes slightly, based on whether they are accented or not, or depending on their position in a word.

THE SEAGULL *Cast of Characters*

Irina Nikolaevna Arkadina:

> Ee-ree′-na Nee-ko-la′-yev-na Ar-ka′-dee-na
>> *("ee" rhymes with the English word "seem")*

Konstantin Gavrilovich Treplev (Kostya):

> Kon-stan-teen′ Gav-ree′-lo-veech Tryep′-lyef (Kos′-tya)

Pyotr Nikolaevich Sorin (Petrusha):

> Pyo′-tr Nee-ko-la′-ye-veech So′-reen (Pye-troo′-sha)
>> *("oo" rhymes with the word "soon")*

Nina Mikhailovna Zarechnaya:

> Nee′-na Mee-khai′-lov-na Za-ryech′-na-ya
>> *("khai" rhymes with the word "why")*

Ilya Afanasevich Shamraev:

> Eel-ya′ A-fa-na′-sye-veech Sham-ra′-yef

Polina Andreevna:

> Po-lee′-na An-drey′-ev-na
>> *("drey" rhymes with the word "grey")*

Masha (Marya Ilyinichna) (Mashenka):

> Ma′-sha (Ma′-rya Eel-yeen′-eech-na) (Ma′-shen-ka)

Boris Alekseevich Trigorin:

> Bo-rees′ A-lek-syey′-e-veech Tree-go′-reen
>> *("syey" rhymes with the word "grey")*

Yevgeny Sergeevich (Sergeich) Dorn:
  Yev-ge´-nee Syer-gey´-e-veech (Syer-gey´-eech) Dorn
    ("gey" rhymes with the word "grey")
Semyon Semyonovich Medvedenko:
  Se-myon´ Se-myon´-o-veech Myed-vye-dyen´-ko
Yakov:
  Ya´-kof

OTHER RUSSIAN NAMES APPEARING IN THE TEXT:
Chadin, Pavel Semyonich (Pashka): Cha´-deen, Pa´-vel Se-myon´-ich (Pash´-ka)
Gogol: Go´-gol
Grokholsky: Gro-khol´-skee
Izmailov: Eez-mai´-lof *("mai" rhymes with the word "why")*
Kharkov: Khar´-kof
Mama: Ma´-ma
Matryona: Ma-tryo´-na
Molchanovka: Mol-cha´-nof-ka
Nekrasov: Nye-kra´-sov
Papa: Pa´-pa
Poltava: Pol-ta´-va
Rasplyuyev: Ras-plyoo´-yef
Rusalka: Roo-sal´-ka
Sadovsky: Sa-dof´-skee
Slavyansky: Sla-vyan´-skee
Suzdaltsev: Sooz´-dal-tsef
Trezor: Tre-zor´
Turgenev: Toor-ge´-nyef
Yelets: Ye-lyets´
Yelisavetgrad: Ye-lee-sa-vet-grat´

UNCLE VANYA   *Cast of Characters*
Aleksandr Vladimirovich Serebryakov:
  A-lek-san´-dr Vla-dee´-mee-ro-veech Se-re-brya-kof´
    ("Alexandre," French pronunciation)
Yelena Andreevna (Lenochka):
  Ye-lye´-na An-drey´-ev-na (Lye´-noch-ka)
    ("drey" rhymes with the English word "grey")
    ("Hélène," French pronunciation)

Sofya Aleksandrovna (Sofi, Sonya/Sonechka/Sonechkina/Sonyushka):
So´-fya A-lek-san´-drov-na (So-fee´, Son´-ya, Son´-yech-ka,
Son´-yech-kee-na, Son´-yoosh-ka)
Maria Vasilyevna Voynitskaya (Matushka):
Ma-ree´-ya Va-see´-lyev-na Voy-neet´-ska-ya (Ma´-toosh-ka)
("Maman," French pronunciation)
Ivan Petrovich Voynitsky (Vanya):
Ee-van´ Pye-tro´-veech Voy-neet´-skee (Van´-ya)
("Jean," French pronunciation)
Mikhail Lvovich Astrov:
Mee-kha-eel´ Lvo´-veech As´-trof
Ilya Ilyich Telegin:
Eel-ya´ Eel-yeech´ Tye-lye´-geen
Marina Timofeevna:
Ma-ree´-na Tee-mo-fyey´-ev-na

OTHER RUSSIAN NAMES APPEARING IN THE TEXT:

Aivazovsky:	Ai-va-zof´-skee *("Ai" rhymes with the English word "why")*
Batyushkov:	Ba´-tyoosh-kof
Grigory Ilyich:	Gree-go´-ree Eel-yeech´
Ivan Ivanich:	Ee-van´ Ee-van´-ich
Kharkov:	Khar´-kof
Konstantin Trofimovich Lakedemonov:	Kon-stan-teen´ Tro-fee´-mo-veech La-ke-de-mo´-nof
Kursk:	Koorsk
Malitskoe:	Ma´-leet-sko-ye
Papa:	Pa´-pa
Ostrovsky:	Os-trof´-skee
Pavel Alekseevich:	Pa´-vyel A-lek-syey´-e-veech
Petrushka:	Pye-troosh´-ka
Rozhdestvennoe:	Rozh-dyest´-vye-no-ye
Tula:	Too´-la
Turgenev:	Toor-ge´-nyef
Vera Petrovna:	Vye´-ra Pye-trov´-na
Yefim:	Ye-feem´
Zhuchka:	Zhooch´-ka

THE THREE SISTERS *Cast of Characters*

Prozorov, Andrey Sergeevich (Sergeich) (Andryusha):
>Pro´-zo-rof, An-drey´ Syer-gey´-e-veech (Syer-gey´-eech) (An-dryoo´-sha)
>>*("drey" and "gey" rhyme with the English word "grey")*

Natalya Ivanovna (Natasha):
>Na-ta´-lya Ee-van´-ov-na (Na-ta´-sha)

Olga Sergeevna (Olya, Olyechka, Olyushka):
>Ol´-ga Syer-gey´-ev-na (Ol´-ya, Ol´-yech-ka, Ol´-yoosh-ka)

Maria Sergeevna (Masha, Mashka, Mashenka):
>Ma-ree´-ya Syer-gey´-ev-na (Ma´-sha, Mash´-ka, Ma´-shen-ka)

Irina Sergeevna (Arisha, Arinushka):
>Ee-ree´-na Syer-gey´-ev-na (A-ree´-sha, A-ree´-noosh-ka)

Fyodor Ilyich Kulygin (Fedya):
>Fyo´-dor Eel-yeech´ Koo-li´-geen (Fye´-dya)

Aleksandr Ignatyevich (Ignatich) Vershinin:
>A-lek-san´-dr Eeg-na´-tye-veech (Eeg-na´-teech) Vyer-shee´-neen

Nikolai Lvovich Tusenbach (Tusenbach-Kronye-Altschauer):
>Nee-ko-lai´ Lvo´-veech Too´-zen-bakh
>>*("lai" rhymes with the English word "why")*

Vasily Vasilyevich (Vasilyich) Solyony:
>Va-see´-lee Va-see´-lye-veech (Va-seel´-yeech) So-lyo´-nee

Ivan Romanovich (Romanich) Chebutykin:
>Ee-van´ Ro-man´-o-veech (Ro-man´-ich) Che-boo-ti´-keen

Aleksey Petrovich Fedotik:
>A-lek-syey´ Pye-tro´-veech Fye-do´-teek

Vladimir Karlovich Rode:
>Vla-dee´-meer Kar´-lo-veech Ro-de´

Ferapont Spiridonich:
>Fye-ra-pont´ Spee-ree-do´-nich

Anfisa:
>An-fee´-sa

Other Russian Names Appearing in the Text:

Aleko:	A-lye´-ko
Basmannaya:	Bas-man´-na-ya
Berdichev:	Ber-dee´-chef
Bobik:	Bo´-beek
Bolshoy:	Bol-shoy´

chekhartma:	che-khart-ma′
cheremsha:	che-rem-sha′
Dobrolyubov:	Do-bro-lyoo′-bof
Gogol:	Go′-gol
Kirsanovsky:	Keer-sa′-nof-skee
kokhane:	ko-kha′-ney
Kolotilin:	Ko-lo-tee′-leen
Kozyrev:	Ko′-zi-ref
Lermontov:	Lyer′-mon-tof
Mama:	Ma′-ma
Marfa:	Mar′-fa
Moskovsky:	Mos-kof′-skee
Nemetskaya:	Nye-myets′-ka-ya
Novo-Devichy:	No′-vo-Dye′-vee-chee
Protopopov, Mikhail Ivanich/ Potapich:	Pro-to-po′-pof, Mee-kha-eel′ Ee-van′-ich/Po-ta′-pich
Pyzhikov:	Pi′-zhee-kof
Saratov:	Sa-ra′-tof
Skvortsov:	Skvor-tsof′
Testov:	Tyes′-tof
Tsitsikar:	Tsee-tsee-kar′
Zasyp:	Za′-sip

THE CHERRY ORCHARD *Cast of Characters*

Lyubov (Lyuba) Andreevna Ranevskaya:

      Lyoo-bof′ (Lyoo′-ba) An-drey′-ev-na Ra-nyef′-ska-ya

      ("drey" rhymes with the English word "grey")

Anya (Anechka):

      An′-ya (An′-yech-ka)

Varya (Varvara Mikhailovna):

      Va′-rya (Var-var′-a Mee-khai′-lov-na)

      ("khai" rhymes with the word "why")

Leonid (Lyonya) Andreevich (Andreich) Gaev:

      Le-o-need′ (Lyon′-ya) Andrey′-e-veech (An-drey′-eech) Ga′-yef

Yermolai Alekseevich (Alekseich) Lopakhin:

      Yer-mo-lai′ A-lek-syey′-e-veech (A-lek-sey′-eech) Lo-pa′-kheen

      ("lai" in "Yermolai" rhymes with the word "why")

      ("syey" rhymes with the word "grey")

Pyotr (Petya) Sergeevich (Sergeich) Trofimov:
    Pyo´-tr (Pye´-tya) Syer-gey´-e-veech (Syer-gey´-eech) Tro-fee´-mof
Boris Borisovich Simeonov-Pishchik:
    Bo-rees´ Bo-rees´-o-veech See-myon´-of-Peesh´-cheek
Charlotta Ivanovna:
    Shar-lo´-ta Ee-van´-ov-na
Semyon Panteleevich (Panteleich) Yepikhodov:
    Se-myon´ Pan-te-lyey´-e-veech (Pan-te-lyey´-eech) Ye-pee-khod´-of
        ("lyey" rhymes with the word "grey")
Dunyasha (Avdotya Fyodorovna):
    Doon-ya´-sha (Av-do´-tya Fyo´-do-rov-na)
Firs Nikolaevich:
    Feers Nee-ko-la´-ye-veech
Yasha:
    Ya´-sha

OTHER RUSSIAN NAMES APPEARING IN THE TEXT:

Anastasy:	A-na-sta´-see
Dashenka:	Da´-shen-ka
Deriganov:	Dye-ree-ga´-nof
Grisha:	Gree´-sha
Kardamonov:	Kar-da-mo´-nof
Karp:	Karp
Kharkov:	Khar´-kof
Kozoedov (Fyodor):	Fyo´-dor Ko-zo-ye´-dof
Lopakhina:	Lo-pa-khee-na
Mama (Mamochka):	Ma´-ma (Ma´-moch-ka)
Papa:	Pa´-pa
Petrushka:	Pye-troosh´-ka
Polya:	Po´-lya
Ragulin:	Ra-goo´-leen
Yaroslavl:	Ya-ro-slavl´
Yashnevo:	Yash´-nye-vo
Yefimyushka:	Ye-fee´-myoosh-ka
Yegor:	Ye-gor´
Yevstigney:	Yev-steeg-nyey´
	("nyey" rhymes with the word "grey")
Znoykov:	Znoy´-kof

Selected Bibliography

The following sources were consulted for some of the biographical information included in the introduction, and for some of the musical and literary illusions in the glossary:

Benedetti, Jean, transl. and ed. *The Moscow Art Theatre Letters.* New York: Routledge, 1991.

Magarshack, David. *Chekhov the Dramatist.* London: John Lehmann, Ltd., 1952.

Magarshack, David. *The Real Chekhov.* London: George Allen & Unwin Ltd, 1972.

Pitcher, Harvey. *Chekhov's Leading Lady.* London: John Murray, Ltd., 1979.

Rayfield, Donald. "Chekhov and the Literary Tradition." In *A Chekhov Companion,* edited by Toby Clyman. Westport, Connecticut: Greenwood Press, 1985.

Rayfield, Donald. "Chekhov and Popular Culture." *Irish Slavonic Studies* 9 (1988): 47–60.

Simmons, Ernest J. *Chekhov: A Biography.* Chicago: The University of Chicago Press, 1962.

In addition to these, the following books are also recommended to actors and theatre artists as valuable source material for enriching their understanding of the four major plays. They are only a few of the many fine sources available in English about Chekhov and his work:

Avilova, Lydia, *Chekhov in My Life.* Translated by David Magarshack. London: Methuen, 1989.

Hackett, Jean. *The Actor's Chekhov.* Lyme, NH: Smith & Kraus, 1992.

Magarshack, David. *Chekhov: A Life.* New York: Grove Press, 1952.

Miles, Patrick, ed. and translator. *Chekhov on the British Stage.* Cambridge: Cambridge University Press, 1993.

Nemirovich-Danchenko. *My Life in the Russian Theatre.* Translated by John Cournos. London: Geoffrey Bles, 1968.

Pritchett, V. S. *A Spirit Set Free.* New York: Vintage, 1988.

Stanislavsky, Konstantin. *My Life in Art.* Translated by J. J. Robbins. London: Methuen, 1989.

Troyat, Henri. *Chekhov.* New York: Fawcett Colombine, 1986.

Valency, Maurice. *The Breaking String.* New York: Oxford University Press, 1966.

The texts of Chekhov's four major plays were newly translated for this collection from the Russian from the following:

Chekhov, Anton Pavlovich. *Izbrannye sochinenia v dvux tomax. Tom vtoroy.* Moskva: Khudozhestvennaya Literatura, 1986.

The excerpted quotations from Chekhov's letters and notebooks, and from Kuprin and Bunin's reminiscences were newly translated for this collection from the Russian from the following:

Chekhov, Anton Pavlovich. *Polnoe sobranie sochineniy i pisem v tridtsati tomax.* Moskva, Izdatelstvo 'Nauka', 1974–82.

Bunin, I. A. "Chekhov", in *Vospominania.* Paris: Vozrozhdenie, 1950.

Kuprin, A. I. "Pamyati Chekhova", in *Sobranie sochineniy v devyati tomax. Tom II.* Moskva: Izdatelstvo Khudozhestvannaya Literatura, 1973.

ABOUT THE TRANSLATOR

Dr. Carol Rocamora, translator, director, and teacher, is a graduate of Bryn Mawr College. She received her M.A. and Ph.D. degrees from the University of Pennsylvania in Russian literature. She is the founder of the Philadelphia Festival Theatre for New Plays at the Annenberg Center, a nonprofit professional theatre, where she served as its Artistic and Producing Director from 1981–1994. In this capacity, she has worked with over 120 contemporary American playwrights in developing and producing their new work for the stage. At Festival Theatre, she directed many mainstage productions of new plays, and, in addition, directed the premieres of the four new translations of Chekhov's plays included in this collection. She has served on the faculties of Bryn Mawr and Haverford Colleges, and the University of Pennsylvania. She currently teaches theatre at New York University's Tisch School of the Arts.